This book given to

_____

on the occasion of

_____

_____

Presented by

_____

Date

_____

COFFEE BREAK MEDITATIONS

260 Devotions for the Workplace

EDWARD GRUBE

CPH.

SAINT LOUIS

To my families:

Renee, Allison, Aaron, and Relma, whose patience
and prayers sustain me.

—

The people of Holy Cross Lutheran Church in Chicago,
who nurtured my young faith through Word,
Sacrament, and fellowship.

—

The children, staff, and parents at
Concord Lutheran School in Addison and Bensenville,
together with the members of St. Paul and Zion.

All Scripture quotations, unless otherwise indicated, are taken from the HOLY BIBLE, NEW INTERNATIONAL VERSION®. NIV®. Copyright © 1973, 1978, 1984 by International Bible Society. Used by permission of Zondervan Publishing House. All rights reserved.

Scripture quotations marked NKJV are from the HOLY BIBLE, New King James Version, copyright © 1979, 1980, 1982 Thomas Nelson, Inc. Used by permission.

Copyright © 1997 Concordia Publishing House
3558 S. Jefferson Avenue, St. Louis, MO 63118-3968
Manufactured in the United States of America

Library of Congress Cataloging-in-Publication Data

Grube, Edward C., 1947–
   Coffee-break meditations : 260 devotions for the workplace /
Edward C. Grube.
      p.   cm.
   Includes index.
   ISBN 0-570-04960-1
   1. Meditations.   I. Title.
BV4832.2.G73 1997
242'.68—dc20
               96-44102
               CIP

1 2 3 4 5 6 7 8 9 10   06 05 04 03 02 01 00 99 98 97

Contents

As You Begin

Have you heard this proverb? "When you burn the candle at both ends, you're not as bright as you think."

So what are you waiting for? Take a break! Whether you work outside your home or in it, whether you get paid or work out of love, whether your chores are difficult or easy, whether you actually work, take a break. And while you're braking (or at least slowing down), do a little reading. Use the brief meditations in this book for the next 260 workdays or weekdays. Perhaps you will find these meditations a refreshing interruption to a year's worth of daily routines—a snack for your soul and a tickle for your heart.

This is a book of meditations. But forget about the wistful (and wasteful) meditation of the New Age. You don't need any Ommmmmms or even Ummmmmms to help you focus. A few HIMMMMMMs will help, though. God will bless your meditiation. Praise HIM. After all, He sent Jesus to take away our sins. Thank HIM. And the Holy Spirit remains at work while you're on break. Trust HIM. God is tireless! Before you meditate on each day's devotion, invite the Spirit to invigorate you. He will enable and enliven you—make you more perceptive about God's involvement in every detail of your life, even the routine or mundane events. And ask the Holy Spirit to roll up your sleeves too, that you may work next to Him, living what you read and believe.

After you read each meditation, you'll want to spend a few moments in prayer. Your own will be far better than any I could provide. Reflect on your personal needs and the needs of others. Take those needs, either on your lips or just in your heart, to God. He has promised to hear you. He has promised to answer you. But be ready. Sometimes He gives unexpected answers!

May God the Father, Son, and Holy Spirit bless your meditation.

Edward Grube

1

They'll Wonder Why You're Smiling

Bless those who persecute you; bless and do not curse.
Romans 12:14

Do you feel their eyes on you? Don't be surprised—especially if you're reading this in a public place or in the presence of your family. Especially if they know you're reading something "religious." Look up, flash a smile, and return to your reading. Even if you're a bit timid about your co-worker's or family's curiosity, you can witness your faith. Let their eyes see it on your lips. Smiles are so powerful. They can even break the ice!

You have much to smile about. Smile as you remember that cooing baby nestled in the hay. Smile as you think about the man mistaken for a landscaper that misty Sunday morning in a cemetery near dark Gethsemane. Then imagine yourself with the disciples, hunkered down in a stuffy room, and suddenly Jesus enters— through a locked door! Go ahead, smile. Perhaps they will wonder what you're smiling about.

Maybe they will ask. Then what will you do? You could tell them you're reading a funny book. After all, our Savior acted "funny." Many who witnessed His ministry laughed at Him. A few laughed with Him. He probably laughed too. (But never at anyone's expense.) He did many funny things—like forgiving His enemies, associating with potentially dangerous strangers, getting within infectious range of contagious people, obeying His Father perfectly, and blessing His enemies.

Reading this book may be risky. Each meditation should make you smile. Sometimes you might even chuckle. At the very least, your heart should be lighter. So be ready. Be ready for inquisitive looks, rolling eyes, even mockery for your devotion. But smile anyway. Who knows? You might ruin the day for a grouch!

Note: This book may not be suitable for people on diets. The first thing dieters usually lose is their good mood!

2

Fine Print I

But because of His great love for us, God, who is rich in mercy, made us alive with Christ even when we were dead in transgressions—it is by grace you have been saved. Ephesians 2:4–5

How do you answer when people ask, "What must I do to be saved?"

If you tell them to find the answer in the Bible, they might page through the Old Testament and get bogged down in all the rules and regulations—the fine print—in Deuteronomy and Leviticus. Like most legal writ, it doesn't make for happy reading. In fact, some of it is downright demanding and frightening. Left by itself, this legalistic fine print can only condemn and destroy any hope of living forever.

Skeptics also look for the fine print in the New Testament. Jesus often said that He is the only thing necessary for salvation. Just believe, and live forever! And how does one believe? Why, it's a free gift of the Holy Spirit! Free! Gift! Still, people look for loopholes—something like successfully observing at least 7.5 of the Ten Commandments to earn eternal life. Or maybe paying God a 10 percent tax to avoid the angelic auditors.

There is indeed fine print involved in answering "What must I do to be saved?" Reread today's Bible passage.

Nothing could be finer! Saved by grace—God's gift of unconditional love. He saves us while we are still sinners. Such love is unheard of these days. Such love was unheard of in Jesus' day too. But true love it is. After all, doesn't the fine print always spell out the truth?

Oh yes, there is more fine print. It's true that believers contribute nothing toward their salvation. Christians don't need a perfect 10 on the Commandment scale, nor are they required to tithe. They don't have to associate with the oppressed or other needy people. If the fine print requires none of this for salvation, why do it? Read the next meditation to find out. The print is fine, but it won't be small.

3

Fine Print II—It Will Make You Dizzy

It teaches us to say "No" to ungodliness and worldly passions, and to live self-controlled, upright and godly lives in this present age, while we wait for the blessed hope—the glorious appearing of our great God and Savior, Jesus Christ, who gave Himself for us to redeem us from all wickedness and to purify for Himself a people that are His very own, eager to do what is good. Titus 2:12–14

Someone said that people rarely get dizzy from doing good turns! While God doesn't require goodness as a prerequisite for faith, faithful people do good because they have faith. Now you could sit down and create a list of good deeds for the day or spend the morning pondering potential situations to which you might contribute your good deeds. *Warning:* Such activities can consume so much time that you won't have any left to actually activate the list.

The best way to do good is to be good. Titus offers reliable advice about the ingredients of a good life. Self-control is the key. The key to self-control is to turn all your sins over to Jesus. He took them away and made you righteous, thereby supplying a means to resist temptation. While Jesus' death and resurrection made us righteous, we still sin as we await that time when He comes again and brings us to complete perfection. The fine words from Titus address that situation too.

We have the blessed hope that Jesus will come again. Living with that hope comforts us in times of pain, sorrow, failure, and sin. We know that despite our own troubles, Jesus knows our needs and He will treat those problems. While we wait for that blessed day, we can be good. We can share His comfort with those in need; forgive as we have been forgiven; care for those who can't care for themselves; support missionaries and charities; help out around church, etc. (The etc. is limited only by your imagination and effort.)

One more thing. If anyone calls you a dizzy Christian because of your good works, take it as a compliment.

4

Rivers

Trust in the LORD and do good; dwell in the land and enjoy safe pasture. Delight yourself in the LORD and He will give you the desires of your heart. Psalm 37:3–4

Pioneers often settled along rivers. Successful riverfront settlements used the water that flowed by (and sometimes through) their front yard. The flowing water brought jobs, transportation, energy, and recreation. The river brought life.

Rivers bring to mind Baptism. Baptismal waters provide a great place to settle down and live. Like rivers flowing on the earth's surface, the waters of Baptism bring jobs, transportation, energy, and even recreation. Settling on the banks of Baptism doesn't station one on Easy Street, however. Baptism leads one to live and share the Gospel each day. That takes work!

The river of Baptism provides transportation—the sole (soul?) transportation between earth and heaven. Yes, this holy river floats us from sin, failure, pain, and shame into the arms of Christ, where we find the other benefits of life on the river. As pioneers used rivers for mills and later, electricity, Christians get their energy from the Holy Spirit, who empowers us to live according to God's will, milling life's produce into useful service to God and others.

Christians rarely think about recreation when they think of Baptism. Perhaps that's because Christians work so hard at being Christians they become like the riverfront laborer who works so hard that he no longer appreciates or enjoys the water. But the River of Life, Christ Himself, wants us to enjoy the baptismal waterfront. Read today's passage again. You'll be delighted!

5

A Perfect Ten

Jesus asked, "Were not all ten cleansed? Where are the other nine?
Was no one found to return and give praise to God except this foreigner?"
Luke 17:17–18

The moral of the passage above is that we should thank God for His blessings. Unfortunately, often our response is to click our tongues at the nine who didn't bother to say thank You.

These verses are relived every day in the modern world. So much good happens to so many people—without regard to their religious background. Have you noticed that God doesn't care whom He blesses? Pagans and unbelievers get their crops watered by the same God who nourishes farmland worked by Christians. Profane, reckless, and rude drivers on the interstate arrive as safely at their destinations as those who practice patience and brotherly love. The seriously ill patient who never uttered a prayer enjoys a miraculous recovery; the Christian in the next bed dies even as a host of believers pray diligently. It's enough to make our tongues click until they're all clicked out!

Why does God love and bless those who don't love Him? Someday we'll understand the depths of His love, but for now this paradox baffles us. For now, God expects us to love as He loves. Listen to Jesus as He says, "But I tell you: Love your enemies and pray for those who persecute you, that you may be sons of your Father in heaven. He causes His sun to rise on the evil and the good, and sends rain on the righteous and the unrighteous" (Matthew 5:44–45).

God bestows His love on all regardless of race, creed, ethnic origin, height, weight, eye color, church attendance, income, language, or breed of dog they own. We don't know how many people recognize His grace and thank Him for His goodness. Perhaps it's only 10 percent. Hopefully, it's higher. Our only task is to remain among the 10 percent and use our tongues to pray rather than click. Pray that more and more people recognize God's grace and come to Him for His final blessing when Jesus comes again.

C

$C_{12}H_{22}O_{11}$

Nehemiah said, "Go and enjoy choice food and sweet drinks, and send some to those who have nothing prepared. This day is sacred to our LORD. Do not grieve, for the joy of the LORD is your strength." Nehemiah 8:10

Do you know what the formula in the title means? Could it be a formula for happiness?

Some define happiness as being too busy to be miserable. Others equate happiness with having everything they want—only to discover they're not happy unless they have more. Some pursue happiness with such vigor that their pursuit is a chief cause of their unhappiness! So where can you find true happiness?

Nehemiah of the Old Testament knew about happiness. Perhaps you're unwittingly taking his advice right now—on coffee break. Let your eyes wander back to the top of the page, and read his words again.

I hope you're enjoying a tasty snack or sipping your favorite coffee break beverage right now. Isn't it wonderful to break from your labor—to tantalize your taste buds and relax your mind or muscles (or both)? But of course, your break will end and you'll return to whatever you were doing—whether you enjoy it or not. Coffee breaks may be one element of happiness, but they certainly aren't the most significant. Nehemiah addressed that issue too: "The joy of the LORD is your strength."

What exactly is the joy of the Lord? A perpetual smile? Endless streams of laughter? Or is it a more subtle happiness, an inner peace? The answer is yes. Joy of the Lord comes from knowing, even in difficult times, that Jesus died to take away your sins. He is the Lord of Life who brings hope for the future even in the face of death. The joy of the Lord provides lasting happiness you don't have to work for. It's free and abundant. It sweetens life just as tiny white grains of $C_{12}H_{22}O_{11}$ sweeten coffee or tea.

Now you know the formula. Use it liberally. And share some with those who don't already have it.

1

Sweet Dreams

When you lie down, you will not be afraid; when you lie down, your sleep will be sweet. Proverbs 3:24

Have you ever noticed that your soundest sleep is the sleep you're in when the alarm clock rings? Or do you find it difficult to sleep—tossing, turning, snoring—working so hard at sleeping that you're too tired to get up? As you have noticed, Proverbs talks about sweet sleep—an unusual topic for a biblical book. Let's examine the context of this piece of proverbial wisdom. (If you have a Bible handy, read Proverbs 3:21–26.)

Solomon begins this section of Proverbs talking about judgment and discernment—two gifts from the Holy Spirit. Solomon says that good judgment and spiritual insight decorate the lives of believers like an ornament. But even more important, wisdom provides safety. And this wonderful security makes it easy to enjoy sweet dreams and refreshing sleep. By now, you may wonder if you have access to this wisdom. If you know the kind of wisdom to which Solomon is referring, you can stop reading and catch a little nap instead. But if you're not sure, read on.

Godly wisdom is believing that God loves you, that He has an angel watching over you right now. And while that angel might not protect you from distressing engagements with sin and Satan, it will keep the devil from taking you away from God. Godly wisdom is knowledge that nothing can separate us from God's love, not even death itself. Godly wisdom is an awareness that we belong to the Savior and not even sudden disaster can tear His hand from ours. God's gift of wisdom lets us see the Savior through blind eyes, talk to Him with mute lips, and turn to Him with paralyzed bodies. When we can't come to Him, He comes to us. After all, that's how we became believers, isn't it?

Loopholes

When their fathers or brothers complain to us, we will say to them, "Do us a kindness by helping them, because we did not get wives for them during the war, and you are innocent, since you did not give your daughters to them." ... In those days Israel had no king; everyone did as he saw fit.
Judges 21:22, 25

The words above from Judges conclude several chapters describing sexual violence, brutal warfare, and a promise to God. The promise to God proved most vexing for the Israelites.

Israel declared war on the tribe of Benjamin over a crime committed against one of their own. They swore that none of their women would ever marry men from that tribe. After Israel devastated the tribe of Benjamin, they felt guilty about attacking their cousins. Some 600 soldiers survived the battle and had no one to marry because Israel killed their women. Now Israel wanted to make amends and provide wives for the survivors. But there weren't enough women to go around, and they had sworn not to intermarry with Benjamin. Israel found a loophole that served both them and the Benjamites, technically circumventing their vows with God. Since God's people had no king, they blindly ruled themselves.

Many of God's people still believe they have no King. In truth, they just don't recognize Him. Strangely, most cultures have codes of right and wrong even though they don't recognize God as their King. American culture itself is awash with laws accompanied by an even larger flood of ways to get around the laws.

One law has no loopholes. It's the law of faith. Failure to believe in Jesus as Savior, for whatever reasons, will receive simple, authoritative judgment from God. Of course, we don't have to worry. Only those guilty of breaking laws excuse themselves with loopholes.

Christ has taken away our guilt. He obeyed God perfectly for us. Then He sent the Holy Spirit to give us faith. So use your loopholes against the devil. Next time you confront him, say, "Yes, I'm a sinner. But Jesus took my sins away!"

9

Backwards

The Pharisee stood up and prayed about himself: "God, I thank You that I am not like other men—robbers, evildoers, adulterers—or even like this tax collector." Luke 18:11

A mother and her son hiked a nature path through a wooded area. The boy asked his mother the names of each tree he saw. She deftly identified the oak, elm, maple, and pine. The boy looked at his mother and said, "Wow, Mom! All these trees are named after streets."

The Pharisee in today's Bible reading got it backwards too. Only his confusion wasn't funny. Making matters worse, he professed his false freedom from corruption to the only one who could release him from his guilt.

People still make the Pharisee's mistake. They may regard themselves in perfect harmony with God's will, and thereby miss their need for forgiveness. Almost as bad are those who think themselves so perverse that they could never address the holy God with their prayers. They are unaware or suspicious of the Savior's powerful love.

Confessing sins is neither popular nor enjoyable. Confess some wrongdoing to one you have offended, and you may hear, "Well, don't let it happen again." Discuss your guilt-feelings with the wrong person and you'll hear, "Oh, there's no such thing as sin. Do whatever pleases you. After all, you only live once." And then we also know the "comforters" who respond to wrongdoing with something like, "Oh, that's okay. … You didn't mean it."

Fortunately, we receive the best response when we confess our sins to Jesus. The conversation goes something like this.

"Dear Jesus, I hate sin. But I sin anyway. Today I _____. Please forgive me and strengthen me to fight sin."

Jesus responds, "I died to take away your sins. You are forgiven and you need not feel guilty anymore. I will send the Holy Spirit to help you fight sin. Go in peace."

10

Changeless Variety

The heavens declare the glory of God; the skies proclaim the work of His hands. Psalm 19:1

Sit near a window today so you can "see" the topic of this meditation. Look out once in awhile even if you're in a place that doesn't seem to "declare the glory of God." What does the sky look like today? What did it look like 12 hours ago? What will it look like 12 hours from now?

Weather conditions change, and the sky differs greatly between noon and midnight. In some locales, the sky smiles or storms on beautiful surroundings, while in others it falls on environments defaced by human folly. Yet, as the psalmist says, "the heavens declare the glory of God." God's glory shines and glistens on His creation and creatures every day regardless of weather conditions. Day after day, night after night, God displays His creative power in a paradoxical mixture of variety and changelessness. Only one thing never changes: Our expectation of change! In a world of change, it's good to know we have a permanent God.

God brings the same glory into our daily lives. His dependable presence soothes our anxieties with knowledge that He is just a prayer away. Better yet, He watches us and knows our changing needs even before we know them. And should illness or accident strike, God doesn't abandon us. He heals, if not physically, then spiritually by bringing us closer to Him—perhaps even making us totally dependent on His love and care.

Some people greet each morning with "This is the day the LORD has made. It must be good for something." No, wait. How about "Let us rejoice and be glad in it" (Psalm 118:24). How true! The Lord makes each day for us to find joy in serving Him—from the kitchen table, the office desk, the factory workbench, the road or rail, the furrows or curbs. So rejoice again. Be glad again. And get back to work again!

11

Wave Your Shoe if You Agree

(Now in earlier times in Israel, for the redemption and transfer of property to become final, one party took off his sandal and gave it to the other. This was the method of legalizing transactions in Israel.) So the kinsman-redeemer said to Boaz, "Buy it yourself." And he removed his sandal. Ruth 4:7–8

Picture this. A strategic business deal worth millions of dollars approaches closure. Company lawyers have dotted every *t* and crossed every *i*. (Then they turned it around and did it the right way.) Hours of negotiation finally reach a climax when one businessman takes off his shoe and hands it to his counterpart, thus sealing the deal. *Warning:* Do not actually try this. You may get the boot in exchange!

That's exactly what happened when Boaz bargained to marry and care for Ruth. (Read Ruth in your spare time. It's only four heartwarming chapters long.) Instead of signing legal documents or conducting a church ceremony, they passed a sandal to legalize the marriage. With that act, Boaz and Ruth became husband and wife.

Don't wave your shoe right now (unless you're alone), but at least wiggle your foot if you agree with the following:

1. God loves me, and I love Him.
2. I will invite God to show me His will as I pray for His wisdom.
3. I will hate evil but pray for my enemies.
4. I will ask God's forgiveness daily.
5. I will forgive myself and others as God has forgiven me.
6. I will spend a few moments each day meditating on God's Word, and I will accept the blessings that come from it.
7. I will bring all my needs to Jesus and gratefully accept His answers to my prayers.

By now your ankle probably aches, and if anyone is watching they probably think you need a clear path to the bathroom. But don't let that bother you. Be like Boaz and Ruth after he waved the sandal. Go off and live happily ever after—in God's grace, of course.

I wonder if Ruth bought Boaz another sandal as a wedding present.

12

Sense-ational I—The Eye Yi Yi

Then He turned to His disciples and said privately, "Blessed are the eyes that see what you see." Luke 10:23

Our eyes contain about 70 percent of the body's sensory receptors. The retina accommodates 127,000,000 rods and cones, which send data to about 2,000,000 optic fibers, which, in turn, carry information to the brain for processing. Eye yi yi, yi yi! As you can "see," the eyes play a major role in our sensory system.

God knew what power He gave human eyes. Today's Bible verse is one of more than 500 references to eyes and more than 700 references to seeing. The Bible mentions eyes filling with tears, witnessing victory and defeat, mocking or honoring God, blinking, closing, getting gouged out as punishment, and seeing things that the eyes of unbelievers couldn't.

Jesus blesses us with eyes that see beyond artists' paintings and sculptures, jeweled crosses, and other religious symbolism. We see Jesus as our very own Savior. We see the Son of God born miraculously in a stable, baptized in the Jordan River, changing water into wine, healing the sick and brokenhearted. We see God Himself in Jesus Christ.

Our eyes mist as we see God's innocent Son nailed to a cross and lifted up to die as a sacrifice for our sins. Then our wide eyes twinkle with merriment as we peer into the empty grave and watch Him appear to His astonished disciples. Blessed were their eyes. And blessed are ours.

Don't take your eyesight for granted. It would be bad enough to be blind, but even worse to be spiritually blind. When unbelievers see art depicting Jesus or crosses hanging on walls, all they see is paint and wood. That's hard to believe when we see so much more.

Share your vision with those who are spiritually nearsighted, farsighted, or even blind. And when you finish reading this devotion, look up and give God a wink. He'll get the message.

13

Sense-ational II—Selective Hearing

Before they call I will answer; while they are still speaking I will hear.
Isaiah 65:24

We all know people whose ears can hear the softest words, but who turn deaf to messages they consider unpleasant. Selective hearing is a man-made disability.

God put the *EAR* in hEARing. His first bit of creative wisdom was to give us two ears and only one mouth. And while God put eyelids on eyes, He created nothing to shut out sounds. Therefore, ears relentlessly monitor life around us. God enabled ears to search where eyes can't—around corners, behind us, the next room, and in total darkness. So when God instructs us to hear His word, we have no excuse for not listening. But like anything else God created, human hearing can become dull, defective, or selective.

Praise God for His perfect hearing. God not only hears our prayers, but He also answers them. He understands all languages and hears us when we mumble, think, or pray silently. He knows what we will ask, and He answers while we pray. Sometimes we don't grasp His answer right away, but He will reveal it to us at just the right time.

How comforting to know that God isn't selective in what He hears or whom He hears. He hears it all, from all of us. He hears the bad news and responds with comforting hope and assurances. He hears our worries and pledges to remain in control of our future. He hears our thanks and praise, and He rejoices with us for all the good He puts into our lives. His hearing provides a model for our life too.

How do you respond when your neighbors or co-workers are fearful, hopeless, or happy? Are you selective in your hearing? Follow God's example. In your actions and words, show how well you hear their suffering, fear, or joy. Tell them about times when you felt the same, and encourage them to tell their troubles to God. Pray with them too. God hears and understands even when everyone talks at once!

14

Sense-ational III—How Does It Taste?

Taste and see that the LORD is good; blessed is the man who takes refuge in Him. Psalm 34:8

Are you munching on something during your break? How does it taste—sweet, sour, salty, bitter, hot, cold, crispy, mushy? Some 9,000 taste buds and other sensory receptors route messages to your brain each time you eat. Too hot. Too cold. Just right. Ugh—cherry pit!

After years of health classes, you're now able to classify foods into at least two groups—those you like and those you don't like. You're able to categorize those foods by personal experience with them. You needed to taste and see which foods appealed to you. That's the focus of Psalm 34:8—experience with the Savior.

Nearly everyone enjoys sweets. Today's psalm tells about sweet Jesus. But to know how sweet He is, we must take refuge in Him—we must rely on Him above everything. Modern people are often do-it-yourselfers. They rely on themselves for success. When failure threatens, the do-it-yourselfers resort to self-recrimination or accusations aimed at others. We usually describe such people as sour or bitter.

Sweet Jesus satisfies and gratifies those who place their faith in Him. His sweetness sends us scurrying for strength or forgiveness when we fail. How sweet it is to know that Jesus closely monitors whatever we attempt—not to see how well we do on our own, but to show us how to trust Him for help. Regardless of what we attempt, we know things will turn out God's way when we ask Jesus for help. *Note:* Sometimes God's way and our way do not agree. In such cases, take refuge in God. His way is better.

Our Savior's willingness to forgive is the sweetest refuge. He made us holy and righteous. He promises a banquet table filled with delectable goodies when He returns. There we'll rub elbows with the likes of Peter, Paul, and Jesus Himself as we savor His divine buffet.

How sweet it is.

15

Sense-ational IV—A Touchy Subject

"Look at My hands and My feet. It is I Myself! Touch Me and see; a ghost does not have flesh and bones, as you see I have." Luke 24:39

Touching was a touchy subject in the Bible. Most often, people were told not to touch something. (Sound familiar?) God warned His people not to touch the very holy, like Himself and the things He touched. He also ordered them not to touch the very wicked, like idols and idolaters. His people moved through history shunning things called unclean. They learned to stay clear of dead bodies, sick people, and certain types of food. God's people wanted to avoid contaminating themselves by contact with such sin-stricken things.

Touching became a more positive subject in Jesus' time. The Bible tells how Jesus wanted little children close enough to touch. How blessed to be touched by the Savior!

Later, Jesus invited the disciples themselves to touch Him. They saw Him die on the cross, and they heard the tomb was empty, but they still thought He was an apparition when they saw Him. Thus the invitation. Perhaps they touched Him with handshakes and hugs, or even high-fives. Jesus lives! Jesus, God Himself, is touchable!

That's our Good News too. Common sinners can touch God. Of course, He touched us first. He reached out and grabbed us by the soul and gave us faith to know Him as our loving Savior. He touches us with the mark of His love so God the Father and all on earth know that we belong to Him. And now we can touch Him with our prayers and worship. Someday the 1,300 nerve endings in each square inch on the hands of our risen bodies will indeed feel the Savior's loving touch. So if anyone says you're a bit "touched" because you're a Christian, tell them they're right!

16

Sense-ational V—Smelly or Fragrant?

For we are to God the aroma of Christ among those who are being saved and those who are perishing. To the one we are the smell of death; to the other, the fragrance of life. And who is equal to such a task?
2 Corinthians 2:15–16

In his Song of Songs, Solomon says his beloved's nose is "like the tower of Lebanon looking toward Damascus" (7:4). (*Warning:* Use discretion before murmuring this "compliment" to your beloved.) Towering noses were once symbols of enamoring beauty. Of course, noses must do more than decorate faces. Like Limburger cheese, noses are worthless unless they smell.

The Apostle Paul spoke of spiritual noses. With a little imagination, you can appreciate the fragrant imagery of today's verse. Paul calls us an "aroma of Christ" to God. Aromas, as opposed to odors, are pleasing smells. God's divine sniffer might be eternally plugged if He had to smell our reeking sins. But Christ perfumes us with His righteousness, and God smells only the cologne of our holiness.

The scent of Christian righteousness isn't pleasing to everyone, however. We are downright offensive to some. We smell as bad as a dead body. How could anyone think of us that way? Perhaps it's because those who are offended by Christians live in a garbage heap of sin. They don't recognize good smells because they haven't smelled any. The best we can do is keep dabbing Christ's righteousness on our life in hopes of infiltrating the stench in which they live. We may also share our perfume—the bouquet of kindness and forgiveness. Then they too may whiff the fragrance of life that we know as our Savior. We may awaken them to the fragrance of Christ's love, brewed fresh daily to quench their thirst for hope and love.

Is your break about over? Sniff the air around you. If anyone asks, just tell them you're enjoying your nose—and the fragrance of life.

17

What the Devil Looks Like

Again, the devil took Him [Jesus] to a very high mountain and showed Him all the kingdoms of the world and their splendor. "All this I will give You," he said, "if You will bow down and worship me." Matthew 4:8–9

A preacher claimed that the Bible identified more than 500 different sins. After the service, several parishioners asked for a list. Apparently, they didn't want to miss anything.

We often blame sin on the devil. If only we could see him coming, we could arouse our defenses. But the devil is hard to see. If only the devil was really that ugly, crimson-skinned, sharp-horned, pointy-tailed character, we could easily avoid him.

When the devil tempted Jesus, he exposed his real character. Jesus had spent over a month alone, seriously contemplating His ministry and what it would require of Him. No doubt He hungered for a break from His routine of fasting and meditation. The devil saw an opportunity to approach Jesus as a "friend" and perhaps trap Him into ruining God's plan. Far from a hideous beast bearing a red-hot pitchfork, the devil approached Jesus with something that would make Him feel better. (Doesn't sin usually start out as fun?) Jesus detected the trap and told the devil where to go.

The devil approaches us the same way. He offers what look like gifts to make us feel better. Unhappy with a spouse? Maybe you should ditch him/her … Too tired to pray at night? Don't—a day without God can't hurt a strong Christian like you … Doesn't it hurt when they mock you? Be like them. Curse and swear more often. Vile language releases your pent-up hostilities.

Yes, the devil may be hard to identify, but the results of his treachery aren't. Sin always brings us down. So thank God for Jesus Christ. We always know Him. He's the one who says, "Come to Me. I'll forgive you. Go in peace, and cling to what is good."

Now go back to work. In peace.

18

Watch Your Language

One day the evil spirit answered them, "Jesus I know, and I know about Paul, but who are you?" Then the man who had the evil spirit jumped on them and overpowered them all. He gave them such a beating that they ran out of the house naked and bleeding. Acts 19:15–16

As we read above, violence erupted when several unbelievers attempted to profit by driving out evil spirits in Christ's name. Unexpectedly, the devils turned on the frauds and knocked them silly. I think it's safe to presume that the frauds watched their language from that point on. They weren't punished so much *for* their sins as *by* their sins.

We hear God's name used most every day. It's used on the loading dock, at the hair stylist, in the factory, and on the farm field. We hear it on radio and TV and in the classroom. God's name even pervades our pastimes—on the golf course (coarse?), in the fishing boat, at the card party. Would that God was really so popular!

Of course, we realize that God's name is used in two ways. As demonstrated by the unbelieving frauds (who probably articulated more "choice" words after their experience), there is the profane way of calling on Him. Unfortunately, this seems the most common use of His name. Worse, misusing God's name is acceptable and even expected in some circles.

When misuse of God's name is so common, isn't it frustrating that proper use invites derision? To utter "Jesus Christ" when something goes wrong seems more acceptable than proclaiming the same name in public prayer or words of forgiveness.

I guess God is used to hearing His name mentioned so often. He always sticks around to listen. Those who call Him in the name of Jesus Christ receive power to overcome evil and live peacefully, knowing that God is good and that He is in charge of every minute of our lives.

You're entitled to use God's name freely. Watch your language. Let others watch it too, for it is the language of love.

19

Good News

Now the Lord is the Spirit, and where the Spirit of the Lord is, there is freedom. 2 Corinthians 3:17

The *Indianapolis Star* included today's passage below the masthead. I wonder how pleased Paul would be with today's news stories.

Someone once quipped that a newspaper was like a circulating library with high blood pressure. Newspapers report the consequences of sin, and it seems to sell well. Wouldn't it be great if reporters consistently found some good news to report?

I have some good news, and I have some Good News. First, the good news. Sorry, but there isn't any! Not without the Good News. Without the Good News, life would be as bleak as the weather forecast during the week you're on vacation. Life would be as corrupt and hopeless as the newspapers report. And the worst news of all would appear on the obituary page. Thank God that He frees us from corruption and despair. He even frees us from death. And what is this Good News? Perhaps a news reporter would outline it like this:

Who: Jesus Christ

What: Freed us from sin so we may live forever with Him.

When: About 2,000 years ago. (But He's still very active today.)

Where: The story began before the world was born and it will never end.

Why: God loves us.

How: God created people to love and serve Him, but they decided to love and serve themselves instead. They broke their relationship with God. Even though He restored that relationship many times, people found new and novel ways of breaking it again. Rather than condemning His people forever, God sent Jesus to earth as a human to live according to God's will in their place. He lived perfectly and died horribly. All because He loves us.

Jesus rose from the dead, and we will too. Then things will be as He originally intended. We will love and serve Him. We will have a happily-ever-after ending. Or is it a beginning?

What Do Christians Look Like?

But the LORD said to Samuel, "Do not consider his appearance or his height, for I have rejected him. The LORD does not look at the things man looks at. Man looks at the outward appearance, but the LORD looks at the heart." 1 Samuel 16:7

Stop reading. (I know. You just started.) Find a mirror, and look at yourself. Take the book with you, and answer the following questions:

1. How would you describe your complexion?
   ❏ Light ❏ Dark ❏ Ruddy ❏ Cosmetically challenged
2. What color are your eyes?
   ❏ Brown ❏ Blue ❏ Gray ❏ Hazel ❏ Red striped
3. How would you describe your overall appearance?
   ❏ Attractive ❏ Plain ❏ In-between
   ❏ I don't use that kind of language
4. If you were a motor vehicle, which would you be?
   ❏ Subcompact ❏ Family sedan ❏ Sport/utility ❏ Beater
5. What expression appears on your face?
   ❏ Frown ❏ Smile ❏ Non-committal

Okay, get your face out of the mirror before someone thinks you're vain.

You just caught a glimpse of what Christians look like. Were you happy about it? If not, don't worry. The prophet Samuel had doubts about one of God's chosen people too.

Samuel was to anoint David as king. In Samuel's time, kings were normally tall, strong, and—well—kingly looking. Samuel went through all of Jesse's sons, several of whom possessed appropriate physical qualifications. But then David stepped forward. He was rather young, and he lacked the general size and demeanor common to kings at the time. But God chose David to lead His people. And God made David the right person for the job.

God worked the same way with us. He chose us to be His people regardless of how we look. Our physical looks are far less important than the beauty that resides in our soul—for Jesus is there. With Jesus in our soul, His beauty radiates through our body, just waiting to escape into the eyes of others.

21

Travel Plans

"I know the plans I have for you," declares the LORD, *"plans to prosper you and not to harm you, plans to give you hope and a future."*
Jeremiah 29:11

Where are you headed, on a guilt trip or a fantastic voyage? Whichever you choose, you'll need a compass and some guidance. Let's examine what a travel guide says about guilt trips.

If you travel the route of guilt trips, you'll follow the compass needle as it points down—the general direction of hell. To be sure, we all make some forays in this direction. We usually don't repeat inauspicious trips, and the same is true for jaunts into sin-filled territory. Our journeys to Faulty Moraland, Sin City, or Idol Valley eventually lead to feelings of guilt. But it's not so much how a trip starts out as how it ends. Guilt is good *if* it points us back in the direction of forgiveness and salvation.

Following this direction, our guilt trip turns into the trip of a lifetime. We pass through canyons of death (Psalm 23) and into the lush fields of God's love. What makes the expedition so fantastic? It's not our travel; it's God's guidance. He leads us to our Savior, Jesus Christ. And once we're with the Savior, we experience the beauty of traveling with Him—*in this life.*

Few people look forward to the end of vacation trips. We Christians have an advantage there too. Our trip won't end. It started when we came to know Christ as our Savior. If we wander off, thinking we can manage by ourselves, Jesus patiently comes looking for us. He takes us down paths laced with righteousness and sends us on side trips to both receive and extend forgiveness. And when we've had just enough travel during our earthly life, He provides a rest stop.

The next leg of our excursion will be an eternal vacation during which we'll enjoy the whole panorama of God's beauty.

Bon voyage.

22

When You Feel Like Shouting

Clap your hands, all you nations; shout to God with cries of joy. Psalm 47:1

You probably know someone who thinks his horsepower is judged by the amount of his exhaust!

The Bible has many examples of shouting. In one New Testament incident, some unbelievers (who thought they were real believers) shouted at Paul, angry because he told them they couldn't obey God's law well enough to save themselves. And Paul shouted back something about their resemblance to poisonous snakes. From Paul's point of view, it was a loud but righteous argument.

Not all the biblical shouting was done in anger. Remember the inspired crowd on Palm Sunday welcoming Jesus with whoops of praise? Psalms and other Old Testament books speak of cheerful shouting.

As modern Christians our shouts can be more delightful. We can attempt to say, "I forgive you," as loudly as others accuse. We can say, "I'm sorry," with the same intensity as we argue our defense. Let God hear your shouts of thanksgiving at the same volume as grumbles of discontent.

If you're too shy or self-conscious to shout out loud, do it in a whisper. You know how a whisper shouts—like when Mom wanted you to stop popping your bubble gum during the movie. Blare out a boldly whispered "Praise the Lord," "Amen," or "Thank You, Jesus" whenever the occasion suggests.

You can also shout without saying a word. A hefty smile on your face, even when you're troubled about something, nearly screams that you have hope—hope in Jesus. A warm handshake or hug for a downhearted person speaks louder than hollow words of comfort.

If you dare, be like David, who often shouted his psalms. Once he even danced so uninhibitedly that he embarrassed his wife. But he just couldn't contain His joy in God. If David could write poems and offer a footloose frolic, we also have freedom to express our joy in Jesus. Shout. Whisper. Or at least offer some polite applause.

23

Right-Hand Man

The Son is the radiance of God's glory and the exact representation of His being, sustaining all things by His powerful word. After He had provided purification for sins, He sat down at the right hand of the Majesty in heaven. Hebrews 1:3

Right-hand" persons usually don't sit around. They busy themselves doing anything that needs to be done. And they have the authority to do it. Bosses in the business world and parents in the family home have right-hands—those on whom they rely to get the job done, to be in the right place at the right time, to cut through obstacles that block the goal. Right-hands are conscientious go-getters, filled with energy and ambition—not for themselves, but for others.

Jesus is a right-hand man. Martin Luther explained just what "sitting at the right hand of God" means. The phrase is traced to language typically used by the Hebrews to express universal authority and presence. We're probably familiar with the authority part. But being God's right-hand also involves being everywhere He is needed. That's good news for us.

While He was on earth, Jesus chose to be at a wedding in Cana and at the attempted stoning of an adulterous woman. He chose to be in the Garden of Gethsemane late one Thursday night. He even chose to breathe His last human breath hanging on a cross. Then He chose to rise.

It's a good thing for us that He chose to go to heaven. The view is good up there. He knows exactly where we are and what we need. And to make things better, He chose us to be His ambitious right-hand people. But be careful. Ambition can get you into lots of hard work!

24

Don't Miss the Boat

Therefore, my dear friends, as you have always obeyed—not only in my presence, but now much more in my absence—continue to work out your salvation with fear and trembling, for it is God who works in you to will and to act according to His good purpose. Philippians 2:12–13

Mackinac Island is one of the Midwest's premier locales for beauty and relaxation. No cars. Every conceivable flavor of fudge. Ample souvenir shops—even for the most devoted shopper. Scenic beauty in rocky cliffs and pristine lake water. Carriage rides and a historic fort. Something for everyone—except for those who tend to wander and lose track of time.

The only way from Michigan's mainland to the island is by ferry. The ferries do not operate on a 24-hour schedule. Oh, there are many opportunities to board and return to the mainland, but eventually the opportunities end. Those who wander aimlessly, fail to watch their watches, or defy the deadlines get stranded up the Straits of Mackinac without a paddle.

Jesus has already claimed us, but we have many opportunities to wander away from Him. It's easy to become sidetracked and miss the boat. We trade one opportunity for another. And when we hear a knock at the door, it's hard to know whether it's opportunity or temptation that's doing the knocking.

How can we recognize opportunity? The passage from Philippians has a suggestion phrased in somewhat curious words. The idea here is to grow in Christ. Jesus died once to save us. But we can miss the boat and lose that salvation if we become disoriented by sin or if we decide to work for salvation without Christ.

Growing in Christ comes from reading and meditating on His Word—like you're doing now. A steady diet of His Word in regular worship and Bible study makes our faith stronger so we can live "according to His good purpose."

Next time you hear opportunity knocking, don't grumble because the noise woke you up. Get up and answer the door. Then again, it might just be one of your relatives.

25

What's It Doing in the Bible?

Warning: The following Bible passage contains violence, sex, and adult themes.

"Bring out the man who came to your house so we can have sex with him." The owner of the house went outside and said to them, "No, my friends, don't be so vile. Since this man is my guest, don't do this disgraceful thing. Look, here is my virgin daughter, and his concubine. I will bring them out to you now, and you can use them and do to them whatever you wish." Judges 19:22–24

It could be a story from the *New York Times*. Worse, it could be a made-for-TV movie. But this true story line comes from the Old Testament. The report ends predictably tragic. The concubine was tossed to the perverts and died from their abuse. The concubine's master wasn't too pleased, either. Revenge was exacted.

The Bible chronicles the history of salvation—and how much people need it. Wickedness is nothing new. Violence and sexual abuse have been around since Adam and Eve vacated the Garden of Eden. The first reported sin was selfish idolatry. The second was murder. Why do these stories appear in the Bible—the *Holy* Bible?

God didn't plant this malice and corruption into the hearts and minds of people. They easily absorbed it through their own flesh and through ardent tutoring from the devil. But God also prevented this depravity from getting in the way of His plans. Many vicious events described in the Bible told of ways the devil tried to prevent God from keeping His promises. And regardless of how ugly and repulsive the sinfulness was, God overcame. Nothing can stand in the way of God's promises.

There was nothing to smile about in today's meditation. Humor has no place in brutality or savagery. But you can leave your chair smiling because nothing can stand in the way of God's promises. The Savior will come again and gather us where the News is always Good.

Filling in the 1040

Therefore go and make disciples of all nations, baptizing them in the name of the Father and of the Son and of the Holy Spirit, and teaching them to obey everything I have commanded you. Matthew 28:19–20

Sometimes you just can't win. When you do things wrong you get fined. When you do things right, you get taxed. But this meditation really isn't about taxes. Instead, it gives new meaning to the numbers 1040.

Ten-forty refers to the land area between 10 and 40 degrees north latitude on the continents of Africa and Asia. Some of the world's most impoverished people live there. Most of them haven't heard about Jesus, or they have rejected the faith. Clearly, this area reflects an urgent need for the Gospel.

Like the IRS' infamous 1040, we can't ignore the world's 1040 either. We usually set aside money to meet our governmental obligations. The connection is obvious. While God doesn't tax our considerable possessions to share with the mission fields, He did leave us an unmistakable command. "Go to all nations. Share the Good News. Teach all who will listen. Tell them how good life is with Me."

Most of us aren't gifted with missionary qualifications. Yet we can help. We can obey the Great Commission by praying for missionaries as they labor under hardship and harassment. We can pray for a great Christian revival among all those who follow false religions. We can also send money. Why not keep a can near this book? Each day before you read, deposit a quarter, dime, whatever you can afford. When the can is full, donate the coins to a mission organization. (If others hear your clinking can, they may help too!)

Taxes may be hard, but they'll be with us all our working years. Mission work is even harder. But read the ending of the Great Commission—"Surely I am with you always, to the very end of the age."

27

Equal-Opportunity Employer

Salvation is found in no one else, for there is no other name under heaven given to men by which we must be saved. Acts 4:12

If you want a humbling experience, open your local newspaper to the job guide section and mark all the jobs you're not qualified to do. Feeling humble yet? Don't go too far. Humility is like underwear. We should wear it but not show it off. Of course, humility isn't always as popular as it should be. Consider the Pharisees in Jesus' time, for example.

Pharisees prided themselves on independence—not needing a Savior to take away their sins. They imagined they obeyed God's Law and lived according to His will. When Jesus pointed out their error, they became angry. They felt quite capable of living perfectly, and they didn't need anyone doing a job they could do themselves.

People of the Old Testament hadn't set a good example either. God wanted them to call on Him for deliverance from their enemies. Occasionally, God's people forgot the source of their strength and went to battle without His help. Their inventory of spears, arrows, and warriors was no match for the enemy on such occasions. Without God they lost and remained lost.

"Equal-Opportunity Employer" is an important phrase today. But it doesn't apply to God's choice of a Savior. Only one qualified for the job. And what a job He did! From birth, to career, to death, to resurrection, to ascension into heaven, Jesus did all the right things to keep us in God's graces.

God is an equal-opportunity employer in one way, though. Regardless of the attributes we possess or lack, we are qualified to share the Gospel with others. Jesus qualified us, and the Holy Spirit authorizes us, to tell others what He has done.

See whom you can recruit for His task force. Tell others the many benefits you have as one of His workers. The retirement plan is especially good too!

Life Begins At …

We were therefore buried with Him through baptism into death in order that, just as Christ was raised from the dead through the glory of the Father, we too may live a new life. Romans 6:4

Today's meditation begins with a fill-in-the blank statement. Life begins at ____. An old slogan suggests 40 as the ripe age. To children and adolescents, life begins anytime, anywhere in the future. And some people are never as old as they want to be. So when does life really begin?

Clinical analysts don't always agree on this deceptively simple question. Most Christians would correctly claim that physical life begins at the moment of conception. But within the context of the phrase "life begins at … ," we might say that life begins the moment a person comes to faith. Good life. Abundant life. Eternal life.

When did life begin for you? People come to life at many different ages. For some, life doesn't begin until it's about to end, and they realize the only hope they have lies in Jesus Christ. Others find life shortly after they are born, even before they can think, talk, or make decisions. Receiving faith as a gift from the Holy Spirit assumes no minimum age or competencies. In fact, faith may establish stronger roots when it's not accompanied by rational thought. Consider the faith of young children. They know and believe it all when they sing, "Jesus loves me, this I know …" We older Christians tend too much toward logic and doubt.

Logic and doubt must die, as the Bible passage implies. They must die together with unbelief. Only then do we begin living. Some day we'll pass from the present life, poisoned with sin as it is, and we'll begin a new phase of life.

When does life begin? It began with a twinkle in God's eye when He knew you would be His. It began when you came to faith.

29

Passing the Buck

God made Him who had no sin to be sin for us, so that in Him we might become the righteousness of God. 2 Corinthians 5:21

Passing the buck" is an old hunting term used in reference to what the doe did with hunters hot on her trail. Okay, so that's too literal. Then it must be what some people do when the offering plate goes by. That one is too cynical, huh? Try this—it's what rodeo champs do to avoid getting kicked.

I hate to pass the buck myself, but you'll have to excuse my feeble attempts at mirth. I inherited my humor from a dead relative. Posthumously.

Passing the buck makes shame, guilt, mistakes, and weaknesses so much more tolerable. Unfortunately, it also dulls our awareness of sin and accountability. Passing the buck is a cowardly way to escape blame, defend against accusations, or shift responsibility to someone perceived as more responsible. Eventually most bucks stop passing. Some even end up where they started. Others continue in ceaseless circles. Let's examine a few common scenarios.

1. The devil-made-me-do-it syndrome. The cause of all our shortcomings is obvious. We would be much better if only the devil would stop tempting us. (The psalmist stopped that buck with Psalm 14:3.)

2. The who-me-a-sinner? syndrome. I'm basically a good person who treats others well and avoids all excesses. (John shot that buck dead in its tracks with 1 John 1:8.)

God passed the buck—from us to Jesus. He transferred all our guilt, shame, weaknesses, depravity, immorality, and defects to Jesus. And while Jesus didn't have any of these on His own, He carried them all to the cross where they lost their power to enslave believers. Once for all, Jesus took sin to the grave and left it there. It festers and rots and continues to stink up life, but it's in the grave nonetheless.

Thank God the buck stopped where it did!

30

Telling the Story

For we cannot help speaking about what we have seen and heard. Acts 4:20

When a terrorist's bomb shattered a federal building in Oklahoma City (1995), more than 10,000 people called the witness hotline with information. People felt compelled to report anything that could help authorities. Eventually, several reports yielded useful information.

That same bomb shook the airwaves with bold Christian witness. People shed their shyness trying to make sense of the tragedy. They knew there was no sense, so they relied on God to work it out— and they shared their trust over national TV and radio networks. In such adverse times, it was refreshing to hear their sincere testimony.

The apostle Peter also felt obliged to tell what he had seen and heard. His story must have warmed many hearts, and it made more than a few angry, or at least uncomfortable. (That's how it is with truth. Some people keep a respectable distance from it!) Peter's passion burned for the Gospel, and he couldn't help but tell the authorities what they needed to know. But it wasn't what they wanted to know, so they told him to be quiet.

Picture this. It's a quiet Sunday morning when a passer-by notices a squad of soldiers flat on their backs, out cold. A huge stone stands beside an open tomb behind the soldiers. The witness peers in and sees nothing. How do you report nothing? Yet that is what Peter did. He reported that nothing inhabited the tomb where Jesus was buried. He told those who would listen, as well as those who wouldn't listen, that nothing could stand in the way of salvation now that Jesus rose from the dead. He was their Savior.

Despite Peter's impassioned testimony, some chose not to believe. But others, like us, rejoiced in the news. Our joy remains even though the event is long past.

Don't wait for a bomb blast to shake your testimony loose. Give it freely. Give it bravely. Tell the story.

31

If the Clothing Fits, Wear It

I put on righteousness as my clothing. Job 29:14

A joy to some and a bane to others—that describes shopping for clothes. Finding fashionable clothing in the right size, made of comfortable material, and priced reasonably is always a challenge. The Bible has some excellent counsel for style-conscious clothing shoppers. It's almost like the departments in a clothing store. Care for a tour?

The first stop is Psalm 45:3, which advises "clothe yourself with splendor." Considering the date of this advice, the psalmist probably isn't talking about evening gowns and tuxedos. But what style could be more magnificent than the look and feel of salvation? What splendor there is in going in style!

The second stop is Isaiah 52:1—the durable clothes department. "Clothe yourself with strength." Nothing lasts as long as life in Christ, does it? It literally lasts forever. You need only one of these garments. Move on.

The next department is Colossians 3:12: "Clothe yourselves with compassion, kindness, humility, gentleness and patience." Christians find compassion always in style, though sometimes hard to find. We can get so caught up in our own spiritual "looks" that we forget what Christians are all about. Take several of these outfits so you can give them to those in need.

The fourth stop is 1 Peter 5:5—perhaps the most confusing department: "Clothe yourself with humility toward one another." Most designers create alluring clothing that attracts attention. Nevertheless, it is good to don this outfit often enough to remind us that the best-dressed people remain sinful and dirty unless they bathe themselves in much-needed forgiveness.

As with any shopping spree, the time comes to pay for the "prizes." If we think the clothes are stunning, they are nothing compared to the bill. It would take a lifetime to pay it. And that's what Jesus did. He gave His life to clothe us in the garments of righteousness. Feel free to fill your closet.

32

Trust Fund

But I trust in Your unfailing love; my heart rejoices in Your salvation.
Psalm 13:5

Trust can be as elusive as a treasure chest filled with priceless jewels. But trust can be quite common too. We trust many things because they are dependable. When you sit down, you expect the chair to be there. Turn the handle on a water faucet, and you expect water. Trust is common when we believe that ordinary (though quite remarkable) things will do what they're supposed to do and be where they're supposed to be. Experience teaches who and what we can trust.

Cynical sages advise us to trust no one. Distrust comes from experience too. Just let the car not start once, and you won't easily trust it again—at least not soon.

We may find God hard to trust at times too. Ardent prayers seem to go unanswered—at least on our terms and timeline. Disease and disaster afflict the believer as well as the heathen. Sometimes we may doubt that anyone could love us as much as Jesus did. Trust can indeed be frail. Perhaps what we need is a good role model to show us what trust is all about.

King David had one of the richest trust funds ever. He often took his task to God for guidance and help. He simply trusted God to support him.

God is a trustworthy fixture in our life too. When we need rest and comfort, we can trust Him to hold us up. If we need refreshment for heart and soul, we can turn our thirst over to Him.

Look around you. Choose an object that is always near where you read this book. Every time you see it, trust that God is always just as common, just as near. Your trust fund is as well supplied as David's.

By the way, someone probably trusts that you'll get back to work now.

You Are What You Eat

Blessed are those who hunger and thirst for righteousness, for they will be filled. ... Blessed are the pure in heart, for they will see God. Matthew 5:6, 8

Have you heard the expression "You are what you eat"? Let's hope you don't make a steady diet of nuts! Perhaps you prefer food that sticks to your ribs. But you know, of course, that's not really where the food sticks. Our tastes might better be served by hash. When it comes to hash, at least we know the cook put everything he had into the dish.

Jesus created some heavenly hash when He mixed ample portions of righteousness and purity. We can't cook up righteousness and purity ourselves. Nor can we buy it. The Master Chef put everything He had into it, even His life. Jesus Christ followed God's recipe for righteousness and purity. The ingredients included a one-of-a-kind perfection commonly known as sinlessness. Jesus' life fulfilled all the daily requirements for spiritual nourishment. His death and resurrection make this a miracle food that sustains those who indulge through eternal life. It's a true miracle food—the miracle is that it's free. All we need for an ample supply is a hunger for it.

The portions of this heavenly hash available to us on earth are only a ration of what we'll receive in heaven. Even though we dine regularly on God's righteousness and purity, we're not completely filled yet. What we are left with is a genuine, insatiable hunger. We want to be exactly like Jesus. We want to be sinless in God's sight. We hate sin and love good. Those are the degrees of righteousness and purity we possess as sanctified Christians. And it's enough for now.

Dietary experts recommend that we stop eating while we are still hungry. That's good advice for ordinary foods, but our spiritual life is sustained by stuffing ourselves with the righteousness and purity served by Jesus.

Are you ready for another helping?

34

Be Attitudes

Blessed are the meek, for they will inherit the earth. ... Blessed are the peacemakers, for they will be called sons of God. Matthew 5:5, 9

The familiar "Blessed are ..." phrases of the Beatitudes introduce some of Jesus' most popular teachings. The Beatitudes describe our new life in Christ. We might think of them as "Be" attitudes.

God's people have always needed to know how to be. The Ten Commandments revealed God's will. Jesus informed us that what we do on the outside must be matched by what others can't see—our real attitudes. To act one way and feel another is hypocrisy. The very best thing you can say about hypocrites is that they regard virtue enough to imitate it.

Jesus blesses us to be meek and to be peacemakers. We can exercise those blessings. In Christ we can be patient, tolerant, and even long-suffering. In Christ we can adopt ways and words that promote harmony and reconciliation.

Through His Word and sacraments He gives us the strength and the endurance we need to put these biblical values into practice. The motivation, the courage, and the perseverance is ours because of the new life we have in Christ Jesus.

The way of peacemaking and meekness is a gift, given to us by Jesus. Is there any better example of meekness than Jesus submitting to His Father's will and suffering for our sins? And how about the time He washed His disciples' feet? But His ability to make peace was even more important. His Gospel promotes genuine harmony. Best of all, He brought peace between God and us. Our sinful selves war against God. We deserve punishment and destruction. But Christ's death and resurrection wiped out our sins. We are at peace with God, and He is at peace with us. Now we are free to enjoy and practice the blessings of peace and meek service to others.

Bless you.

How Are Your Spirits?

Blessed are the poor in spirit, for theirs is the kingdom of heaven.
Matthew 5:3

How are your spirits today—up, down, nowhere? Most often, when we speak of spirits, we refer to emotions. However, it's a mistake to use that connotation for the first of the beatitudes. Then again, if you watch the faces of some people as they worship, you would think they are the most blessed people in the world!

Worded as it is, our beatitude for today presents some challenges. Social scientists might suggest that Jesus' words refer to poor people. Surely, Jesus came to save the poor. But He came for all people regardless of their income. Such an interpretation cheats this beautiful beatitude.

The poor in spirit that Jesus talks about are people who recognize their spiritual helplessness. They know they can't possibly obtain a perfect relationship with God. Their souls, like the wallets of poor people, are empty. The only thing these "blessed" people have to offer God is sin. Now, that they have lots of! The poor in spirit might just as well stand in the middle of a city street holding a sign that says "Homeless—Can you spare a sandwich or some change?" Picture yourself that way. How can that be blessed?

Beggars in Christ really know what it is to be blessed. When you have nothing, any gift at all is reason for profuse gratitude. We spiritual beggars have nothing. We can't even go to work and earn God's love. We just don't have what it takes. God noticed we had nowhere to go—we were homeless and stranded on an island of despair. We were suffering the consequences of sin—ours as well as those who came before us and all those who live around us. But God, through Jesus Christ, gave us what we need. In fact, He gave us more than any beggar could dare hope. He gave us a whole kingdom.

Enjoy your blessings. But keep your spirits poor.

36

Christian Chameleons

To the weak I became weak, to win the weak. I have become all things to all men so that by all possible means I might save some. 1 Corinthians 9:22

Hopefully, you're not one of those people whose weaknesses are the strongest thing about them. Do you know people like that?

Now, if you were to follow Paul's example, how would you reach those who need to know that Jesus isn't some stuffed toga who cares only about people who go to church and read religious books? Does Paul suggest that you adopt sinful ways to attract sinful people to Christ?

Paul's Jewish colleagues thought he was guilty of breaking God's law because he ate with Gentiles—non-Jewish people. He not only ate with them, he ate what they ate. Therein was the problem. Devout Jews restricted their diets to certain types of food; all others were forbidden. But Paul considered none of these old laws as important as winning new believers. All believers were freed from such ceremonial laws by Jesus.

Which religious practices may we ignore and which must we practice? God guided Paul to know where to draw the line. He led Paul to know when to act like a chameleon and when to hold firm to his beliefs and practices. Study Paul and you'll find that he wouldn't compromise when it came to faith in Jesus or acceptance of God's authority over all of life. But he did step away from common traditions and religious practices when it was incidental to real faith.

We don't have to curse with the verbally deprived nor need we dabble with other religions to win others to Christ. We simply need to act like Christ when in the presence of these people. He didn't threaten and He didn't give in. He simply lived what He spoke and taught.

Your break is over. See how weak you can become to win someone for Christ.

Heart Condition

Above all else, guard your heart, for it is the wellspring of life. Proverbs 4:23

We must subscribe to the same school of wisdom as Solomon. The heart remains the seat of desire. Doctors know the heart beats the rhythm of life. Poets and lovers see the heart as the place where affection and emotions dwell. The Bible cautions against hard hearts like the stony one inside Pharaoh when he wouldn't free captive Israel. (It's said that the only thing worse than hard-heartedness is soft-headedness.) And so, as Proverbs indicates, the heart, in whatever context, is a wellspring of life.

Place your hand over your heart. You're not a doctor, but you know you're alive. *Thump thump. Thump thump. Thump thump.* That little thumper is pushing blood through thousands of miles of veins and arteries inside your body. You depend on its operation to keep you alive, yet it works on its own, without your planning or management!

Paul said, "For it is with your heart that you believe and are justified, and it is with your mouth that you confess and are saved" (Romans 10:10). Paul's view of the heart was less clinical, but he recognized its life-supporting significance just the same. He would probably promote activities that maintain healthy hearts too.

First, exercise is vital. Doctors often recommend vigorous walks. Paul might recommend the same—with Jesus for a companion. Although Jesus isn't here to match us step for step, we walk with Him in our meditation and prayers. He's close by, and He promises to guide us.

Second, diet is important. Debates toss about pros and cons of every conceivable food and nutrient, and it's hard to be sure that we're eating the right foods. But Paul's spiritual diet consists of only one item—God's Word. How pleasant to know that we can never consume too much of His nutrition!

Coffee breaks are great times for exercise and snacks, aren't they?

38

Memories

But the Counselor, the Holy Spirit, whom the Father will send in My name, will teach you all things and will remind you of everything I have said to you. John 14:26

You know your memory is failing if you …
- forget the words to "Happy Birthday."
  - can't recall your last mistake.
    - don't remember how long your break lasts.
      - thought the TV rerun was new.
        - go fishing and always catch the limit.

Oh, to be that proverbial elephant that never forgets! Then again, what do they have to remember?

Memories play a prominent role in life. It seems the older we get, the more we live with memories. When you think about it, that's not very profound. Naturally, the older we are the more memories we have. Memory is important from a spiritual vantage point too.

As you read in today's passage, Jesus told His disciples that the Holy Spirit would teach them new things and also remind them of all that He had said. The memories of Jesus preaching, teaching, healing, forgiving, laughing, crying, dying, and rising would come to the disciples when they needed to proclaim Christ. The Holy Spirit would also refresh their memories when they needed to recall all that Christ had done for them. The key to their memories was the Holy Spirit—not their own untrustworthy memory banks. How comforting for us who have a poor or deteriorating memory!

An old friend once worried, "I'm afraid I might get Alzheimer's—then I might forget about Jesus my Savior." As tragic as Alzheimer's is, and as unsettling as normal memory loss may be, we can be certain that we'll never forget our faith. The Holy Spirit just won't let us forget. Besides, He placed faith in our souls, not our minds.

39

It Doesn't Count

Blessed is he whose transgressions are forgiven, whose sins are covered. Blessed is the man whose sin the LORD does not count against him and in whose spirit is no deceit. Psalm 32:1–2

Imagine this newspaper article:

Sin Is Dead

WASHINGTON, D.C.—Today … the courts unanimously and unequivocally declared sin dead and gone. In a cleverly worded decision, the courts have made all sins legal.

David had something else in mind when he declared the words of Psalm 32. He had recently confessed his worst atrocity. In an attempt to cover his lust and illicit affair with Bathsheba, he had her husband killed so he could legally marry her. But God knew exactly what happened. He let guilt play some useful havoc on David's conscience.

David says, "When I kept silent, my bones wasted away. … Day and night Your hand was heavy upon me" (vv. 3, 4).

Like David, we commonly experience guilt for wrongdoing. How many family arguments have kept you awake nights? What have you tried to cover up so others won't know? These are the aching bones and heavy hands David talked about. Good thing David shared with us what he did next. He repented.

Repentance is the gracious loophole through which God lets us escape eternal damnation for Jesus' sake. Repentance begins with sorrow over sins. Sorrow invites confession. David confessed before the prophet Nathan and God Himself. Praise God for accepting the apologies of sinners! He accepted David's, and He will always accept ours too.

Repentance also involves a change of behavior—a desire to do good rather than evil. (This is the hard part. The devil is rather fond of sin, and he'll do everything possible to prevent its extinction!) The desire, like the forgiveness, springs from the Holy Spirit, who empowers us to hate sin and fight it.

The "bottom line" is that God completely forgives and forgets. Why cover up sins ourself when Jesus does such a complete job of it?

40

Welcome Any Time

And you will receive a rich welcome into the eternal kingdom of our Lord and Savior Jesus Christ. 2 Peter 1:11

Peter spoke these words to conclude his teaching on godliness and obedience. He taught believers what to do after they became believers. Like Peter's pupils, we too look forward to the welcome Jesus has planned for all the faithful at the end of time.

We won't be the only ones welcome on Judgment Day. Already we've got a large bandwagon of believers to join, so it would be good to hop aboard without delay. And it's also good to practice some godly manners along the way.

Goodness, knowledge, self-control, perseverance, godliness, brotherly kindness, and love (2 Peter 1:5–7). Those were Peter's principles for the well-equipped Christian. Let's see now, which one are you good at? Peter wouldn't settle for just one, however. His answer would be all of the above. Whoops! That places some burdens on Christians, doesn't it? Don't despair.

The Holy Spirit has already changed our lives with the gift of faith. Now He is blessing us with an ever-increasing ability to practice the virtues of faith. Note the word *practice*. That's what makes perfect. However, before we reach perfection (elsewhere), our practice affects others. God wants us to influence others, to be a kind of spiritual salesperson, offering the Gospel to customers, eager or otherwise. The tools of effective earthly salesmanship are really the tools of practical Gospel pitching.

If people like you because you're good, kind, self-controlled, loving, and hard-working, you'll always be welcome in their company. And you'll always have opportunities to confess why you're so nice. Perhaps they will even come to you when they need greater portions of your godly goodness.

Finally, just as others welcome your presence, Jesus will welcome you to eternal life. Not because you earned it, but because He earned it for you.

41

Together with Thomas

Then He [Jesus] said to Thomas, "Put your finger here; see My hands. Reach out your hand and put it into My side. Stop doubting and believe." Thomas said to Him, "My Lord and my God!" John 20:27–28

Thomas believed his doubts and doubted his beliefs. He put a question mark where God put a period. We, like Thomas, also need to touch the scars of Jesus once in awhile.

The best way to combat doubt is to fortify our faith. Prayer—talking things over with God—is one good way of reinforcing faith. You already know how "talking things out" works with others. For example, one day your daughter comes home and remarks, "I don't think you love me anymore." You would want to know why she felt that way, and reassure her of your love. A heart-to-heart talk, along with further evidence of your love, would likely resolve the situation.

Like Thomas, we need to talk over our doubts with God:

"Good morning, God. I'm on break now, so I have only a few moments to talk to You. I'm sorry, but sometimes You're just unbelievable. So little on earth confirms Your existence. How can You be three Persons, yet only one God? And I don't understand how You could send Yourself to earth so You could actually die, then raise Yourself from the dead! Sometimes I think You've given up on me because I don't feel very holy. That's what You're supposed to do, isn't it—make me holier every day?"

This conversation could continue through many breaks—as long as we have time to think up more doubts. We sometimes doubt because nothing in our present existence equals God's goodness. Instead of relying on experience, we must trust His Word. Through the Bible, God assures us of His love and drives away our doubts. When we pray to God, we need to read rather than hear or see His answers, promises, and comfort. Then we can exclaim together with Thomas, "My Lord and my God!"

42

Who Needs It?

When the Pharisees saw this, they asked His disciples, "Why does your teacher eat with tax collectors and 'sinners'?" On hearing this, Jesus said, "It is not the healthy who need a doctor, but the sick." Matthew 9:11–12

The easiest way to make friends is with a warm heart (as opposed to a hot head). The biggest barrier to making friends is holding your nose higher than your head.

Jesus really knew how to make friends, not that He needed them but because they needed Him. Though He was God in the flesh, He was neither pompous nor conceited. And He wasn't shy, either. He gently but persistently befriended people.

Some Christians seek to shelter their life with only the company of other Christians. Fellowship with other believers is important and desirable, but who benefits from associating only with others of similar beliefs?

It's possible these days to associate exclusively with "announced Christians." Christian business directories lead us to faithful plumbers, contractors, printers, florists, and even used car dealers. (Sorry.) Presumably, this helps Christians share their faith and fees with each other, and that's okay. But carried to an extreme, it can lead to the kind of religious aristocracy Jesus dealt with in today's text.

Dear Christian, you are free to associate with anyone who might be influenced by your faith. So if you employ a pagan plumber, maybe your language, kindness, and the cross on your wall will give him something to stick in his pipe. And you may impress the used car salesperson with your integrity, fairness, and gentle tire kicking.

Don't abandon your Christian companions, and above all, don't let others lead you astray. But don't be afraid to eat lunch or share coffee or do business with sinners. You may even discover that they are just like you—also saints. And even if they are unbelievers, the Holy Spirit can work through your words and actions to bring Jesus into their lives.

Loyal Citizens

But our citizenship is in heaven. And we eagerly await a Savior from there, the Lord Jesus Christ. Philippians 3:20

Ask the boss for a raise. You might convince her it's the company's patriotic duty to raise the income of a loyal citizen like you. After all, the government could certainly use the extra tax money! It would probably take less time for the boss to respond than it took to read this paragraph, so perhaps your time is better spent thinking about your citizenship.

Typically, citizenship involves allegiance to a country. U.S. citizens are expected to pay taxes, support their country with prayers, fight for sovereignty, and sing the national anthem at ball games. In return, the country owes its citizens protection, service agencies, social security, and highway repairs.

Thank God our foremost citizenship is in heaven. Isn't it unusual to maintain citizenship in a place we've never seen? Fortunately, God has revealed enough about heaven to make us yearn for the day when we fully celebrate our citizenship.

How does citizenship in heaven compare with earthly citizenship? No comparison, you confess. You're right. But there are similarities. Take freedom for instance (but not for granted). Our King allows the same freedoms extended to all Americans. We are free to be disloyal if we choose. We are free to leave the borders and seek citizenship elsewhere. We speak freely even if it's offensive to our Leader. The King doesn't make us His puppets.

The King chose to make us citizens, extending the benefits of forgiveness and everlasting life to each of us. What He expects in return is our willingness to serve Him, to dedicate all that we do and say to Him. It may seem like an unfair deal (for God). But the King wants us anyway.

44

Happy Campers

"Watch me," he told them. "Follow my lead. When I get to the edge of the camp, do exactly as I do." Judges 7:17

Camping is the happy pastime of millions of people, but it's certainly not new. Just ask Gideon.

Gideon sounds like a helpful campground director in the brief verse above. But he was about to embark on dangerous business for God in Jericho. The inhabitants of Jericho were God's enemies, and Gideon's job was to defeat them. But Gideon had a unique problem—too many soldiers! God wanted an army of 300 rather than the 32,000 at Gideon's disposal. God didn't want these soldiers to carry conventional weapons either. Trumpets, jars, and the Secret Weapon would do the job. When the day of the battle came, God's enemies crumbled in defeat.

Lest we get sidetracked, the moral of the story is not to look for uncrowded campgrounds. What we learn from Camp Commander Gideon is to trust God, especially when we face powerful, frightening, spiteful enemies. God is our Secret Weapon. The devil and our own human nature are the enemies.

Sin builds a dense wall around itself, but it doesn't stay inside its fortress. It makes well-planned raids against God's people. If all the Christians in the world formed an army to crush sin, it couldn't win. Too many soldiers. God needed only one soldier, and He won the war even though He appeared to lose it.

The war is over, but sin continues its terrorist attacks. To remain happy campers, we need to know who fights our battles because we can't do it alone. Today, we rely on the Holy Spirit as our Secret Weapon. When the Spirit directs us to Christ, we can survive sin's onslaught, even when we become our own worst enemy. The Spirit speaks to our hearts and minds by revealing God's will to us in the Holy Scriptures.

Trust God with all that threatens or attacks you. And don't forget your trumpet and jar.

Christt-Confidence

So, if you think you are standing firm, be careful that you don't fall! No temptation has seized you except what is common to man. And God is faithful; He will not let you be tempted beyond what you can bear. But when you are tempted, He will also provide a way out so that you can stand up under it.
1 Corinthians 10:12–13

Some define confidence as what a person feels before he knows what's really going on! For the average person, confidence is something we have until it's shaken from us. And then we remain shaken—and shaky.

Temptations challenge our confidence. Conversion, Baptism, Bible study, and Christian fellowship all work to assemble and strengthen our faith. We become confident Christians, poised to live devoutly in a sin-filled world. We fend off confrontations with the worst of sins—murder, adultery, witchcraft, rape, and robbery. Confident that we can withstand anything Satan and the world flings at us, we confidently ignore our "little sins"—until they devour our confidence.

Shaken and frightened sinners were part of Paul's world too. That's why God directed Paul to write the words in today's passage. How good for Christian confidence! We can (and must) ask God to help us abandon *all* our sins. (Little sins are inclined to grow like cancerous tumors!) But what about the "bigger" temptations that lead to bigger sins?

Indeed, some temptations are too big for us to face. But when they attack and we retreat, we can be confident that God won't let us be assaulted by anything we can't handle. He keeps those temptations from claiming us.

Confident Christians walk a thin line. We err when we become self-confident, counting on our own noble nature to resist temptation. We walk in complete confidence only when we have Christ-confidence.

46

The Do-It-Yourself Syndrome

"No," said Peter, "You shall never wash my feet." John 13:8

Peter was developing a reputation for denials. But this one was dire. At face value, his refusal to let Jesus wash his feet seems admirable. Why would any devout person permit the King of kings and Lord of lords (Hallelujah!) to perform a task so menial that servants even avoided it? Would you or I tolerate such servitude, say, from the President of the United States? He's too important for lint-picking. How about from someone we love and respect more than anyone else? We love them too much to allow them to stoop so low. We can do it ourselves.

Peter had to be stunned when Jesus responded, "Unless I wash you, you have no part with Me." With that said, a chastised and wiser Peter asked for a whole bath! His story teaches us not to toy with the Do-It-Yourself Syndrome.

Oddly enough, many of us fail to fully appreciate the magnitude of Jesus' humility. We think of Him as gentle, kind, meek, caring, and—humble. But we sometimes miss how humiliating humility was for Him. Washing a pair of filthy feet was one thing. But worse was His bout with the sins of the world. He could have turned this cesspool of sin into pure water with a single command. Instead, He followed the laws that He Himself established for people. He suffered and died in place of sinners because of their self-imposed broken relationship with Him—but only after obeying all the laws for them. Did the gods of any other people ever so humiliate themselves? Of course not. The devil never humiliates himself, either. He only humiliates his victims.

Peter was momentarily the devil's victim. At first he wanted to clean himself. But then he learned that Jesus was the only one who could make him clean enough for God.

Next time you're washing your feet, remember Jesus. Invite Him to give you a whole bath. You'll never be cleaner.

47

Enough Is Enough

Now we see but a poor reflection as in a mirror; then we shall see face to face. Now I know in part; then I shall know fully, even as I am fully known. 1 Corinthians 13:12

"What do you know?" was once a common greeting. Usually the response was brief, and no one gave it serious thought.

Wise people seem unsatisfied with what they know, and they constantly strive to learn more. Ignorance is not bliss. (We can be happy about that.) Is the same true for Christians?

Close your eyes for a moment (but not if you're tired). Think of three things you would like to know about God that you don't know now.

Perhaps you can find the answers to your questions by using a topical Bible or asking a pastor. But the most difficult questions may not have answers readily available. Some examples? How about a practical explanation of the Trinity? How could Jesus rise from the dead? How can anything have no beginning or end? How did God really create giraffes? Did Pontius Pilate repent and go to heaven? What did Jesus really look like? If you're involved in a lively Bible class, you're likely to hear even more questions and speculation as to the answers. To use a religious term, the questions could go on for eternity.

Did you notice anything all the questions had in common? Not one asked anything truly important. None inquired as to how we are saved or what we must do to receive forgiveness. Is it because we don't care about those answers? Hardly. It is because we already know the answers! A truly wonderful thing about the Bible is that it makes us question many things. But even better, the Bible makes the most important information so simple that even children understand it. What could be more uncomplicated than Jesus loves you? He took your sins away. You will live with Him in heaven. Those aren't answers. Those are promises.

Study your Bible. But know when enough is enough.

48

Star Struck

Those who are wise will shine like the brightness of the heavens, and those who lead many to righteousness, like the stars for ever and ever. Daniel 12:3

Today's passage sounds like a poetic goal of someone seeking success. In reality, it's more like the motto of someone who spent a lifetime becoming an overnight success.

These words from Daniel provide a picture of the end times—when earth ends and we join all other believers in the indescribable delights of heaven. Therefore, they don't speak of the present as much as the future. If the words have struck your soul, however, you're headed for stardom yourself.

Most present stars, movie or otherwise, didn't achieve success by sitting around and waiting for it. They discovered that the secret of success is hard work, or as someone put it, they started from scratch and kept on scratching! But we Christians have an advantage—we are successful right now! Christ gave us all the success we need. Now He wants us to use our success to successfully lead others to Him. And He will even help us do it.

If our goal is to become a star, we've missed the point of being Christ's chosen ones. Besides, the sky has so many stars that only astronomers can tell them apart. Christ's chosen stars must shine on those who live in the darkness of ignorance—on those who don't recognize the true star, Jesus Christ. How, then, can we burn brightly?

As God's stars, we burn with energy created by Jesus Christ. We warm those in our presence with love, compassion, and understanding. We light the way through black holes of sin. We share God's warmth and light through our actions and our words. And as we grow in faith—through Bible study, prayer, and the Lord's Supper—we shine even brighter.

Look up at the sky tonight. Think of each star as one of your fellow Christians working to lead others to their Savior.

Twinkle, twinkle little star.

Get the Devil out of Here

Submit yourselves, then, to God. Resist the devil, and he will flee from you. Come near to God and He will come near to you. James 4:7–8

The devil hasn't spent a single minute unemployed. And he certainly doesn't look forward to retirement! Thank God no one will assume his duties once he goes. The problem is that we have to cope with his atrocities from now until Judgment Day.

The devil is real. We don't know what he looks like, but we surely feel his influence. He is a master of attractive disguises, and he plants in human minds plausible excuses for every depravity imaginable. He'll try anything on anyone to sever their relationship with God. He wrapped his coils around Eve and Adam, squeezing innocence from their free will. He appeared through history as stone sculptures, wooden statues, and golden cows. His most foolhardy attack was on Jesus Himself. Theologian Martin Luther recognized his bouts with the devil and had a fitting, if crude, way of dismissing him. (It had something to do with well-aimed flatulence.)

We must be alert when the devil trespasses on our souls. James simply says, "Resist." But resisting Satan can be more strenuous than outrunning a swarm of mosquitos on a forest path at dusk. Gratefully, James adds, "Come near to God and He will come near to you." That's the formula for resisting the devil. Remain close to God; He's here to help.

Prayer and Bible study are like magnets that keep us close to God. Bible study keeps us acutely aware of God's work and His will. It helps us discern right from wrong. Prayer is where we ask God for strength to resist, or we may simply turn the matter over to Him if our resistance is low. "Hey, God, get the devil out of here" is a spiritual 911 prayer to remember. And you might want to add Luther's technique—just to let Satan know how you feel about him.

Party Time

I tell you that in the same way there will be more rejoicing in heaven over one sinner who repents than over ninety-nine righteous persons who do not need to repent. Luke 15:7

Earthly parties could never match the heavenly celebration over repentant sinners. Can you see the banner stretching from cloud to cloud? It says "Welcome Back" in a rainbow of colors.

Do you note any cynicism in today's passage? When Jesus spoke these words, He wasn't conceding that sinners comprise a 1 percent minority of the population. He was referring to people who *think* they are righteous. They are lost until they lose their sense of self-righteousness.

"Repentant sinner" might be an embarrassing name tag to wear in public. Imagine the stares and the snickers. Neighbors might whisper, "I wonder what he did?" Scoffers might comment, "There goes another victim of the church!" Others would dismiss us as unstable fanatics. The repentant sinner label was equally regarded in Jesus' time. Otherwise He wouldn't have spoken these words.

The minority of us who appreciate our title know the importance of repentance. Through repentance Christians take hold of Jesus' invitation to salvation. Much to our chagrin, the angels conduct "welcome back" parties a little too often. Daily, in fact. But God certainly is gracious. Make a fool of yourself at someone's backyard party, and you probably won't get invited again. But God is different—for Jesus' sake. Instead of saying, "Not you again," He says, "Welcome back." And He will say it over and over until that time when you join the angels in heaven.

It's true that repentance includes more than sorrow. We need to abandon our sins. With our human frailty, when we abandon one sin, another usually takes its place. Sometimes the best we can do is just abhor sin, and return to God's profuse forgiveness.

Next time you're outside, aim a wave and a smile into the sky. The angels are holding a party to celebrate *you*.

Separation Anxiety

For I am convinced that neither death nor life, neither angels nor demons, neither the present nor the future, nor any powers, neither height nor depth, nor anything else in all creation, will be able to separate us from the love of God that is in Christ Jesus our Lord. Romans 8:38–39

The little boy peered over the service counter in the department store. An announcement had summoned his mother several minutes ago. As Mom came into view, her little boy raced up and stood squarely, hands on hips, before her. Before she could speak, he asked, "How come you wandered away from me?"

We can get it backwards too. Take the Romans passage, for example. For many, it may seem to guarantee that believers would never fall away from God—you know, once saved always saved. How could this be true when all believers experience lapses in faith?

Christians may regress into a self-centered focus on Bible passages. We do that when we concentrate exclusively on what *we* can do rather than what *God* has done and continues to do. This book, like many others, encourages readers to act on their faith. But I pray that you will always know why you obey God's will. All the good we do is a response to God's love through Jesus Christ. Pray that the Holy Spirit enables us to strike the proper balance between recognizing God's love and applying it.

The affirmation in Romans 8 refers to God's faithfulness. God remains available to us. We must never ask, "Where were You?" Nor may we accuse Him of wandering away. Like the young child in the opening anecdote, we must realize that God is here even when we are there.

Nothing can destroy God's love for us. Our sins may sadden or anger Him, but He still loves us. We may exercise too much spiritual freedom, but He still loves us. Our faith may weaken, but He won't—He still loves us.

P.S. Next time you're out with your Father, try not to wander. But in case you do, He'll find you again.

52

You're Not Getting Older, You're Getting ...

Even to your old age and gray hairs I am He, I am He who will sustain you. I have made you and I will carry you; I will sustain you and I will rescue you. Isaiah 46:4

Don't be discouraged by gray hair. You're not getting older, you're getting better.

We are all headed toward our next birthday. And our next birthday brings us closer to our final birthday. Some may not want to think about that prospect, but we need not fear it. Before we get there, God has promised to care for us. He uses words like *sustain, carry,* and *rescue.*

Sustain means that God will keep us going. (*Note:* This is not the same as prune juice.) Regardless of our age, our Father is always older—and wiser and stronger and everything else that makes a good father. He promises to bolster our faith even though our bodies sag and bend. A newspaper once interviewed a woman who had passed her 100th birthday. When asked how she got that old, she responded, "I think maybe God forgot about me." Isaiah assures us that God does not forget about us. He promises to keep our most important function—faith—in good health.

Carry was another of God's promises to the aging. Many older people fear loss of mobility. Legs weaken, hips break, and strokes paralyze. But God promises to carry us, not to the grocery store or bingo game, but through disappointments, pain, and even death.

Lastly, God promises to *rescue* us wherever we are: living alone, in a retirement villa, from a hospital bed. He also promises to rescue those who've aged only a little bit—from the crib, the classroom, the busy office, or the endless interstates. And, of course, He takes care of all the time in-between.

We're not getting older, we're actually getting younger. We are counting down to the time when we'll open our eyes like a newborn. And we'll never close them again.

Workers Unite!

Slaves, obey your earthly masters in everything; and do it, not only when their eye is on you and to win their favor, but with sincerity of heart and reverence for the Lord. Whatever you do, work at it with all your heart, as working for the Lord, not for men. Colossians 3:22–23

How many people work where you do? (Ask the same question of your boss and the answer may be, "About half of them!")

Today's meditation doesn't address organized labor as the title might suggest. Instead, it deals with the work ethic. Paul makes laboriously clear what God expects from Christian workers. (Paul does not encourage slavery, nor does he treat it as a social issue. He simply addresses those who find themselves in that position. We could substitute the word *workers* in the same way.)

Christian employees should take God's Word seriously. They strive to be honest, fair, and hard-working even when nobody is watching. (Paul also addresses "masters" or employers in Colossians 3. If you are one—a boss or employer, that is—be sure to read it.)

Christian workers advertise the Gospel through their work ethic. They show that their hearts and minds have changed from a what-do-I-get-out-of-it attitude to a what-can-I-do-to-help attitude. Their perspective comes from what they know about Jesus Christ. Never one to stretch His coffee break (Are you watching the clock?), Jesus used every waking moment on the job. He didn't fret about how many days He was away from home. He didn't even have one! He traveled constantly as He preached and taught, healed and forgave, listened and loved. As Paul implies in Colossians, work doesn't always result in fair rewards. But the Christian worker's reward is in heaven even if it doesn't happen on earth.

Why don't you surprise everyone today? Quit your coffee break early, and get back to work. And if nobody is watching, feel doubly blessed. Jesus has awarded you a wonderful bonus—a true Christian work ethic. Workers unite! Unite with Christ!

Pray without What?

Pray continually. 1 Thessalonians 5:17

We do not know what we ought to pray for, but the Spirit Himself intercedes for us with groans that words cannot express. Romans 8:26

"Pray continually" leaves one wondering whether the meaning is literal or figurative. It's a little of both, if that's possible. While we don't need to be on our knees 24 hours a day, we do need to commit our entire day to Christ. Verbal prayers occupy a brief time, but our unconscious commitment and reliance on God occupy the rest.

What we pray for is important too. When in need, we know exactly what we want. We don't, however, always know what we need. (We would be in grave trouble if God answered prayers according to our specifications!) Then there are times when we mistakenly use God as an errand boy or to do odd jobs for us. Proper prayer always includes complete trust in God's will, regardless of what we ask. God takes care of that problem too.

Since we sometimes pray foolishly, or don't know what to pray for, and certainly fall short of continual prayer, the Holy Spirit steps in where only God can go. God surely understands whatever language people speak. But the Spirit's language goes beyond what any human language can express. How comforting to know that God lets nothing stand between our prayer commitment to Him and His faithfulness in answering our prayer. Let's pray right now.

Lord Jesus, thank You for enabling me to speak to our heavenly Father. Please give me wisdom so my prayers ask that His will be done before my will is done.

Dear Father, thank You for listening even though I sometimes babble. I give my whole life to You as a prayer. I trust You to do what is best.

And Holy Spirit, You know me better than I know myself. And thank You for obeying Your own command—You know, "Pray continually"—on my behalf. Amen.

Durable Finish

What does the LORD *require of you? To act justly and to love mercy and to walk humbly with your God. Micah 6:8*

For years, one of the most durable countertop finishes was called Formica. (Warning! Pun ahead.) For Micah, and for God, believers must wear a durable finish composed of justice, mercy, and humility. These traits come not so much from conscious effort as they do from methodical reaction to God's love.

Anyone can be just, merciful, and humble without a personal relationship with God. Some of the world's most generous philanthropists would certainly qualify, even without a declaration of faith. But their mercy and their behavior may be motivated by gratitude for good luck or a belief in the goodness of humanity in general. Micah would probably agree that positive attributes without faith in no way spiritually benefit the giver.

But is it fair for Micah to even ask what the Lord requires of us? After all, didn't Jesus do everything necessary? And isn't faith the only thing required of us? The answer to both questions is yes. However, as we might expect, a loud *but* intervenes. But what?

Jesus did it all, *but* now He expects (yes, *expects!*) us to act like Him. While grace is free and no prerequisites hinder its distribution, grace actually costs us our sinful lives. But, that may not be as radical as it sounds.

Christian workers perform their duties out of love for Jesus. The service may be the same without Christ, but the motivation makes a meaningful difference. Without that motivation, a person would stop serving as soon as that service is unappreciated, unnoticed, ridiculed, or scorned. The motivation of Christ puts a durable finish on relationships—relationships built on love, commitment, and obedience to Christ.

How about you? For Micah, it was justice, humility, and mercy. Micah knew about those things because he received all of them from God. You have too. Be a durable Christian—and don't worry about the scratches or mars.

Who's Who

Who am I, O Sovereign LORD, and what is my family that You have brought me this far? … For the sake of Your word and according to Your will, You have done this great thing and made it known to Your servant.
2 Samuel 7:18, 21

The family that prays together stays together" is a popular expression. After a recent hedge-trimming episode in consort with my wife, she quipped, "The family that prays together stays together, but the family that trims bushes together grows apart!"

God richly blessed David's family. That doesn't mean that his family avoided serious strife. David himself didn't always act like God's gift to his children. So it was entirely appropriate that David, knowing what was behind and suspecting what was ahead, recognized God's Gospel influence in his life. (Even before the word *Gospel* was invented!) Who was he to receive so many blessings? Certainly a miserable sinner with no merit of his own. Yet God loved David and had a purpose for him.

How blessed is your family? (Should that be a question mark or an exclamation point?!) Why should God bother with you? If you're busy thinking of reasons for God's attention, take a deep breath and go back to David's prayer. While you may have no murderers, adulterers, or rebellious children, your family is not without sin. Yet He comes to you and has a purpose for your life too.

God wants to accomplish His will through us. For David, it meant victoriously leading a nation through endless wars. As a result, David made the Who's Who of Kings. But God's will went beyond battle victories. God promised that the Savior would be from David's clan. God's will for us is to bring His Word into the world, and He preserves us to carry out His wishes. Isn't that wonderful news? Even though we're sometimes weak and often sinful, He wants us to bring His Good News to others just like us. And when we do a good job of that, people will really know Who's Who!

Mind Your Own Business

Make it your ambition to lead a quiet life, to mind your own business and to work with your hands, just as we told you, so that your daily life may win the respect of outsiders and so that you will not be dependent on anybody.
1 Thessalonians 4:11–12

Some people just can't mind their own business. Perhaps it's because they have small minds and even less business.

Paul's counsel to those who are tempted to gossip and meddle in other people's business was to keep quiet and keep busy. It was godly guidance too, because we find Jesus observing that practice even as He minded His Father's business. Jesus exercised good timing when He talked. We don't find Him interrupting His friends and followers. He wasn't rude to His enemies, either. And when it came to keeping busy, He was (and is!) the champion. Jesus even knew when someone in a crowd touched His clothing because she believed He could heal her. As He taught on a hillside, He observed that His audience was hungry, so He literally made a meal for all of them. Jesus was even busy under the torture of the cross. He saved a thief, made provisions for His mother, and forgave His murderers. He was too busy to say, "I knew we shouldn't trust Judas," or "You should have seen what I saw in Pilate's house." Jesus' business was God the Father's business.

God's business is our business too. We mind it by doing it. When we see something that others drool to know about, we need to "tell it all"—to God. Oh, He already knows all the dirt about everybody (including us), but it's good to express our concerns and ask Him to intervene or carry out His will.

Minding your own business has fringe benefits too. As Paul said, those who do, often win the respect of others. It's a good thing for people to respect Christians—to say things like "He never has a bad thing to say about anybody." Now that's a good piece of gossip!

The Same Old Story

Finally, my brothers, rejoice in the Lord! It is no trouble for me to write the same things to you again, and it is a safeguard for you. Philippians 3:1

Some people are bored at those Sunday school Christmas pro-grams. They complain, "It's the same old story over and over and over again." You've probably noticed that this book also is redundant. You read repeatedly about what God has done for us. And you're constantly summoned to respond to God's love. That's how it is with life in Christ. The same old thing—over and over again.

We could become defiant or despondent if the "same old story" wasn't such Good News. How horrific if we had nagging replays of Jeremiah's doomsday prophecies or if Lent were not followed by Easter! Such news would tempt us to hate God, or at least fear Him beyond approach. Thank God for His annual reruns of Christmas and Easter!

Regardless of how often we hear it, God still loves the world so much that He sent His only Son to save it. Jesus' story always includes His unconditional love for sinners. And though few stories survive retelling without losing meaning, the narrative of Jesus' life, death, and resurrection always means that we who live in Christ will die in Christ and rise to live with Him forever.

If we ever get bored with the Good News, we can always look at the disgusting repetition of bad news. Newspapers assault our val-ues with graphic accounts of violence, murder, cheating, and steal-ing. When we review our own life, we recognize our feeble attempts to live according to God's will as well as our outright refusal to obey Him. And yet the Good News persists. For each sin and every crime, Jesus offers forgiveness. Redundantly! And as often as we repeat the phrase "I'm sorry," we hear Jesus say, "I forgive you." The same old story remains the same old story. It's God's way of safeguarding us. So "Rejoice in the Lord always. I will say it again: Rejoice!" (Philippians 4:4)

Take Me to Your Leader

In the beginning God created the heavens and the earth. Genesis 1:1

Dateline: July 13, 1994—NASA reports that its Galileo spacecraft released the Jupiter space probe. It will free-fall more than 50,000 miles into the gaseous atmosphere of Jupiter, delivering previously unknown data. One reporter comments, "We hope the probe teaches us more about the origin of the universe." Scientists also hope to use the Hubble Space Telescope to trace the history of the universe.

I don't know the enormous price tag on our persistent endeavors to discover earth's roots. We might be better served if evolution-influenced scientists reformed and tried to answer useful questions, such as how birds know exactly when we've washed the car. And it's a shameful waste when you consider that both our past and our future appear in the Bible. You don't even need to read the whole Bible—just the first and last chapters.

The Bible isn't very scientific, it's true. Readers need to believe in a real God who so far surpasses human intelligence that we can't explain how He functions. We need faith in Jesus Christ to believe that God is so good that He saved us from ourselves. Our faith also sustains our acceptance of how the Bible says the world will end (bad) and what will happen to us (good).

No, the Bible isn't scientific. Or is it? Science is built on many theories. Theories are beliefs built upon fragile human knowledge and speculation. Beliefs! The Bible rests on stories told by God through those who believed in Him. Beliefs again!

I don't mean to disqualify scientists from God's grace. As with anything, science harms or helps depending on how it's used. And if scientific "knowledge" takes precedence in your life, please don't close these pages in disgust. But do consider one thing. When an awesome figure descends through the clouds someday, I pray that you beat me to the site. Ask Him to take you to His Leader.

Get Your Kicks

But for you who revere My name, the sun of righteousness will rise with healing in its wings. And you will go out and leap like calves released from the stall. Malachi 4:2

In the good old days, dancing tested a person's agility in moving feet nimbly and accurately—mostly to avoid your partner's prancing. Modern dance seems more an exercise in wearing out clothes from the inside. For some of us, the best way to describe our dancing is to watch a calf finding its first legs! They don't do very well. But they surely are happy doing it.

It is good for Christians to kick up our heels once in awhile. For those who can't or won't dance with their feet, there are alternative forms of dancing.

Alternative 1: Dance with your eyes. As you consider all God has done, let the joy travel up your optic nerve. Let it shine on those whose glance (or glare) meets your gaze. Eyes can twinkle as well as toes! I suppose it's no coincidence that you see similar looks in the eyes of lovers as they discover the exhilaration of unconditional, unexpected, and unmerited love. That's like our relationship with Jesus. (Solomon thought so too. Read Song of Songs sometime.)

Alternative 2: Dance with your lips. Lips dance in several ways. Obviously, singing gets the lips moving. God likes many different kinds of singing—the praise can be soft, loud, beautiful, or discordant. The Bible says the angels dance with their lips, and they're probably good singers. But our lips need only move to the rhythm of our heart to stay in step.

Lips also dance when they pucker out humor. Good humor. The kind that laughs at self or human foibles but never destroys with cruel snickers. Too bad the Bible doesn't record Jesus' laughter as it does His tears. Surely He laughed when He healed the sick, welcomed little children, and rose from the dead. Our lips too can dance with jovial verbs and jubilant nouns. If life gets dull, just picture yourself leaping like a calf!

Rising to the Bottom

*Whoever wants to become great among you must be your servant, and who-
ever wants to be first must be your slave—just as the Son of Man did not
come to be served, but to serve, and to give His life as a ransom for many.*
Matthew 20:26–28

D o you have any secret goals in life? Some people aim at their
goals, but they're lousy shots. Take Jesus' disciples, for
example. The mother of two of them aimed high. She wanted her
sons to have the highest ranking among His followers. Jesus warned
that such high status was no picnic. It would cost them their lives.
Then Jesus told them the real secret of success in the company of
Christians. Aim low.

Modern corporate executives might reject Jesus' protocol for
rising through the ranks. But Christians are in the business of serving others. Jesus was able to start out at the bottom and stay there.
He was the perfect servant, obeying God and serving people. He was
the only one who could reach low enough to save us, and His job
was successfully completed on the first Easter. Now, as any good
leader does, He inspires us to ever lower levels of service.

As we labor and grow in the company of Christians, we do well
to imitate those who founded the company. The apostles weren't
just a bunch of junior executives making decisions for others. They
went into the field and cultivated new Christians. They sometimes
ended up with dirtied hands and bloodied bodies. Several of the
most prominent execs were killed on the job.

Thousands of Christians have retired, and we're here to replace
them. What service can we offer? Will it be driving Mr. Thomas to
church every Sunday? Will it be reading a preschooler the story of
Josiah—743 times? Will it be cleaning the seats in church? Will it be
suffering scorn and mockery as we try to outdo one another in kindness? One thing is certain. To reach the top, you have to strive for the
bottom.

Horn Tooters

One who puts on his armor should not boast like one who takes it off.
1 Kings 20:11

Flattery gets you nowhere; especially when you give it to yourself. Some people even brag about their humility! We all know a few horn tooters, and perhaps we even see one each time we pass a mirror. Boastful people might be compared to monsters with heads full of I's. The king's advice in the passage above applies equally well to us. Don't toot your horn unless you play in the band.

Braggarts usually feel insecure about who they are. They fear nobody will notice or value them unless they point out their worthiness. Often this leads to a vicious circle in which acquaintances avoid the boaster so the boaster feels an even stronger need to gain attention. Braggarts, even occasional ones like ourselves, need prayer.

We can be confident that Jesus notices us. He chose to befriend us—and even more! He knew that we were born sinful, that we would remain sinful, and that we would lose our life as a result. And there was nothing we could do about our condition except, perhaps, talk about it. But no amount of talk could make us worthy or righteous. We could brag that we were sinless or that we could do enough good deeds to make up for our sinfulness, but that would just be empty talk. So Jesus said, "I love you, *(insert your own name)*. You don't need to toot your own horn in front of Me. I'm the whole band! I'll play the tune for you, and I won't flub a note or miss a beat. Yes, _____, you are Mine."

We don't need to flaunt our goodness before God. When the world ends and we appear before God, we won't need to invent stories about how good we are. Instead, we will tell God how good Jesus is—for us. In fact, maybe some bragging is good. Paul advocated boasting to the Corinthians. He said, "Let him who boasts boast in the Lord" (2 Corinthians 10:17).

Just Like the Grocery Store

Dear children, let us not love with words or tongue but with actions and in truth. 1 John 3:18

Where do you buy groceries? Do you make a list, or are you an "impulse" shopper? What do you do when you get them home? How often do you return to the store for more?

Do you go to church? What do you take home, and what do you do with it? How often do you replenish your supplies?

When you go to the grocery store, do you wander aimlessly and leave with an empty cart? Or if you buy groceries, do you take them home, unpack the sacks, and never look at the goods again? Of course not! Except for that jar of caramelized anchovies way back in the cabinet, you consume most of what you purchase. What good is uneaten food? The same is true for regular visits to church.

How tempting it is to leave God in church! If we don't take Him home with us, we don't have to use Him. We don't have to watch Him getting dusty on the shelf. Of course, most people don't go to church and leave God there. They at least leave the building with Him. But does it surprise you to find gossip, slander, and perhaps even a few adulterous glances right outside the church door? It's so easy to put God on the shelf and leave Him there.

A well-stocked church service always reveals God's love for us. And well it should! But we can't leave God's house simply feeling good because we're stocked with mercy and grace. We need to digest His love so that He makes us live and move.

Actions speak louder than words. Unfortunately, they just don't seem to speak as frequently! And when it comes to church, when the sermon and the Word are said and done, there is usually much more said than done. May God grant us the ambition and the ability to practice what He preaches.

64

All the Same

This is how you can recognize the Spirit of God: Every spirit that acknowledges that Jesus Christ has come in the flesh is from God, but every spirit that does not acknowledge Jesus is not from God. This is the spirit of the antichrist, which you have heard is coming and even now is already in the world. 1 John 4:2–3

"It doesn't matter what you believe, as long as you're sincere." "I can worship in any church. All religions are the same anyway." Tolerant attitudes, for sure, but dangerous ones. Such statements come from those who claim no religious prejudice, but the dismal truth is that no prejudice often equals no religion.

What Christians need to do, according to John, is to be intolerant (as opposed to intolerable). This doesn't mean that Christians should desecrate Jewish synagogues, Muslim mosques, or Buddhist temples. But they shouldn't credit those places as dwellings of God either. As John says, unless Christ is confessed, the religion is phony and evil. Note that John didn't use the word *harmless*. He calls the priests of false religions antichrists—against Christ! Pray that the Holy Spirit reaches these lost people before it's too late!

Christians must be alert to even more subtle and subversive religions, though. Some religions look like Christianity but fail to qualify with the only thing that counts: Christ as the only Savior from sin. Watch out for churches devoid of crosses. (Sometimes they just don't want to scare visitors away with religious symbolism, but who except the devil fears the cross?) Stay away from those who concentrate exclusively on you at the expense of Jesus and what He has done for you. Be cautious about churches that focus on success rather than humility and service in the name of Jesus. If it doesn't proclaim Jesus, it serves the devil.

Slow Down

For rulers hold no terror for those who do right, but for those who do wrong. Do you want to be free from fear of the one in authority? Then do what is right and he will commend you. ... Therefore, it is necessary to submit to the authorities, not only because of possible punishment but also because of conscience. Romans 13:3, 5

It seems we have more laws than we could ever possibly break, but we manage to test a few anyway. Although ignorance is no excuse, it sometimes does provide a plausible alibi.

Both Jesus and Paul knew about civil laws and strongly supported them. Apparently, their support was important because God chose their counsel to appear in the Bible. (Too bad the government doesn't support God as much as God supports the government!) We might question this mix of Church and state, but one good reason exists for the Bible's support of civil authority. "The authorities that exist have been established by God" (Romans 13:1).

Paul wrote those words during some of the more tolerant years of Roman rule, but he wrote them about a pagan government nonetheless. Other examples from the Bible seem to suggest similar deference to the law. Even Daniel facing the lions didn't call for revolution. He refused to obey a law directly contrary to God's will, and he willingly faced the consequences in God's name. What the Bible suggests is that God empowers governments to provide an orderly life for their citizens—not necessarily a good one—but an orderly one.

So what shall we do about laws, authority, and government? The same thing Jesus did. Proclaim what is right in God's eyes. Obey the laws (even to death), and don't do anything Jesus wouldn't do. Forgive as Jesus forgave when officials do wrong. And prayer is always a safe (and mostly legal) practice too.

As Jesus obeyed God's Law to bring us life, liberty, and happiness, cooperate with the governmental authorities as they bring order to our lives. And when you get a chance, tell them why you're so cooperative.

Chip Off the Block

Praise be to the God and Father of our Lord Jesus Christ, the Father of compassion and the God of all comfort, who comforts us in all our troubles, so that we can comfort those in any trouble with the comfort we ourselves have received from God. 2 Corinthians 1:3–4

Have you ever felt like knocking the chip off somebody's shoulder? Is there someone at work or in your neighborhood who needs a good kick in the pants? What they really need to displace that chip is a little comfort. There's nothing like a pat on the back to knock a chip off the shoulder. And while a pat on the back is only 18 inches higher than a kick in the pants, it works better.

God is the greatest source of encouragement and comfort. When God's Old Testament people fell (or leaped) into bad times, they retreated to God for counsel and aid. God's admonishment was always the same: Return to the Lord, give up your evil ways, and He will help you. Another way of putting it was "Return to Me, and I'll return to you." When Christ came to earth, the command was similar as Jesus invited people to follow Him and evade sin.

How can we help others to find this comfort? A curt "Go to God with your troubles" is likely to place a whole log on that person's shoulder. When someone is distressed or angry, we can help by getting that person to talk to us—especially if he or she is not accustomed to talking to God. Once the problem has been "confessed," it's time to relate with compassion. Tell the person that you know how it feels to be bitter, depressed, or frightened (without going into details), and that you find relief in prayer. Share your trust in God— your absolute confidence that He will work things out. Offer to pray with the troubled and afflicted. And if the person wants to talk more after praying, make time to do so. Maybe you're God's answer to his or her prayer—and a chip off the divine Block.

Oh yes, when you're all done, give Him a big pat on the back.

Take a Vacation

The apostles gathered around Jesus and reported to Him all they had done and taught. Then, because so many people were coming and going that they did not even have a chance to eat, He said to them, "Come with Me by yourselves to a quiet place and get some rest." Mark 6:30–31

Vacations are when you send postcards saying, "Wish you were here" to people you traveled hundreds of miles to get away from. Most of us eagerly anticipate vacation time. Americans have actually increased their work week by six hours in recent years. Maybe you're one of those people who puts in 80-hour work weeks. And if you work in the home, your job is no picnic either. Stress and strain affect your emotions and health in negative ways. Jesus tells you the same thing He told His other friends: Take a vacation.

Some may enjoy vacations off by themselves, but many others want the company of those they love. And like it or not, many vacations find the family car bloated with luggage, panting pets, and one-too-many kids wedged in the backseat. But whether alone or with others, it's good to make room for one more. Take Jesus along. (He won't even mind Rover's wagging tail and bad breath!)

Make room for the Savior by packing your Bible. Just as you do things out of the ordinary on vacation, choose something unusual to read. Take a tour through the "little" books like Titus, Philemon, the three Johns, or Jude. The Psalms have some great vacation passages too. Look for those that praise God for His wonderful creation. And if you're on a romantic interlude with your spouse, try Song of Songs. (*Note:* Song of Songs is a poetic expression comparing love of a couple with love for their Savior. What a unique way of meditating on our love for Jesus and His love for us!) Wherever you go, don't just wish Jesus was there. Take Him along.

Call Me in the Morning

Elisha sent a messenger to say to him, "Go, wash yourself seven times in the Jordan, and your flesh will be restored and you will be cleansed." But Naaman went away angry and said, "I thought that he would surely come out to me and stand and call on the name of the LORD his God, wave his hand over the spot and cure me of my leprosy." … Naaman's servants went to him and said, "My father, if the prophet had told you to do some great thing, would you not have done it? How much more, then, when he tells you, 'Wash and be cleansed'!" 2 Kings 5:10–11, 13

Have you visited a doctor's office lately? It seems they found a cure for what to do with old magazines!

Today's Bible selection finds Naaman indignant when Elisha (a prophet, not a physician) refused to see him personally regarding a disease. Naaman heard that Elisha worked many miracles, and he hoped that Elisha would work one on him. But Elisha simply pronounced God's prescription of washing in the Jordan River. Elisha's prescription must have seemed like an impersonal "Take two and call me in the morning." Naaman was so angry that he stormed off without filling the prescription—and he hadn't even seen the bill! Later, Naaman reconsidered Elisha's presumably preposterous proposal, and he was cured.

We are sick too—sick with sin. The symptoms include everything that makes us miserable. It's a terminal disease for which there is only one cure, and only one Physician can work the miracle. Yes, miracle.

Many of us might think miracles happen only to others or exclusively in Bible history. But each of us have received the healing miracle of forgiveness from Jesus Christ, the Great Physician. None of us have yet seen Him face to face, so we—like Naaman—rely on His word. If He says we're forgiven, we're forgiven! Jesus does comprehensive surgery on our souls. He removes the sin, and we are healed.

Thank God for sending Jesus on house calls. And thank Him for footing the bill too.

Hard Heads

For I knew how stubborn you were; the sinews of your neck were iron, your forehead was bronze. Isaiah 48:4

Car makers would make history if the government forced them to recall defective drivers! While that seems improbable, governmental agencies do seem determined to protect people from themselves. You probably have your own opinions about seat belts, cycling helmets, four-way railroad crossing gates, and other such devices. But have you stopped to think about why we don't exercise common sense in protecting ourselves—without government intervention?

God and Isaiah saw the same flaws in people. (Didn't Isaiah have a unique expression for hardheadedness?) The people in Isaiah's time also refused to practice common sense and self-preservation. God promised His people that He would be their God and they would be His people. God would protect them and make them flourish. That was an excellent deal and certainly more than fair. But like drivers buzzing along at 85 sans seat belts, they refused to protect themselves. They took chances.

Seat belts confine and restrict movement. Obeying God limits our normal activities and keeps us in line with all that God has provided to keep us happy and safe. And when we collide with major temptations, God's will keeps us in place. Why would He bother to protect us that way? Especially when we so often have bronze foreheads!

God loves us. He saw our helplessness and took our safety into His own hands. He placed Jesus at our disposal. God continues to send the Word accompanied by the Holy Spirit. Many heed His direction and submit to the safety of His law and love. Yet others rebel. The rebels and the careless need our prayers even more than those who refuse protection from earthly harm. As for ourselves, may God always keep us from sin and the devil, and may the Holy Spirit ever give us the faith to take advantage of God's love.

Remember, each time you awaken to a new day, buckle up with Jesus.

70

Safe Deposit

Guard the good deposit that was entrusted to you—guard it with the help of the Holy Spirit who lives in us. 2 Timothy 1:14

You know you're a success if your bank loan is sanctioned because you're able to prove you don't really need it. On the other hand, you know you're in trouble when your checkbook has a sad ending.

What about our spiritual credit rating? Someone estimated, with uncertain accuracy, that by the time a person is 50 years old, he or she has accumulated 2,000,000,000 sins! Just one sin is enough to condemn us. But 2,000,000,000? Only one resource grants us a good credit rating, even when we fall into hopeless debt. Through Jesus, God gave us His grace at our Baptism. We have enough grace on deposit to cover the cost of our sins. And did our sins cost! They cost Jesus His holy life.

When we consider that Jesus is God, we might begin to understand how He could pay the massive debt of all sinners combined. (The first couple racked up at least 4,000,000,00 alone in their first 50 years, and Adam lived to be 930. Let's see, 930 divided by 50 times 2,000,000,000 = A LOT OF SINS!) God, and only God, has the power to forgive. And Jesus Christ as God was the only one who could pay for sins. Only He could supply grace in enough abundance to provide all believers a credit balance on God's Book of Life.

Our credit balance includes God's Word. We might regard the Bible as a guide to our spiritual finances. In it, God commands us to invest grace in others, showing them the same generosity He showed us. God's Word also instructs us how not to squander His grace.

As we seek to obey Him and resist temptations, may He empower us to follow His will. And the next time we're tempted to keep an account of someone's sins, remember this: You're a billionaire yourself!

71

Sensitive Issue

When men tell you to consult mediums and spiritists, who whisper and mutter, should not a people inquire of their God? Why consult the dead on behalf of the living? Isaiah 8:19

Would you like to know your future? It probably wouldn't do much good. As many old-timers would tell us, the future isn't what it used to be! But that doesn't dampen the zeal of those who closely follow the astrology column in newspapers.

Admittedly, some Christians read horoscopes for "fun." They don't really believe this form of fortune-telling, but they might find it curiously strange how often the charts seem to "predict" the future. Fortune cookies at Chinese restaurants probably fall into the same category. But how easily everyday conversations become peppered with phrases like "good luck," "how fortunate!" "bless you" (in response to a sneeze), or even "may the force be with you." Of course, we don't actually believe that stuff, but ...

During the prophet Isaiah's time, fortune-telling, or future-telling, was also popular. Isaiah's words were probably considered insensitive by those who consulted or tolerated mediums. But Isaiah revealed the real story about futurists. They were no better than talking to dead people! And as Christians with a mission to witness the Gospel, do we really want to sound like we're talking to dead ears, even if we're only making casual remarks?

If only we could erase such language from our vocabulary as easily as stroking the delete button on a computer keyboard. We can, however, be sensitive in our speech.

May the Holy Spirit guide us to find alternatives to phrases like "good luck." "I'll pray for you" might be a natural. In place of "fortunate" we can say things like, "God was really watching over you." And of course, what's a "bless you" without God? Occasions like these open windows of opportunity to witness sensitively during common situations. Use your words so others know that the past hasn't escaped God's notice and that the future is in His loving hands.

Never in Need

The Lord is my shepherd, I shall not be in want. He makes me lie down in green pastures, He leads me beside quiet waters. Psalm 23:1–2

Psalm 23 is one of the most famous chapters in the Bible. Perhaps we can relate to sheep because we know their reputation for helplessness. (They also score low on the intelligence scale, but we would rather not identify ourselves with that!)

If you're not a shepherd, perhaps you can identify with a pampered pet dog or cat. Kind and conscientious owners provide food, most often a healthful diet supplemented by treats. They provide shelter, often a soft, warm place to sleep with a fresh bowl of water nearby. All this without the pet doing a thing to meet its own needs or contribute to its own welfare. But there is something even more important than physical needs. Without love, a pet's life is incomplete.

We need love too. Family and friends provide for our needs, but the Savior's love is perfect, constant, and plentiful. In fact, in the worst of times, we need nothing more than His love. Sin deprives us of days in green pastures beside still waters. Disagreements, arguments, and revenge may taint love in the family and among friends, but it never affects Jesus' love for us. Illness and accidents may sap our strength and depress our spirits, but that's also when we realize how close Jesus is to us and we to Him. Jobs may be lost and less food may fill our platters, but we can get by when we're full of God's love.

Jesus offers a shepherd-size supply of love even at times when we stray. Our willingness to blindly, even stupidly, follow wherever sin leads is a major fault in our spiritual character. Like a watchful and resourceful shepherd, Jesus comes after us. When we see Him, we can't help but wonder why we would go anywhere without Him.

73

For Christ's Sake

He restores my soul. He guides me in paths of righteousness for His name's sake. Psalm 23:3

If we try to walk the path of righteousness alone, we will find ourselves going downhill.

In Psalm 23, David clearly announces that the Good Shepherd restores or renews his soul. And where does it lead? Up the route of righteousness. David traveled that route from the time he tended his father's sheep until he rested on his deathbed. That's not to say that David avoided unwise detours along the path, but by God's grace he always responded when his Good Shepherd restored his soul.

What's the condition of your soul? You can't restore it yourself. Only the Holy Spirit, working through God's Word, can restore our soul. The results of a restored soul are always the same. It returns us to the road of righteousness where we serve our Shepherd in all that we do—until we "detour" and find ourselves needing restoration again. The Shepherd believes in keeping a capital *RE* in restore!

Have you wondered why the Good Shepherd does all this for us? We know we're undeserving and beyond earning His care. David said that God guides us up the path of righteousness "for His name's sake." For years, phrases like "for Christ's sake" puzzled me. (What do I know? I'm just a dumb sheep!) Has it perplexed you too? (Join the flock!)

All our righteousness comes from God for Christ's sake. He resisted all temptation—for our sake. He agonized on the cross and died—for our sake. And by His godly power He came to life again—for our sake. God would never waste all that work. He restores our soul and leads us to follow His will for the sake of Jesus Christ, who gave His life for us.

Waste not. Want not. That's why we're never in need—for Christ's sake.

74

What Lurks in the Shadows?

Even though I walk through the valley of the shadow of death, I will fear no evil, for You are with me; Your rod and Your staff, they comfort me. You prepare a table before me in the presence of my enemies. You anoint my head with oil; my cup overflows. Psalm 23:4–5

Welcome to the third installment in the miniseries on Psalm 23. The plot darkens here, though. What lurks in those shadows? Sin, evil, and death itself. Have you walked there? Most Christians walk there every day.

The "valley of the shadow of death" may be on a street shadowed by soaring skyscrapers. It can be located between rows of corn, in a dark alley framed by broken-down garages, or in a rugged gorge lined by sheer cliffs. And sometimes the shadowy valley is between the bedroom walls, the kitchen cabinets, or rows of office desks. Every day, death's shadows lurk around us. And behind those shadows is the bloody smile of Satan. He likes to see us scared. Even more, he likes to see us contented. Then he can really shock us! He wants us to die before we're dead.

Just when the devil thinks he's got us, we hear a tremendous thump. It's the sound of the Shepherd's rod and staff connecting with Satan's skull. He drives the wicked enemy back into the shadows. No wonder His rod and staff bring us comfort! But it goes even farther than that.

In the Lord's Supper the Good Shepherd furnishes a banquet table for us. The devil sees us enjoy the body and the blood of our Shepherd—so much spiritual food that our plates and glasses overflow. And he sees who we're eating with—the King of kings, Lord of lords, Shepherd of shepherds. This goes beyond ordinary gloating. This is victory! Victory over sin, death, and him who lurks in the shadows.

Laugh and enjoy yourself. But if you're smiling right now, look out. It's making the devil even madder! Be sure to see tomorrow's conclusion to the Psalm 23 series.

75

How Long Will It Last?

Surely goodness and love will follow me all the days of my life, and I will dwell in the house of the LORD forever. Psalm 23:6

David ended Psalm 23 with a most welcome assurance, one that grew from his experience and hope in God. I wonder if he repeated Psalm 23 as often as we do. Can you imagine this Psalm being a one-time thing? Certainly our life experiences parallel David's. It's a psalm we need often because we find ourselves in need often, tramping repeatedly up the path of righteousness but always among sinister shadows. In addition to dreading threats from the shadows, we have ourselves to fear. We surely like to sin! We're usually open to alternate routes around the path of righteousness. We need to feel the Shepherd's crook around our neck, gently pulling or even fiercely yanking us back to safety. Then He patiently prepares another feast table for us, and we celebrate the victory all over again.

God's goodness and love stay close to us. Wherever we are, He is. Whenever the devil swipes at us, He doesn't spare the rod. If we lead ourselves astray, He snatches us back to the flock. Since we're unable to stay close to Him, He goes the extra mile and remains close to us. But how long will this last?

Together with David, we can be confident that He will stay close forever. While we're living on earth, Jesus will continue to chase us around and fight our battles with the devil. One day, God will send Satan to his final defeat. That's the day God has set aside to send Jesus back to earth so we can meet the Good Shepherd face to face. That's the day that will never end.

Get ready for the banquet!

Hop to It

Then he said, "Take the arrows," and the king took them. Elisha told him, "Strike the ground." He struck it three times and stopped. The man of God was angry with him and said, "You should have struck the ground five or six times; then you would have defeated Aram and completely destroyed it. But now you will defeat it only three times." 2 Kings 13:18–19

The setting of today's reading was a somber room in which God's prophet Elisha was about to die. Israel's king had come to pay his respects and also get some of God's power through Elisha. Now Elisha seemed a man of few but potent words, so his conversation with the king was brief—as you can see in the passage. The king half-heartedly struck the ground with the arrows. He probably thought this was a silly exercise ordered by a feeble man. His lack of enthusiasm, however, was really reluctance to trust God. Elisha predicted the outcome of the king's indifference and then died. (Maybe he was killed by the king's jaw dropping open!)

As we might guess, there's a lesson here. When the Lord empowers us, we need to hop to it. And keep on hopping! One benefit of faith is forgiveness. God commissioned us to forgive as we have been forgiven. Translated loosely, that means a lot. How angry God must get when He sees us half-heartedly attempt to carry out His will, or when He sees us forgive only a few times. How many more battles we could win with forgiveness than with anger and bitterness! Isn't that the way He won us? We didn't come to Jesus because we feared what He would do to us. Instead, the Holy Spirit delivered His words of invitation and forgiveness. It was love that drew us to Him, and it's His love that we can use to draw others.

Hopefully, you're fired up and ready to strike a few arrows. Get the point?

77

Call on Line 1

And you also are among those who are called to belong to Jesus Christ.
Romans 1:6

Seventy-five percent of people called by the Lord today would probably subject Him to answering machines or voice mail.

We know, of course, that the Lord doesn't use a telephone when calling people to faith. However, His call is just as real as the calls we receive on Bell's invention. Perhaps it's not out of line, then, to image the following scenario!

Ring. Ring. Ring. Ring. Ring. Ring.

"Hello, this is Ed."

"Hi, Ed, this is the Lord Jesus."

"I've heard of You, Jesus. Some people claim that You're the Savior. Others say that You're a nice man in history. Some say You're only a legend."

"Who do you say I am?"

"C'mon, Jesus. You took those words from the Bible. But okay—I, I, I … don't really know."

"Hang on, Ed. I'll put the Holy Spirit on the line."

"Ed, I'm the Holy Spirit, and I'm calling to say that you're a winner! Jesus saved you, and I'm making you a lifetime member of the family of Christians. What do you think of that?"

Sound too good to be true? We've become so jaded by telemarketing that we're probably suspicious of the offer. But the Spirit's truth is just too good—period. He gave us faith and brought us to Christ. Do you remember the event?

If you were baptized as an infant, it's unlikely your memory reaches back that far. That doesn't mean your Baptism was ineffective, though. Baptism is powered by the Holy Spirit, not our intellect. If you came to faith later in life, perhaps you remember learning about God's goodness. In days of such evil and selfishness, it's hard to believe that Jesus lived and died to make us part of His family. Now, He wants us to make Him part of our family.

The gift of faith is free. Christ now lives in us and sends us to others. Perhaps you should go now. I think you have a call waiting.

78

Litterbugs

When we were overwhelmed by sins, You forgave our transgressions.
Psalm 65:3

The window descends, an arm extends, and from a hand some trash offends. (Littering isn't very poetic, is it?) Litterbugs! They leave trash everywhere but the garbage can. I suppose they become overwhelmed by trash. When your dashboard litterbag bulges, what can you do but pitch it from the car?

Some of us accumulate quite a cache of sins too. When our conscience becomes bloated, we are overwhelmed. Where can we dump our trashy sins? One technique works like the litterbag. We store our sins until we can store no more. Then what? We probably get another litterbag. Another technique avoids the inconvenience of storage and appropriate disposal. We simply toss off our sins like gum wrappers out the car window. Out of sight, out of soul. But this simple "redistribution" method doesn't clear up the problem either.

The Bible tells us where to place our trash. Give it to Jesus. Now it might sound disrespectful to talk about loading Jesus down with the garbage of our lives, but that's the only way to properly dispose of it. In fact, Jesus gave His life for our sins at a place adjacent to the city dump.

Unlike litterbags or even huge Dumpsters, Jesus has unlimited capacity to remove our sins. His death and resurrection have incinerated our transgressions beyond a trace. Then He recycles our sinful self into an entirely new creation, designed to serve Him and others.

We don't need to stockpile our sins because we don't know what else to do with them. Jesus takes out the trash every time we call, not just when we're weighed down. So place your sins at His disposal. And open your heart to the Holy Spirit that you may help others take out their trash.

Three Crosses

Carrying His own cross, He went out to the place of the Skull (which in Aramaic is called Golgotha). Here they crucified Him, and with Him two others—one on each side and Jesus in the middle. John 19:17–18

Ready for another miniseries? This is the first of three meditations on crosses. Not the three crosses on Golgotha, but three crosses we readily see today. Our first cross is the crucifix—the cross with Jesus nailed to it.

I don't like crucifixes much. They're too real and not real enough at the same time. How they remind us of our sins! There we see Jesus, arms stretched and ribs protruding. We see the holes dotted with blood on His hands and feet. And what you don't see hurts too. There, on His bare and scrawny shoulders, lie the sins of the world. All that weight pulling on His arms, crushing His lungs, pushing down on His feet. It's almost too repulsive. Yet we must gaze on this cross, the crucifix.

Although they realistically depict the Savior's suffering, somehow crucifixes can't fully symbolize the pain and agony. We can close our eyes and we won't hear the labored breathing or gasps of anguish. We can touch the crucifix and it's cold and hard, not clammy flesh on splintered wood. Good thing it's not. We couldn't bear to know just how much He languished on that cross. Yet the fact remains, we must take a distressing look at the crucifix now and then. But not to make us feel guilty.

Jesus removed our guilt on the cross. All of it. He doesn't want us in the throes of extended mourning either. He has prepared a place for us where tears will be extinct. But the crucifix does serve one excellent purpose. It makes us thankful. It could be us up there, for hell holds equal terrors for unbelievers. Jesus did in six hours what would have taken us an eternity.

Now get back to work, and have a good mourning.

Clean Cross

Later, Joseph of Arimathea asked Pilate for the body of Jesus. Now Joseph was a disciple of Jesus, but secretly because he feared the Jews. With Pilate's permission, he came and took the body away. John 19:38

As decorations go, crosses are often the pride of Christian churches. Some are cut from rare and expensive imported wood. Others are cast in gleaming steel or aluminum. Often, their towering presence becomes the focal point of our attention. And well they should. This instrument of execution is a symbol for Christ Himself.

The empty cross reminds us that Christ's story—and ours—doesn't leave us hanging. And the bare beams of wood or steal imply much more than we read in John's report above. True, some of Jesus' admirers didn't want to leave Him suspended there like some common criminal. Finally, one of the wealthy believers risked the contempt of his peers to bury Jesus in his own plot. But that was one body that would not decay into dust. Jesus would simply not go away.

The clean lines of modern crosses remind us of what Christ did for us. His death on the cross made us clean. When God looks at us, He sees squeaky-clean Christians, polished by Jesus' love and sacrifice.

The vacant cross would mean nothing if the tomb had remained occupied two days later. Neither brutal cross nor damp, dark tomb can defeat God. So unoccupied crosses also remind us of Jesus' resurrection. We can almost hear the words of God's angels: "Why do you look for the living among the dead? He is not here" (Luke 24:5–6). The same might be said of us someday. The empty cross and the risen Savior mean that we won't remain dead either. Perhaps we'll rest in the grave beyond the third day, but we will rise, never to fall again.

Look around. Find any object that resembles a cross. Look at it several times each day. Christ isn't on it, is He? He's in heaven. He's someplace else too.

Cross my heart.

Take It with You

Then Jesus said to His disciples, "If anyone would come after Me, he must deny himself and take up his cross and follow Me." Matthew 16:24

I'm certain that Jesus wasn't talking about lapel pins or necklaces in the verse above. But at least those are crosses we can easily wear—on our lapel, around our neck, on our finger, or pinned to our ears. Crosses are not just banal jewelry. People notice the difference when we wear the cross on our heart.

To wear His cross worthily, we must meet the requirement that Jesus established for His disciples. We must deny ourselves as we take up the cross. That's what Christ did. He denied His divine power to serve us and to die for us. Would we not have cheered if Jesus struck the taunting high priest dead? Would it not have served the crowd right if Jesus pronounced a plague of muteness as they chanted, "Crucify Him! Crucify Him!"? And certainly we would have rejoiced had Jesus sprung from the cross and tossed His antagonists straight into hell. That would have served them right. Jesus would have done Himself a favor too. But the Savior wasn't self-serving. He served His Father and us instead.

When Jesus tells us to deny ourselves, He means that we can't be the center of our own life. The Savior doesn't want us to deny ourselves through seclusion or solitude. He doesn't want us to devote our time exclusively to singing hymns and chanting prayers. Who would ever see our crosses that way? Serving Jesus means serving others. Sometimes the service involves simple acts of kindness or assistance. At other times, it may entail private or public prayers for someone in need. Service may consist of giving some of our treasures to the needy. And yes, we must also serve by telling others what we believe. Maybe if you wear a cross, someone will ask.

The Naked Truth

But the LORD God called to the man, "Where are you?" He answered, "I heard You in the garden, and I was afraid because I was naked; so I hid." Genesis 3:9–10

The truth hurts, especially when it's about us. Adam and Eve uncovered (excuse the pun) this conventional wisdom after they both succeeded and failed to become "number 1." Let me explain. As you know, this young couple was the first to sin. They sinned because they wanted to be "number 1"—not at sinning, but more like God than He intended them to be. God knew about evil. Adam and Eve didn't. At least they didn't until they ate the forbidden fruit. Then they saw the whole picture. The naked truth hurt. They were sinners and there was no hiding it.

God found a way to hide their shame. He made the first articles of clothing for Adam and Eve. But even more important, He also promised them a way to cover the sinfulness that would otherwise condemn them to eternal evil. God promised them a Savior—someone to give them new garments, to clothe them in righteousness. To properly appreciate the righteousness Jesus proclaimed for sinners, we must see the naked truth about ourselves. We must be exposed, so to speak.

Sin certainly has a way of exposing us. Often, others notice our sin sooner and keener than we do. But even if we succeed at hiding our sins from others, we can never hide them from God. God knows the naked truth about us, and He sent Jesus to dress us in holy righteousness. As we confess our sins and receive forgiveness, we can be sure that everything is all right—right with God. Now go out there and make a fashion statement.

Don't Look Down

Brothers, I do not consider myself yet to have taken hold of it. But one thing I do: Forgetting what is behind and straining toward what is ahead, I press on toward the goal to win the prize for which God has called me heavenward in Christ Jesus. Philippians 3:13–14

For many people, the future comes too soon! If the future frightens you, think of it as climbing a rope to the top of the gym. You'll be okay if you just don't look down.

Looking down or looking back shows where we've been rather than where we are going. The sight may not be pretty. As we age, we store many memories. Some of those memories are things we might want to forget or that make us dread the future. But, to paraphrase what St. Paul told the Philippians, don't look down. Look up. Press on. After all, the future is looking up.

Try this sometime when you're frightened or feeling low. Whistle a happy tune. No, wait. That's from a movie. Look up, for that is the direction of heaven. As you look up, imagine Jesus looking down at you. Picture Him saying the words He put into Paul's mouth. He calls you heavenward to receive your reward.

Don't be misled. Your reward isn't something you earned or won on your own. Jesus earned your right to live with Him here on earth and later in heaven. But by faith you believe that Jesus is your Savior. Faith too is a gift of the Holy Spirit. God wants us to use our faith to face the future. He wants us to grow in faith so we can continue our climb into the future. The reward for faithfulness is everlasting life, but it's a life that begins right now. So keep climbing, and if you're afraid, don't look down. Jesus is at the top, urging us on. Things certainly are looking up, aren't they?

Select the Best Answer

You, then, why do you judge your brother? Or why do you look down on your brother? For we will all stand before God's judgment seat. ... So then, each of us will give an account of himself to God. Romans 14:10, 12

Ready for a multiple choice quiz? Select the best answer. What will you answer when you stand before God's judgment seat?

A. I didn't know any better.

B. What? I was just having a little fun!

C. You'll have to talk to my lawyer.

D. How did you find out about that?

The Bible says that God will require an account of our lives when we stand before Him. Will God want to know why we should be allowed into heaven? The answer is easy for Christians: "I believe that Jesus Christ is my Savior." Yes, that's a super answer. But maybe God will examine us in more detail. Suppose He pulls out a file filled with official-looking forms. We ask, "What's that?" (Even if the sweat on our forehead suggests we don't really want to know.)

God answers, "I wrote a ticket every time you exceeded the speed limit and the police didn't catch you. If your belief in Jesus was genuine, you would have obeyed Him. Remember? He's the one who told you to obey the government's laws."

God undoubtedly owns several fat file folders on every Christian. He won't miss the "little sins" that we often toss aside and forget. Every lie, vengeful thought, speeding violation, tax claim, and bitter word lies there festering in the file cabinet. What will we answer?

The best answer confesses belief in Jesus as our Savior. God will burn the files forever when we plead, "Have mercy on me for Jesus' sake."

Better the files than us!

You're Elected

For He chose us in Him before the creation of the world to be holy and blameless in His sight. Ephesians 1:4

Want an inexpensive way to trace your family history? Run for office. Reporters and opponents will expose every skeleton in your closet! And then, if you win the election, people will criticize every decision you make. Don't let all this influence your reaction to the biggest (and perhaps only) election that lists you in the winner's circle.

God elected you. As Paul said in Ephesians, He chose you even before He created squash or Saturn or sea cucumbers. God didn't research our relatives to determine our worthiness either. He is at the very root of our family tree.

We didn't deserve to win the election. An examination of our past would uncover pits filled with sin. What we deserve is an eternal term in hell. But Jesus cleaned up our record and placed us on His winning ticket. He won the election for us even if the election was unfair—unfair to Him.

It's one thing to begin with a clean slate, but quite another to maintain it. Did you notice why God elected us? Like politicians who make promises they can't keep, we're in trouble. So it's Jesus to the rescue again—erasing our slate of sins and forgiving us far more than voters forgive those whom they elect. Each time the Lord forgives, He renews our will to lead blameless and holy lives.

There is only one way to be blameless and holy. Locking yourself away with the Bible, isolating yourself from all that might tempt you is not it. Instead, we are blameless and holy when our sins are washed away from us by Jesus Christ.

Go out there now and shake a few hands and kiss a few babies. Take out your neighbor's trash and give shut-ins a ride to church. Help anyone in need. Do favors—especially for your family. After all, you've been elected!

How Do We Do It?

How great is the love the Father has lavished on us, that we should be called children of God! And that is what we are! 1 John 3:1

A certain man was praying in public. A passer-by noticed the folded hands, closed eyes, and moving lips, but he didn't hear anything. He said, "Speak up. I can't hear you." The man opened his eyes and replied, "That's okay. I wasn't talking to you."

The disciples were, at first, equally confused about prayer. They wanted to know to whom they should pray and what they should say. Jesus taught them words that have been on the lips of millions of people throughout history. If you're like most Christians, the Lord's Prayer is a staple in your spiritual diet. This and the next six devotions focus on what we say each time we use the most perfect prayer.

"Our Father in heaven, hallowed be Your name" (Matthew 6:9). Jesus wants us to call God "our Father." How that must have stunned His early followers! For centuries, people didn't believe they could directly address God. God was so mighty that sinners calling on Him would perish if they spoke of anything but the somewhat distant "Name of the Lord." Jesus changed all that. He made it possible not only to call God God, but also to call Him Father. It takes only a small assumption to realize how we're related to the Savior if Jesus was God's Son. As if that relationship isn't good enough, the Bible even tells us that we're friends with Jesus! (See John 15:13–15.) When Jesus took away the sins of His friends, He brought us into His Father's family. And what a name that family has! Not just any name—but a holy (hallowed) one.

Call your Father every day—for praise, help, or thanksgiving. You know how to do it. After all, you had a good Teacher.

Dual Citizenship

He who testifies to these things says, "Yes, I am coming soon." Amen.
Come, Lord Jesus. Revelation 22:20

Even liberty has limits beyond which we may not take liberties. Historically, most kingdoms were led by kings who gave their subjects the liberty to pay outrageous taxes and swear absolute allegiance or else spend lots of free time in a cold dungeon. Is this the kind of kingdom for which we ask in the Lord's Prayer?

Let's realize at the outset that we hold a dual citizenship. Jesus considered our earthly citizenship important. He told people to pay taxes and obey laws. Jesus wants us to understand that God empowers governments to keep order. Some governments keep order in oppressive ways. Others outlaw God's Word. And some want to make God's Word available but keep it out of the government.

"Your kingdom come." Our other citizenship is in God's kingdom, where we live now. (Our move to the mansion comes later.) God made us His subjects when He sent the Holy Spirit into our heart. We might call His kingdom the Church. (Notice the capital *C*.) His Church is believers in all time and all places. We are subject to His will and commands, but He is most merciful. He even forgives our acts of weak loyalty and occasional consorts with the enemy.

Good citizenship in God's kingdom means much the same as good citizenship in earthly kingdoms. We strive to lead a godly life by regularly honoring our King in everyday language as well as in worship. Since He is a good listener, we talk to Him and tell Him our needs. We can be sure that He has our best interests in mind as He meets those needs. We also want to tell everyone the good He does for us so they too will recognize Him as our good God.

God's kingdom is a great place to live. And we don't even have to pay taxes!

88

Willpower

*I do not understand what I do. For what I want to do I do not do, but
what I hate I do. And if I do what I do not want to do, I agree that the
law is good. As it is, it is no longer I myself who do it, but it is sin living
in me. I know that nothing good lives in me, that is, in my sinful nature.
For I have the desire to do what is good, but I cannot carry it out. For
what I do is not the good I want to do; no, the evil I do not want to do—
this I keep on doing. Now if I do what I do not want to do, it is no longer
I who do it, but it is sin living in me that does it. Romans 7:15–20*

Do you, like Paul, also argue with yourself when it comes to
problems of willpower? Martin Luther said that willpower
is the most powerful power we have. The dynamics of willpower present some stubborn problems. Willpower inevitably results in clashes. Take a moment to consider your own involvement in each of the
following conflicts.

Sometimes the contest is between my will and the will of
someone else. (Maybe you already had one of these today.) At other
times, the conflict is between God and me. Still other occasions find
me experiencing the "Paul syndrome." The peace treaty in any war
of wills demands an application of a short phrase in the Lord's
Prayer—"Your will be done."

We pray it all the time. We ask God to do His will. When His will
overpowers our will, then we're bound for spiritual serenity. Right?

Not exactly. The sin within us won't die easily. And that's exactly why we pray "Your will be done." God's will is to keep sin out of
our life. He also wants to save us. He wants to keep our faith strong
so we can praise Him and live with Him forever.

Now go out there and practice some willpower. Try some
"won't power" too—the power God gives to battle and hate sin.

Enough Daily Bread

Give me neither poverty nor riches, but give me only my daily bread. Otherwise, I may have too much and disown You and say, "Who is the Lord?" Or I may become poor and steal, and so dishonor the name of my God. Proverbs 30:8–9

The words flow so smoothly. "Give us today our daily bread." Of course, we would like it buttered on both sides, and some cake would be nice too. And make sure we have enough to last us the whole week, Lord.

With or without prayers, God supplies food to the world—even to unbelievers. That's just the way God is. He cares for everybody. The difference is that believers know who to thank and praise for all good things.

Bread is sometimes called the staff of life. When we pray for daily bread, we acknowledge that God provides everything our bodies need. In addition to food (even cauliflower!), God provides the roof that shelters us, family and friends to provide affection, jobs, good weather, and even coffee breaks. God grants it all!

When you think of the amount of edible food trashed from American tables and the acres of farmland that purposely remain unproductive, it's a miracle of mercy that God gives us anything. It's also a shameful sin that hunger reigns in the bellies of so many. Good thing God doesn't say, "Enough is enough!" and strike us all with famine.

Christians need to know when enough is enough. Have you noticed how we pray, "Give us *today* our daily bread"? Our prayer takes us beyond greed or stockpiling. It expresses confidence that God will provide what we need each day. History suggests that when God's people have more than they need, they tend to forget where they got it. When enough is enough, we are more likely to keep our focus on God.

Isn't it good to know who butters our bread?

90

Perilous Prayer

Be kind and compassionate to one another, forgiving each other, just as in Christ God forgave you. Ephesians 4:32

Some people find forgiving much easier after they've gotten even! Others forgive because they know it really annoys the trespasser. Of course, the only proper motivation for forgiving is that we ourselves have been forgiven.

If we really concentrate when we say, "Forgive us our sins as we forgive those who sin against us," we recognize the serious deal we make with God. We give up our eternal life if we reject God's forgiveness by refusing to forgive others. Rather than dig through archives of sins committed against us, fearing that we forgot to forgive some, let's complete our "deal" with God right now.

Dear heavenly Father, sometimes I'm a real flop at forgiving. I still store some bitterness in my heart from things past. Warm my heart with kindness for those who have done wrong to me. And fill me with compassion for those who will sin against me today, tomorrow, and next year. I don't deserve Your mercy or grace any more than those who do wrong to me. Yet, as You forgive me, strengthen me to forgive others. Fill me with the peace that comes from forgiving, even when it's not appreciated or acknowledged. Make me more like You. Amen.

Forgiveness feels good. It lightens our heart both when we get it and when we give it. God's forgiveness enables us to pray with a clear conscience. Forgiveness is also evidence that we believe God's forgiveness is real. To know that reality, we must recognize and confess the huge inventory of sins we garner each day. Only then do we also grasp the magnitude of God's grace and realize our obligation (yes, obligation!) to forgive others.

Is the Lord's Prayer truly perilous? It can be. But God's forgiveness gives us power to forgive too. Do some forgiving today. Then forget it.

Let's Have Some Fun

Consider it pure joy, my brothers, whenever you face trials of many kinds, because you know that the testing of your faith develops perseverance.
James 1:2–3

Temptation is patient. It always gives a second chance. How wise Jesus was to instruct us to pray, "Lead us not into temptation."

God is the last one we would suspect of enticing us with temptations. Would He really do that? Of course not. Between the unholy trinity of the devil, the world, and our own flesh, temptation abounds in all shapes and sizes. Jesus knew all about those temptations because He encountered them Himself—with very personal attention from the devil. Jesus wanted His disciples—us included—to pray for strength to resist temptations.

Take a moment—an agonizing moment—to recall your most persistent temptations. Now take another moment to recall what happened the last time you foiled your tempter. Check out the Bible passage at the beginning of this meditation. The best thing about temptations is what happens when you repel them.

Temptations test our faith. Now God was and is prone to testing faith even if He refuses to tempt us to evil. He did it to Abraham in the incident when Isaac, Abraham's long-anticipated son, was to be the family sacrifice. What faith it took for father Abraham to wield the knife, trusting that God knew what He was doing. The story ends with God providing a substitute sacrifice for Isaac. "Lead us not into temptation." Will God answer this prayer? Listen to what Paul says:

No temptation has seized you except what is common to man. And God is faithful; He will not let you be tempted beyond what you can bear. But when you are tempted, He will also provide a way out so that you can stand up under it. (1 Corinthians 10:13)

Shipping and Handling

But He said to me, "My grace is sufficient for you, for My power is made perfect in weakness." Therefore I will boast all the more gladly about my weaknesses, so that Christ's power may rest on me. 2 Corinthians 12:9

When we have problems, we often either try to bury them or blame them on someone else. Paul didn't appreciate his problems either, so when he prayed "Deliver us from evil," he expected an answer. He shares God's answer in the passage above. God delivered Paul from much evil, but he also endured much more than most of us would want to face—beatings, jail, shipwreck, and eventually death. Paul had another mysterious problem. He simply called it a "thorn" and asked God to take it away. God let him live with it instead.

We know that God doesn't lead us into temptation and that He fortifies our faith through tests tailor-made for us. And although we ask Him to deliver us from evil, He sometimes says, "Live with it." (Of course, we never know just how much evil He delivers us from!) It's all part of God's shipping and handling plan to take us from birth to eternity.

Make no mistake. God has already delivered us from the worst evil through the sacrifice and victory of His Son, Jesus Christ. Now He commands His angels to protect us as we move toward our final destination in His mansion. They handle us well, but they allow us to experience bumps, bruises, and detours along the way. Those problems are good if we respond as Paul did. He recognized that Jesus keeps us close to Himself through our weaknesses. We don't ever want to forget that we need Him. And we also don't want to neglect our praise for Him.

Thank God for your weaknesses. Boast if you must—especially if someone questions how a sinner like you can be a Christian. Then run to the Savior who has paid all the shipping and handling charges for your delivery.

Think of Yourself

For by the grace given me I say to every one of you: Do not think of yourself more highly than you ought, but rather think of yourself with sober judgment, in accordance with the measure of faith God has given you.
Romans 12:3

It's time to think of yourself. You say we already do more of that than we should? You're probably right. If you browse the self-help section of most bookstores, you'll see title after title of self-help, self-evaluation, self-promotion, and self-esteem books. Self-esteem is a popular subject these days, so we must be careful not to confuse self-esteem with selfishness. (We all know people who are all wrapped up in themselves. They're grossly overdressed.)

Psychologists tell us that we need to love ourselves before we can love others. Does that also imply that we must serve ourselves before we can serve others?

Let's think of ourselves for a moment. Do we count our assets before we identify a few token liabilities? Do we find more faults than "goods" about ourselves? Chances are good that we hope someone will come along and give us a little esteem. And that's what we can expect from others—little! But God comes along and gives us lots of esteem. He loves us though we don't deserve it. He loves us even when we don't love ourselves.

Why should we possess self-esteem? God loved us so much that He sent Jesus to live and die and live again to save us. If God loved us, we can love ourselves. He gave us faith to accept and use our strengths to love and serve others. He gave us faith to forgive ourselves our shortcomings too. After all, why shouldn't we forgive what He forgave?

Think of yourself for a while. Not too highly, though. But love yourself as Jesus loves you.

94

What a Friend!

I no longer call you servants, because a servant does not know his master's business. Instead, I have called you friends, for everything that I learned from My Father I have made known to you. John 15:15

A true friend is one who remains your friend, even after getting to know you!

It's no wonder that "What a Friend We Have in Jesus" is a favorite hymn of many Christians. Believers through all ages have benefited from the presence of their divine friend. Jesus befriends sinners by taking them into His confidence, as friends often do. What does He tell them?

Jesus withholds no important information. While we may wonder about His private life—the years unrecorded in the Bible—He doesn't consider that to be important. We might like to know about our friend's background—the games He enjoyed, the pets He kept, names of His childhood friends (everybody!), the foods He enjoyed most, and how other kids treated Him. But that information would neither build our faith nor save us. Instead, Jesus tells us how to be saved, how to pray, how to serve, and how our friendship will grow.

Jesus tells us some important things about Himself. He says He is God, the Savior inside a body like ours. He taught us how to talk to Him. Jesus also insists that we make friends with others—even our enemies. No secrets here. Jesus tells it all. And much to our delight, He promises to remain friends forever.

Most of us are pleased when some important or popular person claims friendship with us. We're willing to do almost anything to please, and we're proud to be seen in his or her presence. That's how it is with Jesus too. We're happy to be near Him—most of the time. And when we abandon Him in favor of lesser friends, He's always willing to forgive and restore the relationship. He is happy to be with us too.

I guess we might feel the same if we died for someone.

Partly Cloudy

The priests could not perform their service because of the cloud, for the glory of the LORD filled the temple of God. 2 Chronicles 5:14

It happened so fast that it took them by surprise. Then, as now, people weren't too surprised by sudden shifts in the weather. But *inside* a building—in the days before sports domes with their mini-environments?

The occasion for the interior cloud was the dedication of God's temple built by Solomon. Years of hard labor yielded a magnificent building—a house for God. The project was financed freely by God's people. When he dedicated the temple, Solomon admitted that even this magnificent building couldn't really confine God, but he asked God to remain with His people anyway. God was so pleased with the righteous intent of Solomon that His spirit filled the temple, appearing as a cloud so thick the priests couldn't see what they were doing.

Solomon's temple vanished long ago, but God still lives with His people. In fact, He lives *in* His people. So what's the weather like in your "temple"? Today's Bible passage hints that good weather conditions include clouds.

Sin beats down on us like a blistering August sun in Arizona. Without clouds to shield us, we're inclined to wither and die. Since we can't create friendly clouds, we linger under the control of a force beyond us. No, it's not the meteorologist. Only God can provide a holy cloud to shelter us from the torrid climate of sin. He filters out sin's scorching rays by filling us with Jesus the Christ. And while we enjoy the complete cover He provides, we always push the cloud partly aside, allowing sin to burn us over and over again. Every time we do so, He returns to fill us once again. May God fill our life with the clouds of His Spirit as He did in Solomon's temple!

P.S. Maybe now you can enjoy the next cloudy day.

In over Your Head

O my God, I am too ashamed and disgraced to lift up my face to You, my God, because our sins are higher than our heads and our guilt has reached to the heavens. Ezra 9:6

In some places, garbage landfills are being used for sledding hills. Throngs of young and old dot those hills riding inner-tubes, toboggans, sleds, snow saucers, and squares of cardboard. What a novel way to cope with our garbage! Otherwise we might be over our heads in junk-food wrappers and Styrofoam artifacts.

The prophet Ezra had some trash predicaments to deal with too. Sins. Heaps of sin and guilt. In a way, those unsightly piles of trans-gression were a recreation area for Ezra's people. They enjoyed their sinfulness. Only when they were in over their heads did they com-prehend that sin's brief satisfactions brought them long-term blight.

Have you ever felt buried beneath the rubbish of your sins? Have you felt like Ezra, who confessed that the sins of his people were more than God should ever have to forgive? Take heart. Remember, while Ezra confessed the magnitude (or should I say alti-tude?) of their sins, he was indeed talking to God. Although he knew mercy was undeserved, he also knew God was merciful.

Our God is the same God who listened to Ezra centuries ago. As He listened to the confessions of Ezra's followers, He listens to our repentance too. Never do Christians need to feel their sins are too numerous to forgive. Never do Christians need to think they are beyond hope or help. The same God that forgave Ezra's congrega-tion forgives us. After all, God takes His word seriously.

God always promotes repentance and forgiveness. His own Son died near a dump in a sacrifice that ended all sacrifices. If all our sins have been trashed by Jesus, where are the landfills? Jesus might answer, "Oh, they're around. I just forgot where I put them."

97

A World without Sin

*For the time will come when men will not put up with sound doctrine.
Instead, to suit their own desires, they will gather around them a great number of teachers to say what their itching ears want to hear. 2 Timothy 4:3*

We can tell when we're dealing with sensible people. They
always agree with us. Unfortunately, that's the concept
behind the "itching ears principle." Even more unfortunate is that
itching ears affect people seeking God too.

A whole new "church" movement, known by critics as "feel
good" churches, has gained popularity in our culture. People flock
to services to hear what they want to hear, and they worship their
favorite people in the process. Preachers and teachers in these popular venues tell their congregation how to be successful and happy—
how to tap the vast potential that resides inside them. They're so
good at "soft-soaping" that their followers see nothing but the suds.
Rarely, if ever, will you hear talk of sin. That would be offensive,
humiliating, and otherwise unpopular.

Our entire culture is moving away from the concept of sin.
Some mainline churches even prefer to use a synonym like *weakness*
to take the repulsive edge off sin. It certainly sounds good to itching
ears. Yet, as we shun a word like *sin*, we endanger ourselves. We
become callous toward sinfulness even as it abounds around us. We
forget that sin is the work of the devil, our surroundings, and even
ourselves. Gradually, we may come to believe that we live in a world
without sin. But if we believe that, we're as foolish as those who
tried to build a tower to heaven.

Let sin be sin in your life. Confess it boldly. If we forget the
heinous nature of sin, we also forget the vital need for a Savior. A
world without sin doesn't need Jesus. So believe in sin, and believe
in your Savior. And if your ears itch too much, scratch them. Even in
public.

Champions

As for God, His way is perfect; the word of the LORD is flawless. He is a shield for all who take refuge in Him. 2 Samuel 22:31

Wouldn't you love to see it? The camera pans the sidelines. Several behemoth linemen and a couple of toothless runningbacks hop in front of the camera. Each holds up four fingers and chants, "We're number 4. We're number 4." Allow the scene an instant replay in your mind. You'll never see it for real. Everyone wants to be the champion.

We Christians know the real Number 1. It's none other than God the Father, Jesus, and the Holy Spirit. But through the mystery of divine teamwork, they're all rolled into one Number 1. We are their devoted, victorious fans.

God does everything right. When He battles treacherous rivals on our behalf, it's good to know He always wins. His first victory came in the Garden of Eden, when He had only two fans. The devil briefly won their loyalty, but he couldn't claim their lives.

Later in history, God went to war for those He called the Children of Israel. He fought the Hard-Hearts of Egypt in a series of lopsided plagues that freed His fans from their losers' plight. His greatest victory, though, came in sudden death when everything was at stake. Fans who saw it undoubtedly thought the contest was over when Jesus, sprawled over the cross, closed His eyes, gasped, and stopped breathing. But before His evil opponent could gloat, Jesus sprang back to life and crushed the devil's wicked power.

Warfare with the enemy continues today. But the victory is already ours even when our score lags behind the enemy's. And we cheer the Holy Spirit as He continues to win our contests with the devil.

We are champions—number 1. But not because we won the bout. We're number 1 because the Number 1 won. Isn't that one-derful?

99

Even If …

Though the fig tree does not bud and there are no grapes on the vines, though the olive crop fails and the fields produce no food, though there are no sheep in the pen and no cattle in the stalls, yet I will rejoice in the LORD. I will be joyful in God my Savior. Habakkuk 3:17–18

Bad news. Newscasters sling it at us every night. Most news is so bad that we're tempted to watch the soap operas just to cheer up. In fairness, it's not the anchorperson's fault any more than the meteorologist is to blame for the weather. Sin rages and storms through history, and we're making history right now.

Bad news is nothing new. The prophet Habakkuk witnessed much of it thousands of years ago. As bad as things were for God's people in those days, Habakkuk didn't let the news depress him. As you can see by his psalm, Habakkuk was armed with dozens of "even ifs." Read the verses above again.

You probably don't worry much about barren grape vines, empty olive trees, or vacant sheep pens unless you make your living by them. But our lives remain filled with an abundance of other bad news. We might say, "Even if floods destroy homes and farmland, even if hurricanes shred our coastlines, even if AIDS decimates our population, even if terrorists unnerve our tranquility, even if domestic violence saturates our floors with blood, even if we lose our jobs, even then we will be happy with our Lord and God who saves us."

In fact, God saves the best for last. The last thing we'll ever experience is eternal life. Why not conclude today's meditation with Habakkuk's prayer?

LORD, I have heard of Your fame; I stand in awe of Your deeds, O LORD. Renew them in our day, in our time make them known; in wrath remember mercy. (Habakkuk 3:2)

100

Name Dropper

Those who know Your name will trust in You, for You, LORD, have never forsaken those who seek You. Psalm 9:10

Politicians, junior executives, and salespeople benefit from knowing names. Drop the right name in the right place and move one rung up the ladder. Of course, name droppers also can become tedious. There are times, however, when dropping the name of Jesus Christ is fundamental. Indeed, we must rely on His holy name instead of our own paltry identity. Consider the following scenarios.

You tell someone that sex is God's gift for enjoyment in marriage. He insists that his relationships hurt no one and that what he does is his business. Who are you to impose your standards on him, anyway? Such a challenge calls for some name dropping. It's God Himself who establishes the rights and wrongs for every situation. God made the rules and offers neither apology nor exception for them.

Scenario two. A co-worker or neighbor asks, "How did you become a Christian?" You might credit years of hearing Bible stories from your mother or how you studied religion in school. But note the emphasis on you. It's time to drop a name again. This time, mention the Holy Spirit who placed faith in your heart. Just think how important you must be if the Holy Spirit would make *you* a believer. You are important to God.

Your last opportunity to drop a name will come on Judgment Day when God will ask, "Why should I let you in heaven?" Time to drop a name again. You'll want it to be a name you can trust. More important, you'll want it to be the only name that God will trust. Today's psalm reveals the only name that saves us. Just tell God that you and Jesus are friends. Tell Him how much Jesus did for you. You'll get to heaven based on whom you know rather than what you know.

101

Gone Fishing

As Jesus was walking beside the Sea of Galilee, He saw two brothers, Simon called Peter and his brother Andrew. They were casting a net into the lake, for they were fishermen. "Come, follow Me," Jesus said, "and I will make you fishers of men." Matthew 4:18–19

Peter and Andrew probably told lots of fish stories. They were professionals who worked hard at a job they enjoyed. Jesus knew just how to reach them. He had a knack for making ordinary people into disciples. Tax collectors, tent makers, physicians, and homemakers all followed Him when He called.

Jesus called you too. Jesus wants you to do a little fishing, so look at the pond around you and make some plans. If you work or live with other Christians, fishing isn't so challenging. However, Christians need to share their bait!

If unbelievers inhabit your pond, you have some challenges ahead. But if you recall Jesus' words to Peter and Andrew, He said that He would make them fishers of future believers. You're not in the boat alone. Jesus provides energy and vigor for the task. Pray for the angler's chief virtue too—patience. As we share what Christ means to us and invite others into Christ's creel, some will only nibble at the prospect, afraid to commit. Gentle perseverance blessed by the Holy Spirit will eventually win their confidence. Others will take us at our word—hook, line, and sinker. What a joyful catch when the Holy Spirit latches onto those eager to feed on God's Word! Of course, every fisher encounters the ones that refuse to bite.

Go fishing today. Right after coffee break. Whatever you do for a living, you can fish too. Every catch is a keeper regardless how small. Ask Jesus to guide you. And don't be afraid of getting skunked once in awhile. It happened to the disciples too. Both in the boat and out.

Say Grace

Do not let any unwholesome talk come out of your mouths, but only what is helpful for building others up according to their needs, that it may benefit those who listen. Ephesians 4:29

Even in our violent society, we never need fear getting killed with kindness. No wonder Jesus and His disciples so strongly promoted kindness! And long before Jesus preached on earth, our heavenly Father commanded that we be kind to His children. (Moses had that as item eight on the tablets.)

It's easy to say "grace" at our tables, so it shouldn't be too difficult to speak words of grace at other times. Yet gossip, slander, and "trash talk" remain chronic problems for most of us. It's so much easier to tear people down than to build them up. We need a good example to follow.

Jesus was a master builder. Not that He didn't know how to aim a well-placed *whap* upside the conscience when needed, but divine kindness was a hallmark of His ministry. For example, consider His choice of friends and eventual followers. Matthew the tax collector was a prime example. If Matthew was like most others in his business, he skimmed profits at the expense of taxpayers. This did not make him popular. But Jesus was kind to Matthew anyway, and invited him to teach God's Word. The tax collector ended up writing a best-seller—to God's glory.

Zacchaeus must have heard how Jesus even collected a tax collector. He climbed a tree to see the Savior and ended up having dinner with Him.

Jesus says grace to each of us too. Regardless of our occupation (or preoccupation!), Jesus invites us to follow Him. How can He build up such conspicuous sinners? He forgives us. Is there any other way? His kindness, mercy, love, and compassion focuses on poor, pathetic sinners and makes us rich, cheerful disciples. His kindness commissions us to show the same kindness to the same kind of people He loved. Namely, everybody!

Be sure to say grace today.

103

Life Savings

Do not store up for yourselves treasures on earth, where moth and rust destroy, and where thieves break in and steal. But store up for yourselves treasures in heaven. Matthew 6:19–20

Aaron was depressed. Asked what he learned in school today, he replied, "I learned that some Americans are so poor that they have only one car and one TV."

On the serious side, a 1995 study of American savings habits revealed that an alarming number of citizens have insignificant or no savings accounts. With easy credit available, it seems that banks are making more deposits in people than people in banks. The words of Jesus recorded in Matthew offer a quick economics course for people of our era.

Jesus says something we may find hard to swallow. He says that true wealth is beyond our reach. It's in heaven. The question is, how do we get it? How can we get rich quick? And the answer is almost too easy. Jesus hands it out to us.

We are spiritually homeless, starved for something to sustain us. Only Jesus has what we need—and lots of it. He doles out the treasures of heaven in His Word. His treasures fill us with awe and love and sometimes fear for His great power, which protects us from the devil. His treasures load us full of forgiveness so sin need never bankrupt us. Then there are the heaps of hope on which we may freely draw when troubled, threatened, or endangered. Yes, the Bible is the biggest bank book in the universe. These meditations only scratch the surface of God's vault of goodies. Make time to look through the investments He has made for you. The New Testament is especially rich. And if you're already in awe of your Savior, read the books after Matthew, Mark, Luke, and John. You have a personal fortune stored there—a treasure of truth and joy on which you can bank.

104

It Happens So Quickly

Hezekiah and all the people rejoiced at what God had brought about for His people, because it was done so quickly. 2 Chronicles 29:36

The future seemed bleak. God's people forgot Him. They trusted their lives to fate, false gods, and other futile fads. Then Hezekiah became king and, with helpful hints from the Holy Spirit, rediscovered God. He led his people to repentance and worship. They asked God to help them rebuild the long-abused temple. Contributions rolled in to support the project, and the temple was rededicated in a grand festival. Hezekiah and all the people marveled at how quickly it all happened.

Change—especially change perceived as good—remains popular. You probably know people who practice change religiously. They change spouses, friends, cars, homes, and jobs. Of course, they wouldn't think of changing themselves. But that's exactly what Hezekiah and company did. They were amazed at how their change changed their lives.

We can't change God. Sometimes we try with our prayers, but it doesn't work. Then there's the technique that suggests if we just ignore Him maybe He'll go away—but hopefully not too far. When we do those things, we usually fail to recognize just how good He is.

Another change needs to occur every day. We need a personal repentance routine. Put more bluntly, we need to change for the better. We can do it with God's help. The change begins as the Holy Spirit moves us to see how we daily forget God. It happens so quickly. The curse, the meal without prayer, the "one more for the road" drink, the submission to ways of ungodly people. Next, we feel the weight of our godlessness and grieve over our behavior. What a blessing! It leads us to confess our sins. And God forgives us. It happens so quickly!

God will help us make our change more lasting. Just ask Him to keep you in mind when He has some spare change.

Stifled

It is for freedom that Christ has set us free. Stand firm, then, and do not let yourselves be burdened again by a yoke of slavery. Galatians 5:1

We may claim to be born free, but hospitals usually charge for the birth. Besides, from a spiritual standpoint, "born free" is a faulty concept.

As much as we condemn slavery, we still practice it. All people are born slaves to sin. Left on our own, not only do we remain slaves, we may actually think we enjoy our enslavement. We may depend on the devil to satisfy emotional and physical needs. Sometimes we don't need much help from the devil; we're effective at enslaving ourselves, following our own self-serving desires rather than God's will.

Jesus is the Emancipator. He set us free when He died and then returned to life. He sent the Holy Spirit to share freedom with us. It happened the moment we became believers. We were born sinful slaves to the devil, but Jesus gave us a new birth, one in which we were truly born free. As Paul told the Galatians, Christ freed us to enjoy the advantages of freedom. He warned them—and us—to resist the slavery that once stifled us. Furthermore, freedom is a package deal that implies responsibility.

We are free—free from sin's power to condemn us and free to enjoy a life of service to God and others. We're even free to make mistakes because God will forgive us. We're free to praise Jesus by singing hymns from a book or by making up our own little songs—even if they're off-key. We're free to pray the Lord's Prayer and proclaim our faith with the Apostles' Creed or we can make up our own ineloquent prayers or simple declarations of faith. So enjoy your freedom. And if you ever yearn to return to slavery, call on the Holy Spirit for some quick help. He will help you stifle it.

Back behind the Wheel

So do not throw away your confidence; it will be richly rewarded.
Hebrews 10:35

Confidence is that calm security we feel just before we fall flat on our face! We take much for granted each day, and that's sometimes confused with confidence.

Another word for confidence is faith. We may take it for granted too. After all, we have a routine supply of it and we use it every day. Occasionally, our spiritual confidence collides with the harsh realities of life. We can recognize these times of shaken confidence when we find ourselves asking, "Is there really a God?"

What tempts you to ask that question? Airplane crashes? Earthquakes? Furious storms that destroy homes and families? Drive-by shootings? Fatal wrecks caused by drunk drivers? Perhaps your confidence-shakers are more personal—a son with AIDS, a promiscuous daughter, a cheating spouse, a failing career, a dying parent. Is there really a God? So many people don't believe in Him—are they right? Is God just a psychological crutch to help us cope with difficult times? Are we only complex globs of proteins and acids as the evolutionists would have us believe? Talk about confidence-shakers! We even let schools shake our children's confidence in God. After all, isn't God denied by most popular authors of scholarly books?

Another book fights to maintain our confidence. The story is simple. Jesus died to save us from our sins. We live in His kingdom now, and He takes care of us regardless of headlines or personal tragedies. Someday we'll move in with Him in His heavenly kingdom. For now we need to read the story often. Through the Bible, the Holy Spirit gives us faith to know Jesus and confidence about what He has in store for us.

The Key to Success

Do not let this Book of the Law depart from your mouth; meditate on it day and night, so that you may be careful to do everything written in it. Then you will be prosperous and successful. Joshua 1:8

The key to success doesn't always fit our door! If it's any consolation, failure is a far better teacher than success—as long as we actually learn and improve from our mistakes. (Not that we should go out and make better mistakes!)

The success formula recorded in Joshua outlines a difficult road of hard work. In fact, Joshua makes success look impossible. The Book of the Law contains no exceptions, but solid rules for perfect behavior. A person would be prosperous and successful, if only …

What is the greatest success anyone could accomplish? Making a billion dollars? Two thousand years from now both the billionaire and his dollar bills will be forgotten molecules of dust. How about discovering a vaccine for cancer? As with the dreaded smallpox, some other fatal disease will replace it. Immortality? God already announced the way to escape death. No, the greatest success is to be perfect. Or at least latch onto someone who can do it for you.

That someone is Jesus Christ, and we're already hanging onto His sandal straps, riding the wave of His Easter success. God does not make us successfully complete a list of requirements for salvation. Jesus has already fulfilled those requirements for us. The success of Christ is now attributed to all who believe. We are successful only because Christ was successful for us.

Jesus is our key to success. He has opened the door to heaven.

108

Overtime

Hezekiah spoke encouragingly to all the Levites, who showed good under-standing of the service of the LORD. For the seven days they ate their assigned portion and offered fellowship offerings and praised the LORD, the God of their fathers. The whole assembly then agreed to celebrate the festival seven more days; so for another seven days they celebrated joyfully.
2 Chronicles 30:22–23

Lots of people would like an occupation that didn't occupy so much of their time. American workers are working more and vacationing less, according to some recent studies. An alarming number of people work overtime just to keep their jobs. And with cellular telephones and other communication technology, overtime can come in the middle of the night, on a fishing trip, during an anniversary dinner, or on weekend outings with family or friends.

Is overtime a good work ethic? We can point to Jesus, who labored overtime serving those He loved (everybody!). Some criticized Him for working on the day of worship. He even died on the job. But Jesus' job was absolutely vital to the welfare of countless people. Regardless of our position, we're not quite so important and neither is our work. If we want to spend some worthwhile overtime, we can take a hint from Hezekiah and his people and take worship into overtime.

When we think how God loves us so much that He sent Jesus to take away our sins, we can't help but adopt a festive mood. Now staying overtime at a festival—that's more up our alley. So you probably won't mind adding a few thank-Yous to your prayers. And while you're at it, add a few more people to your prayer list. Tack an extra 15 minutes to the end of your day to learn more from your Bible or other devotional reading. The pay is great.

Revealing Secrets

Jesus left that place and went to the vicinity of Tyre. He entered a house and did not want anyone to know it; yet He could not keep His presence secret.
Mark 7:24

Can you keep a secret? Probably. It's only the people you tell it to that can't! Why would Jesus want to keep His whereabouts secret in today's text?

Jesus had just fed 5,000 people. That news didn't stay secret for long. People were looking for Him—especially His enemies—who wanted to silence Him and end His miracles. But Jesus wanted time alone with the disciples so He could teach them how to carry on His ministry.

There were other times when Jesus' disciples preferred secrecy. Peter was a notable example. This brash follower claimed to love Jesus more than anyone else. He pledged unflappable loyalty. Yet, when Peter had three successive opportunities to testify about his Savior's innocence and power, he kept it to himself (Mark 14:66–72).

We can't be too hard on Peter. (He was hard enough on himself when he realized what he had done.) Some of us are very good at keeping Jesus' presence a secret. Unlike the episode in today's Bible passage, Jesus doesn't want to be hidden anymore. He wants everyone to know what He did and how they have salvation in Him.

Do we throw a blanket over Jesus in tough times? It's much safer sometimes to keep the shades drawn than to reveal His light in our heart. Like Peter, we're often afraid of what others will think if we say we know Jesus. We tremble to think how others might ridicule us or label us as some sort of religious nut. Just as threatening, they might like what they hear and expect more support, compassion, hand-outs, or better behavior from us!

It's time to tell your secret. Who knows? Maybe others have a few secrets of their own.

Something to Chew On

For Moses writes about the righteousness which is of the law, "The man who does those things shall live by them." ... For with the heart one believes unto righteousness, and with the mouth confession is made unto salvation. Romans 10:5, 10 (NKJV)

P. K. Wrigley was a successful failure. He sold soap and baking soda. Attempting to increase sales, he gave customers an incentive to buy his products. With each purchase, customers received sticks of chewing gum. Chair bottoms and sidewalks haven't been the same since! A new business grew in ways that even the Wrigley family didn't expect. The story of salvation has some similar twists (but less sticky an ending).

Moses didn't invent God's Word, but he distributed it to God's people by telling them that God wanted to be their God—their one and only God. If they wanted to be His people, they needed to obey His laws wholeheartedly. They could live happily ever after through perfect obedience.

This didn't work well for Moses or God's people. The people angered Moses and vice versa. Moses literally broke God's commandments and had to go back for another set. People grumbled for years about obeying God. Perhaps we would grumble too. That often happens when guilt encumbers people. Moses wanted people to know God's love and concern for them, but often the people missed the incentive supplied to bolster their faithfulness.

Then things took a turn for the better. Christ came to redeem all humanity. But what is free for us came at an enormous price to Jesus. He had to leave the comforts of heaven for a brief life on earth. Then He died to take away our sins and conquered death three days later.

Next time you chew a stick of gum or see someone blowing a bubble, think of God's incentive. Take Him home today. He lasts a long, long time.

111

The Only Good Christian

For the trumpet will sound, the dead will be raised imperishable, and we will be changed. 1 Corinthians 15:52

The Roman Emperor Nero might have said, "The only good Christian is a dead Christian." Of course, some Christians have been dead for years—they just don't want to admit it. But Nero would only laugh at that kind of Christian. He was more concerned with Christians who conspicuously lived and proclaimed their faith. Nero's bloody and cruel persecutions are true horror stories. But Nero only *seemed* to have his way. King Herod also seemed to have his way against God. Try as he might to kill young Jesus, and succeed as he did in killing many innocent children, he was actually doing what God's prophets said he would do many years earlier. Some thirty years later, Jesus' enemies succeeded in killing Him, but only to fulfill God's plan for our salvation!

Nero may have been right too. The only good Christian is a dead Christian. Christians try hard to be good—for Jesus' sake. We know how good our Savior was and is to us, and we want to copy His goodness. How far we fall short! Sin keeps trying to slay us. While it can't really accomplish that, it surely can hobble us and slow us down. We might think we are "pretty good" Christians, but we never come close to attaining the goodness required to earn a room in heaven.

When we die, we become truly good Christians! Good Christians are good because Jesus earned perfection for them. We die corrupted but forgiven sinners. We rise incorruptible, imperishable—better Christians than the devil imagines possible. He seems to win, but he really loses. He doesn't realize how right he is when he snarls, "The only good Christian is a dead one."

112

Good Luck

*Early in the morning they left for the Desert of Tekoa. As they set out,
Jehoshaphat stood and said, "Listen to me, Judah and people of Jerusalem!
Have faith in the LORD your God and you will be upheld; have faith in
His prophets and you will be successful." 2 Chronicles 20:20*

Jehoshaphat may be remembered for many things, but we
would do well to note a motto he lived by: "Faith, Not Fate."
Some people easily confuse the two.

How often haven't you (a fine and faithful Christian) wished
someone good luck? Frequently, it's a phrase that just slips out—as
common a saying as "Have a good day." But some people take luck
seriously.

A cross sits atop a well at a Russian village. Those who live
around the well think the cross will bring good luck. Of course,
baseball fans are familiar with players who cross themselves before
each at bat. Perhaps I shouldn't be suspicious, but I wonder if they
do it to proclaim their faith, bless their bat, or bring "good luck."

Luck is an impotent substitute for faith. It's another four-letter
word we should erase from our vocabulary—even if we don't mean
anything idolatrous by it. Consider Jehoshaphat's words for today in
the context in which they occurred. He and his army faced oppressive odds. By military standards, they had little hope of winning the
battle. Only God's awesome power and Jehoshaphat's genuine trust
could win the victory.

That's how it always is. Fate is nothing; faith is everything. We
may not know the future, and perhaps we fear the battles that might
embroil us. But have faith that God will win for us. He might not
always win in the manner we would like, but a single is better than
a foul ball any day.

Snakes and Scorpions

Which of you fathers, if your son asks for a fish, will give him a snake instead? Or if he asks for an egg, will give him a scorpion? If you then, though you are evil, know how to give good gifts to your children, how much more will your Father in heaven give the Holy Spirit to those who ask Him! Luke 11:11–13

Pet stores sell enough snakes and scorpions to suggest their popularity, but many of us sprout goose bumps the size of Mount Sinai just thinking about them. At the very least, we wouldn't gift wrap them. As popular as these pets may be, the gist of the passage from Luke suggests that people give presents with good intentions.

If you're like most gift-givers, you spend considerable time choosing "just the right thing." We give gifts from our hearts because we want the recipients to know how we feel about them. On the giving side, thoughtful people might even ask future recipients what they would like. What would you request if someone asked?

Would you be afraid to ask for something expensive? What would you fear—not receiving it? Perhaps you wouldn't want to impose on anyone by asking for something specific or precious. Would we ever fear that someone who loves us would give something harmful? Probably not.

Young children—and even some older ones—usually don't feel such restraint. I think Jesus would suggest that we become more like them when we ask for spiritual gifts. The Holy Spirit is the most versatile gift we could ever want. We may possess different quantities of His gifts, but the quality is always tops. Jesus bought the gift of the Holy Spirit at a going-out-of-business sale, but it wasn't a bargain. He put sin out of business and paid for it with His life.

Before you end your break, ask Jesus to send you the Holy Spirit. You've already got Him but ask for more. Ask like a little kid, and trust Jesus to give you just the right size and color. You won't have to shake the package to see if it hisses first!

114

Fragrant Relationship

Pleasing is the fragrance of your perfumes; your name is like perfume poured out. No wonder the maidens love you! Song of Songs 1:3

My mother wouldn't let me read Song of Songs (or Song of Solomon as it was called then) until I was 21 years old. Even then I had a hard time figuring out why this spicy love poem was in the Bible. It seems so out of place until you make the love connection. What a fragrant parallel the Bible draws comparing the relationship of Christ and the Church (us) with an amorous marriage! It says a lot of what God thinks about marriage and even more of Christ's love for believers.

Our marriage to Jesus began as a gleam in His eye, as He knew He wanted us long before we ever knew His name. He proposed on the eve of our faith, and the marriage was consummated with Baptism. We are now united with Him forever. Unless, of course, we break our vows or go chasing after another lover.

The devil is a shameless flirt, and he enjoys making those married to Jesus unfaithful partners. He plies us with cheap perfume that only masks his foul stench. Jesus, however, purchased a one-of-a-kind fragrance that sweetens our love for Him.

Love, by true description, is sacrificial. Jesus died to keep our love alive. Instead of mourning, however, we celebrate because our love lives on and so does Jesus. We are blessed with perpetual bliss. Like any good marriage, these blessings affect our everyday life.

Hold hands and take long walks with Jesus. And when you begin to stray (or turn your head), you'll feel a gentle tug on your soul-strings as He gently pulls you back to His matchless love.

Every day is an anniversary with Jesus. He never forgets it, even if you do. So when you wake up, thank Jesus for being with you as you slept, and ask Him to stay close during your waking hours too. Just think, this is one honeymoon that never ends.

All I Need

But as for me, my feet had almost slipped; I had nearly lost my foothold.
For I envied the arrogant when I saw the prosperity of the wicked. ...
Whom have I in heaven but You? And earth has nothing I desire besides
You. Psalm 73:2–3, 25

Advertising is the science of making us think we've wanted something our whole life, and now it's finally available. If ads are believable, there is even a way to borrow enough money to get out of debt! If only we owned what ads offered, we would be smarter, happier, sexier, and more successful.

We can't completely blame advertising for leading us to want more than we have. We can't impute blame for the desires and greed that normally infect our all-too-human hearts, either. Nor should we be quick to equate wealth and prosperity with evil, even though we may know of several people with ill-gotten affluence. Money isn't evil—only the exclusive love for it. The psalm for today focuses on the real problem. It's us.

Envy often pushes us until we stumble. Worse yet, we frequently envy what is wicked. We watch others "enjoy" all the sins of life. Does God strike them with lightning bolts? No. Suddenly, we begin to feel like we're missing something in life.

What do we enjoy? The Bible? Humming hymns? Frank, though one-sided, conversations with God? How exhilarating! Exciting? Would you believe satisfying?

Attitude is everything. While earthly delusions of pleasure pull us in one direction, true pleasure beckons quietly from the opposite side.

The psalmist tells us where to find absolute and total satisfaction. We have it in Jesus. As long as we have Him, we need nothing else. Even if we lose our treasures, suffer paralyzing accidents, or lose our senses, we still have all we need. So yearn for whatever good you want, subdue the desire for wicked pleasures, and hold on to all that you need—Jesus.

Minor Keys

I will heal their waywardness and love them freely, for My anger has turned away from them." … Who is wise? He will realize these things. Who is discerning? He will understand them. The ways of the LORD are right; the righteous walk in them, but the rebellious stumble in them. Hosea 14:4, 9

We would rather listen to the music than face it. With that, we have something in common with God's rebellious people of long ago. It's to them that the so-called Minor Prophets like Hosea, Amos, and Haggai ministered. Their preaching and prophesying would probably be played in sad and haunting minor keys if set to music.

Have you ever considered it odd that among the Bible's prophetic books, the Minor Prophets are in the majority? Their messages aren't minor either. God considered the themes proclaimed through these men key information for all His people in all times. Therefore, the next 11 days will find us meditating on what the Minor Prophets had to say.

If you haven't read the Minor Prophets, take some brief excursions to these tiny islands of prophecy in God's Word. But not on an empty stomach. These prophets portray God at His angriest since the great flood. God talked through these prophets, but His stubborn people refused to listen and obey. But even as God pronounced grisly judgment on the traitors, He graciously offered them an "if only." If only they would repent and return to Him, they could be His people again.

Do the Minor Prophets have anything major to say? Look at the verses from Hosea again. We hear that God indeed is liberal with forgiveness. But Hosea also has a word to the wise. God's ways are still right even though they receive heavy criticism from those who believe that only we ourselves know what's right for us.

Our God hasn't changed since the time of the prophets and neither have people. They still rebel. He still loves and offers forgiveness. Now that's something we can profit by!

Holey Hearts

Rend your heart and not your garments. Return to the LORD your God, for He is gracious and compassionate, slow to anger and abounding in love, and He relents from sending calamity. Joel 2:13

You can't always judge people by what they wear. Sometimes there just isn't enough evidence!

People living in Old Testament days lamented their sinfulness by ripping their clothes. Left with little to wear after such episodes, they changed into fresh sackcloth to further demonstrate their repentant hearts. While the prophet Joel was no fashion critic, he was savvy enough to know that torn clothing might still hide hardened hearts. That's when he suggested that people should rip their heart rather than their raiments.

Echoing the key theme of other Minor Prophets, Joel demanded that people change their mutinous hearts and defiant behavior. God isn't fooled. To be truly repentant, says Joel, we need to bare our hearts and soften the hard parts.

God's people are frequently guilty of the fatal flaw of hardheartedness. Each time we choose to act in ways that God wouldn't approve, we harden our hearts. Perhaps the greatest contributor to stoney hearts are our "pet" sins—the ones we commit so often that they don't seem serious anymore. Joel might say, "Poke a few holes in your hard heart. Soften up and come back to God!"

We can trust Joel's teachings. God told him what to say—not only to ancient believers but also to modern Christians. He describes God's reaction to our repentance with words like *compassion*, *grace*, and *love*. We receive those blessings not through some outward expression of sorrow or desperation, but through contrite hearts that seek to do God's will. And when He forgives, our hearts no longer weep and cower before Him. We can celebrate, adorned in His grace.

(I wonder what Joel would have to say about bikinis.)

118

Who Did It?

He who forms the mountains, creates the wind, and reveals His thoughts to man, He who turns dawn to darkness, and treads the high places of the earth—the LORD God Almighty is His name. Amos 4:13

It's a marvel that He did all the above without benefit of a diversified holding company or manufacturing empire. And He didn't quit there. He assumed human form and became one of us. He offered immortality by dying and coming back to life long before Ponce de Leon searched for a fountain of youth. He sent Paul on business trips that changed the lives of millions of people without using a scheduled airline or rental car. And now He keeps the earth tilted at just the right angle without the help of cranes or scaffolds. He knits cells together into the cutest bundles even though He lacks a degree in molecular biology, and He gathers thousands into His kingdom without immigration or equal opportunity quotas. Who is He? You know Him already. He is God, of course. His name is one to both fear and revere.

Fearing God suggests we recognize His ultimate authority for what it is—authority! How modern society rebels against authority! We want the right to make decisions that directly affect us—even if we haven't a clue about long-term consequences. We often want God's love, but not His rule in our lives.

God doesn't flaunt His authority, though. Nor is He secretive. Instead, as Amos points out, God tells us His thoughts. His thoughts carry more weight than human opinions. His thoughts were the very power that created the heavens and earth and preserves them yet today. He reveals His thoughts about us too. He loves us so much that He's willing to forgive and forget our faults. He wants us to love Him and be happy—and He tells us how: Believe in Him who died on the cross for our sins.

Who is "Him"? Why Jesus, of course.

119

Minority Report

The day of the LORD is near for all nations. Obadiah 15

Each tick of the clock brings us closer to judgment, or as we read in Obadiah, the day of the Lord. Some people deny the reality of Judgment Day. Perhaps that's an easy way to live, never admitting that we'll need to account for our actions someday. That viewpoint is as foolish as killing some time because the boss isn't around—at the time. Very risky.

Others joke about judgment. Perhaps you've heard some Judgment Day jokes, complete with verbal imagery of pearly gates, St. Peter monitoring the entrance, and devilish creatures rubbing their hands in ghastly anticipation of heaven's castoffs.

Sadly, some people dread the coming judgment. They fear they won't have a good enough lawyer to protect their reputation. Or maybe they fear that God really knows their reputation is true! But saddest of all are those who know their unworthiness in all its expansive dimensions, and either hate God or despair because of it.

Christians can welcome Judgment Day because we know what will happen. The Bible says that Jesus will return suddenly, with the sound of trumpets blasting the air. All people shall rise from the dead. All. Not just believers, but all the rebellious unbelievers as well. They, together with all those still alive, will appear before God for His judgment. Not that He doesn't already know where we belong. The Bible says God will thumb through the Book of Life to find our name. If we're registered, we proceed to everlasting bliss. If not, we spend eternity suffering in hell. We're also told we need to account for our behavior. (No excuses accepted.) And we better have some answers.

Are you ready to answer? Remind God (respectfully, of course) that although you're a weak sinner, you're also a firm believer that Jesus took those sins away. Just ask God to check the book under *F* for *forgiven.*

120

Shucks

He prayed to the LORD, "O LORD, is this not what I said when I was still at home? That is why I was so quick to flee to Tarshish. I knew that You are a gracious and compassionate God, slow to anger and abounding in love, a God who relents from sending calamity." Jonah 4:2

Have you ever prayed for something and then complained when God delivered what you wanted? Look at Jonah's prayer above. As you might remember, Jonah never wanted to take God's business trip to Nineveh—even if God would have sent him first class.

Nineveh was a horrid city filled with fierce opponents of God. Jonah wasn't about to go overboard telling them to repent—or so he thought. When, after a soggy detour, he ended up telling the citizens they were miserable sinners, Jonah was disappointed that they actually repented. Jonah's prayer came at that point. It's as if he was saying, "Why did I go through all this trouble to tell these sinners that You would destroy them when we both knew that You would extend Your mercy and grace to spare them?"

For those who repented in Nineveh, and millions of other sinners, what better news could we have? God is merciful. He spares us from calamity. God's grace even goes further back than Jonah and Nineveh. He had every right to wipe out Adam and Eve for infecting the world with sin, but instead He gave them some new clothes and promised them a Savior. (This greatly disappointed the devil!) And well after Nineveh, sinners continued their old tricks. All creation should have trembled the day God's Son hung on the cross. But that was just another act of grace and love. Once again, the devil was heaving out puffs of smoke and yelling, "Shucks!" (It's possible the devil used some other words.)

The moral of this story? Pray for unbelievers, even if you would rather see them get what they deserve. If you think about it, we don't get what we deserve either. Nineveh isn't too far from our own neighborhood.

121

Stamp Out Sin

Who is a God like You, who pardons sin and forgives the transgression of the remnant of His inheritance? You do not stay angry forever but delight to show mercy. You will again have compassion on us; You will tread our sins underfoot and hurl all our iniquities into the depths of the sea.
Micah 7:18–19

Picture this: A large crowd marches around the county building. You squeeze your way in to read the demands scrawled on their placards: "Stamp Out Sin!"

Unlikely, you say? Sadly, you're right. Today, anyone demonstrating to stamp out sin would face ridicule. Besides, there isn't much we can do about sin, can we?

Sin is a fact of life. A fact—not a figment of radically religious imagination. For centuries, people have tried to stamp out sin with laws. (Even people who weren't religious.) The result? Millions of people apply rules and regulations to daily life—especially the daily life of other people. But the only law that everyone obeys is the law of gravity!

If we really want to stamp out sin, we must lobby with the only one who can do anything about it. In fact, He already has done something about it. God sent Jesus to abolish sin. In so doing, He abolished our sins forever. Jesus obeyed all the laws for us and summarized them with only two. Love God and love others. Love springs from a godly heart and soul, with a willing desire to serve and show mercy.

Because God has "tread our sins underfoot," He has prevented sin from claiming our lives. God stamped out sin, not in some violent confrontation with the forces of evil, but through self-sacrifice on the cross. When the world ends, there will indeed be a final, fatal confrontation with the devil. Until that time, we live with the comforting words of Micah. God is delighted to show mercy. And most of us sinners surely bring Him much delight!

Ho Hum

The LORD is good, a refuge in times of trouble. He cares for those who trust in Him. Nahum 1:7

Would you believe that Nahum had a younger brother named Ho? (Think about it …) There was nothing ho-hum about Nahum. From the sound of his words, he didn't take God's care and protection for granted. Are we sometimes guilty of spiritual complacency?

Consider this scenario. The alarm clock summons us from our beds. We wipe the sand from our eyes and process our bodies for another day of work. We begin our chores with various degrees of enthusiasm, and we usually sense relief and relaxation at the end of our work day. In a few hours, our heads burrow into the pillow as the alarm clock once again waits to perform its once-a-day ritual. Ho hum.

Such a ho-hum existence lulls our senses and numbs our awareness of God's presence. We may forget that He and His angels accompany us in the routine times, the good times, and the times we're unaware of how much we really need Him. Then something happens to take the hum out of the ho. Perhaps it's serious illness or just a nagging toothache. Maybe it's financial problems or a brutal argument with someone we love. Whatever intrudes on our ho-hum routine usually sends us straight to our Savior's side, where we can expect comfort, security, and hope.

In some ways though, perhaps it's okay to have a ho-hum trust in God. Our trust in Him can be as routine as the alarm clock waking us every morning. What else, who else is more trustworthy? Horoscopes and rabbits feet can't compare. They differ little from the impotent idols that people trusted in Old Testament days. And saving for the proverbial rainy day is futile in a full-fledged flood. Our only hope is the constant, routine, habitual, even ho-hum hope in the Lord.

Isn't it great to have a God who cares? Aren't we contented knowing we can always count on God? What else is new?

123

Speak Up!

Your eyes are too pure to look on evil; You cannot tolerate wrong. Why then do You tolerate the treacherous? Why are You silent while the wicked swallow up those more righteous than themselves? Habakkuk 1:13

In some large cities, you can walk a mile and never leave the scene of a crime! Headlines mourn the loss of children killed by an abusive mother. Our cries of injustice usually prompt a flurry of activity by legislators hopeful of averting more violence. But such "solutions" are only temporary. And how rightfully indignant we get when a guilty party escapes the justice system on a technicality. Surely, it would help if God would only speak up.

Things were indeed bad in Habakkuk's time: rampant crime; random violence; deadly marauders; masses of wicked sinners refusing to worship and obey the true God. Habakkuk would feel right at home in our society. But he probably wouldn't get much press if he brought up the issue of people unfaithful to God. And if he asked God to speak up, people would dismiss him as a religious fanatic. Yet the root of our problems is our refusal to conform to God's way of life—and our resistance to acknowledging that God is God. But before we complain to God about His silence, we better think of a response in case He turns the question back to us.

God gave us His Word. We know what it says. As in Habakkuk's time, God's words often fall on deaf or mocking ears. Yet we must carry on the tradition of believers. Being motivated by the power of Christ we can speak up and let God's Word be heard—heard in the ears of our neighbors, co-workers, civic leaders, and everyone else. Let those ears hear words of hope, words that extend the forgiveness that we know so intimately. Remember, God speaks to us too.

124

A Refreshing Thought

The LORD your God is with you, He is mighty to save. He will take great delight in you, He will quiet you with His love, He will rejoice over you with singing. Zephaniah 3:17

We all like people who come right out and say what they think—especially if they admire us. Then there are those less high on our list who probably know us better. Regardless of what happens to us, they knew we had it coming. How refreshing, then, it is to read what Zephaniah said about us! Go ahead, read it again.

God breaks into song because He's so delighted in us! God's love quiets us—calms and soothes our troubled soul and body. Yet once in a while, isn't it normal to feel disquieted—to hear loud clanking coming from the vicinity of our soul?

An honest appraisal of ourselves can't help but suggest one thing—God has little to rejoice and sing about. We have trouble imitating Jesus' attitude toward other sinners. Even if forgiveness comes easily, forgetting doesn't. Not much for God to croon about there. We have those temporary but persistent lapses in our language and thoughts—the kind that integrate disobedience of the Second, Fifth, and Sixth Commandments into one fiery ball of sin. God is anything but delighted.

Time to turn to Zephaniah again. As much as we like to hear God's joy about us, it makes no lasting sense unless we remember the real reason God is happy. Jesus Christ the Savior is our Lord God. He wiped out sin's power to control us. True, we're not completely empowered in this matter yet, but we're on our way to perfection. In the meantime, our Savior dabs our guilty brows with forgiveness in equal measure to our sins.

God is indeed happy with us for Jesus' sake. How else could a Father feel about His children?

125

Get Back to Work

"But now be strong, O Zerubbabel," declares the LORD. *"Be strong, O Joshua son of Jehozadak, the high priest. Be strong, all you people of the land," declares the* LORD, *"and work. For I am with you," declares the* LORD *Almighty. Haggai 2:4*

I hope you didn't attach any immediacy to the title. After all, you deserve a break, don't you? Just don't stretch your break too long. (You wouldn't want to miss quitting time.)

We may find it hard relating to Zerubbabel or Jehozadak's son, but God's word to them is also good for us. That's why God kept this message in the Bible. Perhaps we can relate to these two men if we consider a little background information.

Zerubbabel and Joshua were land developers of sorts. They were to manage the building of a temple to replace the one destroyed earlier by the Babylonians. That task might not seem overwhelming except for one thing: Solomon built the original temple. It was a huge, ornate, and splendid edifice.

The new builders worked with a drastically smaller budget. After they completed the foundation, some people complained about how it was shaping up. Naturally, their reaction discouraged Zerubbabel and Joshua. That's when God stepped in and said, "Be strong. I'll be with you. Now get back to work."

Do you find your work satisfying? Granted, not everyone has a job they enjoy. Is there anything else that you would rather be doing?

However you feel about your job, God's Word comes to you through Haggai. Your work is important, and you need to get busy again. God promises to be with you, and that implies much about the attitude and effort that you'll put into your work. So get back to work now. It's okay to smile. The best Helper is with you. Together you'll do a great job.

Singed, Soiled, and Saved

Then he showed me Joshua the high priest standing before the angel of the LORD, *and Satan standing at his right side to accuse him. The* LORD *said to Satan, "The* LORD *rebuke you, Satan! The* LORD, *who has chosen Jerusalem, rebuke you! Is not this man a burning stick snatched from the fire?" Zechariah 3:1–2*

It's probably no surprise that whatever their working role, everyone is the same in God's sight. What we might not be so eager to confess, however, is that everyone is the same in the devil's sight too! Take Joshua, for example. Even a high priest couldn't escape the devil's indictments! How Satan must have contemplated his dramatic affect! He was really living up to his name, which, not surprisingly, means "accuser."

If there was one time when we would welcome Satan's lies, it would be when he prosecutes us before God. But the devil doesn't have to lie about us. The truth is enough to damn us to a death sentence. Like Joshua, we're nothing but a burning stick and one without a legitimate defense, at that.

Accusations are always unpleasant and even frightening. More so if they're true. Thank God we share something else with Joshua. Though singed by Satan's fire and soiled by our own dirty life, we're also saved. Jesus always has a ready ear for our self-accusations. We can confess all that we've done wrong—not that He doesn't already know. But as we tell Him how sorry we are and how much we hate our sins, we can also be confident that He forgives and energizes us to go on living in freedom. So next time the devil points his fiery finger at you, tell him to stick it in his ear. He'll be able to hear the Judge better.

127

Little Change

I the LORD do not change. So you, O descendants of Jacob, are not destroyed.
Malachi 3:6

D o you know anyone operating under the delusion that if they wait long enough, God will change? Kids are experts at applying this principle to parents and teachers. They know that the longer they ignore a request or command, the greater the likelihood that adults will abandon their efforts.

This, the last meditation in the series based on the Minor Prophets, features Malachi. Actually, like all other prophetic books, it features God speaking through a prophet. God is telling us what He has done for us and what He expects from us. God still expects people to love one another as He has loved them.

God really doesn't need our dollars and cents. However, He blesses us with money and expects us to support ourselves and share with others from what He gives. He knows that true giving doesn't come from the wallet, but from the heart. That was Malachi's message to God's selfish people too. A few verses after the ones above, we hear God accusing His people of robbery! Not only did they allow greed to govern their giving, but they gave half-heartedly.

God tells people of all generations what He has done. He tells us in plain English that He loves us and that He sent Jesus to take away our sins. That story will never change! But another story never changes either. It's the one where God's Word tells us to send missionaries throughout the world. And He doesn't want us to forget the physical needs of poverty-stricken people either. And while the tithe, or 10 percent, rule is an Old Testament law, giving from the heart is a changeless rule for all ages.

At your very next opportunity, give generously to God's work. And don't ask for any change—except a change of heart.

Independence Day

You, my brothers, were called to be free. But do not use your freedom to indulge the sinful nature; rather, serve one another in love. Galatians 5:13

The Constitution of the United States guarantees many freedoms. Though not explicitly stated, this includes the freedom of people to make fools of themselves—a right that is profusely practiced.

Had we lived in Old Testament days, we would be faced with hundreds of rules established by God. He wanted His people to know how to treat Him and how to treat others. As it turned out, the rules were too many and too difficult for anyone to obey perfectly. So God sent Jesus, not only to obey the rules for us, but to suffer the consequences of our disobedience. The result? Easter became our first Independence Day. Jesus reduced the "too" rules to two rules—love God and love others. Within those two rules, we are free to live as we want.

The question now is, "How do we want to live?" Will we enjoy our freedom to do whatever pleases us, to follow each tantalizing temptation, to disobey God and the authorities, knowing that Jesus responds freely and favorably to every request for pardon?

Just as good citizens respond to their independence with responsibility, good Christians honor their freedom with love. Love of God. Love of others—yes, even those who are hard to love. Yes, even those who don't know Jesus or refuse to believe that He is their Savior. Yes, even our competitors or irritating neighbors. And we can even love ourselves. He knows what we're really like and loves us anyway. He died and rose to empower us with new life. In whatever time remains of our freedom on earth, we can live responsibly—and responsively. So take care of yourself. And take care of others too.

129

We Just Don't Know

Do you not know? Have you not heard? The LORD is the everlasting God, the Creator of the ends of the earth. He will not grow tired or weary, and His understanding no one can fathom. Isaiah 40:28

By the time you read this, you're probably a bit fatigued. That's why you're taking a break. Can you imagine what would happen if you worked seven days a week, 24 hours each day? That's exactly how God operates.

We can't understand it—how God works, that is. Consider these questions: **Q:** Where did God come from? **A:** We just don't know. **Q:** How is the Trinity possible? **A:** We don't even understand the question, much less the answer. **Q:** How can anyone put in the time God does creating and maintaining the world? **A:** His ways aren't our ways. (Now you know.) **Q:** If Jesus is God, and Jesus died on the cross, how is it possible that God could die? **A:** Huh?

God left many things unknown. For our purposes, those things either aren't important or they are left to faith as opposed to proof. What God wants us to know is in the Bible. And it's all the important things. Consider these questions: **Q:** Does God really love *me*? **A:** Yes. **Q:** Why? **A:** Now we're back to unfathomable things once again. **Q:** What did Jesus do for me? **A:** He took away your sins through His life, death, and resurrection. **Q:** Why? **A:** Because He loves you. **Q:** Me? **A:** Yes, and don't ask why. **Q:** Am I now His disciple? **A:** Yes. **Q:** What should I do? **A:** Tell others that Jesus died to save them too. **Q:** What happens next? **A:** Jesus will come again and take us to heaven. **Q:** How long will we be gone? **A:** Forever. **Q:** You're not making this up, are you? **A:** No. It's all in the Bible.

Q: Should I read it now? **A:** Not unless you want to stretch your coffee break all the way to the unemployment office.

He Must Hate Me

And you have forgotten that word of encouragement that addresses you as sons: "My son, do not make light of the Lord's discipline, and do not lose heart when He rebukes you, because the Lord disciplines those He loves, and He punishes everyone He accepts as a son." Hebrews 12:5–6

Millions of modern parents are doing something about discipline. They're reading about it! Our Father (who art in heaven) wrote the book, and He liberally applies it to His children (who art on earth).

Useful discipline originates in love. We adults could point out ample examples from child-rearing—taking away the bicycle that's ridden blindly into the street, restricting diets to healthy food, grounding the young person who violates curfew. But when discipline comes to us, we often react the same as our children. It's not a pleasant subject.

Sometimes discipline comes from God Himself as He seeks to make us more reliant on faith or compliant with His plans. At other times, discipline may actually be applied by wicked, sinful agents who hate God and His followers. What our enemies intend as affliction, God turns to discipline that strengthens and tempers our faith.

As with any situation involving discipline, we can "make light" of it or "lose heart." Both involve misuse of what God wants to do for us. We can imagine what would happen to the child who was indifferent or rebellious about careless bicycle riding. And we place ourselves in the same deadly position if we're indifferent about the discipline God applies to us. Discouragement is just as deadly as indifference because we're tempted to forget God's grace and forgiveness.

Our loving Father provides neither more nor less discipline than we need. His discipline keeps us close to Him. Our faith matures each time He applies His loving hand. Someday we'll thank Him for it.

Close for Comfort

But those who suffer He delivers in their suffering; He speaks to them in their affliction. Job 36:15

Few things draw people closer to God than bad health. Think about it. Prayers fairly fly from our mouths when we're sick, endangered, or otherwise suffering. When we feel out-of-control and helpless to change our condition, we discover (or rediscover) the reality that we are indeed out-of-control and helpless.

God never promised to spare Christians from suffering. But He did promise to stay close through our suffering. Today's Bible reading comes from the Old Testament book of Job, one of the most dramatic sagas of human suffering ever recorded. The words you read were not, however, spoken by Job. A man named Elihu was openly criticizing Job. Much of what Elihu said about God is as true for us as it was for Job.

God helps us through suffering even though He may not actually ease our physical pains or remove our problems. It happens when we get close to God, when we talk to Him more frequently and depend exclusively on Him for help. Affliction and distress make us seek God with an intensity unrealized in more routine times. And how God welcomes us!

We often picture faithful Job as so strong in faith that he never had doubts. A careful reading of his story, however, reveals otherwise. Job punctuated his powerful faith with question marks and exclamation points. He sometimes felt abandoned by God and, worse, too good to be suffering like other sinners. Job needed to hear from Elihu. So do we. When life unravels, God invites us to listen to our suffering. It moans, "Come close to God. Come into Jesus' arms." That's one place that's never too close for comfort.

You Are Here

For if you remain silent at this time, relief and deliverance for the Jews will arise from another place, but you and your father's family will perish. And who knows but that you have come to royal position for such a time as this? Esther 4:14

Don't you love those signs in public places that proclaim "You Are Here"? If you get lost easily, the signs may offer token comfort. At least you know you are here even if you don't know where "here" is!

Have you sometimes wondered why you are here? Perhaps God has you in the right place at the right time just as He had Queen Esther.

Esther was one of many women "collected" into King Xerxes' harem. The king's crown must have twirled when he saw Esther because she immediately became his favorite. Xerxes made her his queen, but they probably never discussed family on their dates because the king didn't know Esther was Jewish. (This might have doomed their marriage from the start!) Some wicked officials plotted to exterminate the Jews, but Esther's uncle uncovered the conspiracy. He reported the evil to Esther, who probably said something like, "What can I do?" Her wise uncle answered her in the words of today's Bible reading.

Surely, you are here for some vital reasons too. Your mission is to work for the Holy Spirit, saving or sustaining the lives of your co-workers, family, and neighbors. You see, there is a devilish plot to exterminate them, and you're in the right place at the right time. You are here to declare and live the Gospel. You know that Jesus died to take away the sins of the world. You know that His sacrifice guarantees everlasting life to all believers. And now that you are here, you can share it all. Tell you friends, family, and co-workers about your Savior—even if they already know. Life is even better when everyone knows where they are.

Nomads

My brothers, if one of you should wander from the truth and someone should bring him back, remember this: Whoever turns a sinner from the error of his way will save him from death and cover over a multitude of sins.
James 5:19–20

Sometimes you need to let your conscience be someone else's guide. Every Christian spends some time as a spiritual nomad in need of a guide.

James doesn't mince words. (Just read his short book if you don't believe me.) He says that calling mutual believers to repentance will cover a multitude of sins. In other words, we are responsible for helping others see how they've wandered. Most of them already know their way back and can probably return without our preaching, nagging, or any other -ing except praying. The flip side, of course, is that we tend to wander too. (Have you noticed that enormously attractive person over by the water cooler? Did that extra glass of wine make you happier? Did you break the speed limit today? What did you say under your breath when you made that last mistake? Repent, you sinner!)

While neither God nor James wants us to assist the devil in prosecuting other sinners, our role is to watch out for others *for their own good.* Pointing out every sin isn't the way to help others, but if we notice a trend away from faithfulness and obedience, it's time to act. Spiritual wandering usually begins in such small ways that wanderers don't even realize how nomadic they've become. Being moved by the love of Christ we can pray and point the way. We can remind the wanderers how much Jesus loves them, and ask them if they really want to stray. We can always invite them back to the forgiveness that Jesus so freely offers. And we can always share stories about the times we wandered away and what we found when we returned.

134

The Other Side of the Ditch

But a Samaritan, as he traveled, came where the man was; and when he saw him, he took pity on him. He went to him and bandaged his wounds, pouring on oil and wine. Then he put the man on his own donkey took him to an inn and took care of him. Luke 10:33–34

Ancient Jews despised Samaritans; Samaritans weren't especially fond of Jews either. So when Jesus told about a wounded, pain-racked Jew who lay dying in a ditch, the last person you might expect to help was a Samaritan.

I wonder if anyone listening to Jesus that day dared to ask, "Why help?" Why risk helping others in such a dangerous and prejudiced society? Perhaps we can understand why if we get on the other side of the ditch. Lie down in the cold, stagnant water. See your blood mix with water and mud into a color God didn't include in the rainbow. Feel the mosquitos and flies stick to your wounds. Try to crawl up where someone might help you. But how it hurts to breathe, much less move! What's that in the distance? Someone is coming! Perhaps … Well, I guess he was late for an appointment or something. Someone else is coming, perhaps …

Sin has beat us bloody. Satan has left us wallowing in filth with no hope for help. Modern society and science have many remedies and cures, but all are powerless to treat sin. The only one who can and will help is really foreign to us. He's perfect. A resident of heaven. Will He really stoop low enough to pick us up?

We already know the answer. God stooped all the way from heaven to give us Jesus. And Jesus stretched across some rough timbers to heal us. Now He leaves us in the care of the Holy Spirit, who delivers healing doses of the Gospel every day. Our Lord raised us from the ditch to love Him and serve others. Are there any better reasons for being a "Good Samaritan"?

Terrific Tootsies

How beautiful on the mountains are the feet of those who bring good news, who proclaim peace, who bring good tidings, who proclaim salvation, who say to Zion, "Your God reigns!" Isaiah 52:7

If you can get away with it, take a close look at your feet. You may not want to bare your feet right now, but at least consider the naked foot and its appendages. How would you describe yours? (*Warning:* Avoid laughing while looking at your feet as it might draw stares.)

Isaiah, Old Testament prophet by trade, greatly admired feet—even the dusty and calloused ones that transported messengers over the mountains. He thought feet were beautiful, and he treasured every toe of those who sped the message of victory: "Your God reigns!"

The most beautiful feet that ever delivered the Good News belonged to Jesus. While we can't hear the patter of His holy soles on the dusty paths of Samaria or on the sandy beaches of Galilee, we can read His messages in the Bible. We can almost hear His good tidings as He welcomed people to sit and hear His Good News that He is God and that He came to save them. We can almost see the peoples' toes excitedly wriggling against the dry ground.

Do you remember the beautiful feet that delivered the message to you? Maybe it was a parent who carried you to the baptismal font. Perhaps friends or relatives told you about your Savior. The Good News may have arrived via the feet of those who work full-time for the church. It's even possible that the invisible footprints of the Holy Spirit led you to find the Good News in other ways.

Thank God for beautiful feet—those that led you to Jesus as well as those that occupy the space between your own ankles and toes. Be sure to give them a good workout today.

Multiple Choice

This day I call heaven and earth as witnesses against you that I have set before you life and death, blessings and curses. Now choose life, so that you and your children may live. Deuteronomy 30:19

How many decisions do you make each day? Obviously, some decisions are more important than others. Choices are made at various levels of confidence too. Sometimes we make final decisions. (Sometimes our final decision is "maybe"!) Multiple choices make decisions difficult, but when the choices are potentially disastrous, our decisions are critical.

God allows no room for bad choices when He offers to be our God (John 15:16). As we see from His words in Deuteronomy, He made that clear many times to many people. Risking nothing to human wisdom or integrity, God even told us the right choice. In a way, it was a nonchoice. Very clearly, God explained the life and death decision in terms everyone could understand. Choose life and live. Choose death and die. No "maybes" here.

Some decisions are easy to make—especially when they have already been made for us. God decided, even before He created the world, that we would be His—that He would love us, care for us, and provide for our every need (Ephesians 1:3–6).

Now we can live in His grace and reflect His love in the way we live. His love can be seen and felt in the way we treat our spouse, our children, or our co-workers. *Or* we can choose to turn away from His love, cut ourselves off from His grace, and wither and die like a branch that is cut away from the vine (John 15:4–6). What a disastrous decision that would be!

It's comforting to know that we don't have to deliberate long and hard when it comes to Jesus. He chose us without second thoughts long before Deuteronomy. Now we trust Him to guide our lives and care for our eternal future. Hard decision? Not at all. It's really a snap.

Buzz Words

Give beer to those who are perishing, wine to those who are in anguish.
Proverbs 31:6

Some scientist once defined liquor as the liquid state of trouble. And one old adage advises that one drink is enough, two drinks are too many, and three are never enough!

Out of context, today's verse might put some sparkle in blood-shot eyes. But the verse concludes a paragraph advising leaders to avoid alcohol because it impairs their judgment and leadership. The verse you see above suggests that beer and wine be left to those who need to lighten their burdens. Note, of course, that these words fall short of compulsory drinking for troubled hearts, minds, and bodies. We're left to ponder this verse's application to modern life.

Back in Bible days, fresh and healthy water supplies were rare. Wine was safer, and the drink of choice. The Bible mentions several occasions when people drank too much and did stupid, God-displeasing things. Clearly, alcohol abuse is nothing new. On the other hand, Jesus Himself performed a helping miracle when a wedding party ran out of spirits. Clearly, moderate use of alcohol must be permissible for those who choose to drink it. As with everything else, trouble begins when we relinquish control to that which we should be controlling. And alcohol leads to serious trouble when it is abused by those responsible for leading, making rules, and rendering important judgments.

Overindulgence of anything displeases God, whether it's beer, wine, cheese, beans, or broccoli. If we fall to this temptation, we're not beyond hope. Even the most severe overindulger isn't far from forgiveness—and help. Jesus Himself is a virtuous example to follow. Even as He agonized with the weight of a sinful world on His shoulders, He refused the potion offered to Him on the cross. The power of the Spirit is the greatest elixir for pain relief. That's one Spirit that makes for a real happy hour!

Lifetime Guarantee

Being confident of this, that He who began a good work in you will carry it on to completion until the day of Christ Jesus. Philippians 1:6

Is your automobile covered by an extended warranty? Three miles or 30 minutes (whichever comes first) after the warranty expires, so will your car!

God guarantees His workmanship. We can read the terms of the warranty in Philippians. Note the period of coverage—until Christ returns. (Most of us probably don't think the warranty expires any time soon, but Christ may return before our next coffee break!) Like any guarantee, we should read this one closely.

Christ began a good work in us—the work of setting us free from sin. He placed faith in our hearts and gave us the Bible, Baptism, and the Lord's Supper to carry on that good work. All this makes us confident that we will continue to work as Christians until He returns and retires us from earthly service. But while the warranty has its short form in Philippians, we find a complete edition of it in the rest of the Bible. We find that this warranty, like most, is limited.

The only unlimited part of the warranty is that Christ died to take away our sins. And it's true that the Holy Spirit brought us to faith and helps us grow. But we can violate the warranty by abusing God's workmanship. The Bible chronicles many sad events when God's people decided they didn't need the good work started in them. They followed other gods, refused to obey the real God, and, in one very tragic instance, even betrayed the Savior. Since history tends to repeat itself, we must guard against breaching our own warranty too.

Put your confidence into action. Continue to study God's Word and worship Him. Confess your sins and accept His forgiveness. Thank God for giving you a lifetime warranty.

Scum of the Earth

We work hard with our own hands. When we are cursed, we bless; when we are persecuted, we endure it; when we are slandered, we answer kind-ly. Up to this moment we have become the scum of the earth, the refuse of the world. 1 Corinthians 4:12–13

Picture this. You rise early in the morning, read your Bible, say your prayers, brush your teeth, and dress for the day. Doesn't it feel good to start your day with God? You go about your daily routine wearing the bright smile and airy attitude that Jesus' love placed in your heart. You treat those around you with dignity, respect, and friendliness. With Christ in your heart, your day is bound to blossom into fragrant, beautiful fruit of the Spirit—until someone poisons the atmosphere with ridicule or slander. "Wait," you say. "Something is wrong here. I'm a Christian. I'm nice to you and you appreciate it so much that you're nice to me. At least it's supposed to be that way, isn't it?"

St. Paul would understand. This letter to the Corinthians expressed the same experience, so we're in good company if some consider us the scum of the earth. Jesus understood too. While some welcomed and worshiped Him, others spit, slapped, mocked, and conspired. Persecution is a way of life for Christians. If you display and proclaim your Christ-centered focus on life, some will love you, some will tolerate you, some will avoid you, and others will persecute you.

Don't be afraid. Jesus stands with you. Remember how He answered jeers and reacted to the violence? He endured, blessed, and forgave. Christians like you have been doing this for centuries. Go ahead. Keep the Gospel evident in everything you do. You're in good company even when you're in bad company.

140

The Good Old Days

We remember the fish we ate in Egypt at no cost—also the cucumbers, melons, leeks, onions and garlic. Numbers 11:5

Remember the good old days? For the most part, a poor memory greatly enhances the good old days. However, some people have such perfect memories of the good old days that they even remember things that never happened! Let's review the good old days to see if we can find something truly good about them.

The best place to start is the beginning. Now those really were good old days. Husband and wife living in perfect harmony with each other and with God—in complete freedom. They were even free to disobey God. And that's where the trouble began. The first couple wasn't satisfied with their blessings. Eve was curious about the snake's invitation. Adam was curious about Eve's invitation. One bite into the forbidden fruit forever destroyed the good old days. But God remained good. He protected Adam and Eve, promised them a Savior, and gave them children.

The children of Israel longed for some good old days as they slaved in Egypt for Pharaoh. After 400 years God sent Moses to rescue them. But they soon forgot how precious their freedom was. As today's Bible text tells, they yearned for the bad old days. Later, God sent prophets to remind them of His good old promises. But the Israelites tried to relive the old days, to their own destruction.

The good old days aren't all bad, though. Among the best are Christmas, Good Friday, Easter, and Pentecost—good old days we fondly celebrate yet today. As you remember the good old days, be sure to remember just how good they were. And confidently face the future knowing that the best days are yet to come.

141

Who Do You Think You Are?

God said to Moses, "I AM WHO I AM. This is what you are to say to the Israelites: 'I AM has sent me to you.' " Exodus 3:14

As candidates for nomination to the Republican Party's 1996 presidential slate vied for recognition, politicians and news media aimed a spotlight at the Christian Coalition. Suddenly, everyone wanted to hear what supposedly religious people had to say. Or did they? A prominent newscaster interviewed Christian Coalition leader Ralph Reed. The newscaster cynically asked Reed something like, "Who are you to dictate how the rest of the country should live?" Reed confidently offered a tactful, politically correct response. He confessed that he wasn't in a position to impose Christian views, but he insisted that many Americans supported the Christian Coalition's political platform and, therefore, deserved a hearing.

Have you ever found yourself squirming in Mr. Reed's shoes? Has anyone challenged your Christian and Bible-centered principles? Perhaps it happened at the workplace, on the patio, or in the doorway to your son's bedroom. "Who are you to tell me what to do?" Even God's children wanted the answer to that question. God's answer seemed almost cryptic. "I AM WHO I AM." (God often spoke in capital letters!) Of course, if Reed or you tried an answer like that, you would get little more than a cynical snicker or a counseling session with a psychiatrist. Moses, delivering that message to the Israelites, got a similar reception.

God was so powerful and magnificent that Old Testament people couldn't even whisper His name. Doing so meant death. Therefore, God just said, "Because of Who I am, just call me I AM." When others question our Christ-centered judgment or authority to speak on issues, we have at our disposal a good stock answer: "God says so." (Be sure you know where in the Bible "God says so." Otherwise, you may just be fostering a weak opinion!) And if they ask, "Just who is this God?" I guess we're back to "I AM WHO I AM." Believe it or not.

142

Cobwebs

Woe to those who go to great depths to hide their plans from the LORD, *who do their work in darkness and think, "Who sees us? Who will know?"* Isaiah 29:15

It started as a few specks of dust. Soon it had grown into a gossamer cobweb. No time to take care of it now; you'll get it later. A week later you see it again and remember your pledge. But it can wait. Nearly anything is more important than cobwebs. Months pass and the cobweb remains. In fact, it has grown, perhaps so much that it's also strung between your ears! Ah. Ignorance is bliss and it's so good to be happy.

Let cobwebs remind us of sin. Sins may begin small, like specks of dust. It's hard to notice them, and they're nearly impossible to combat until they accumulate and knit together like a cobweb. At first, they may seem an illusion, just a shadow of unavoidable human nature. Then the illusion becomes a delusion. "What harm will a few sins do? Let them build up, and when I have enough, I'll take them to Jesus for disposal." But then, like cobwebs, our sins pile up, ignored and looming larger every day. We procrastinate, forget, or risk total disregard.

When it comes to sinfulness, we can't let "forget" come before "forgive." Jesus invites us to clean up our sin-filled corners daily. He knows all our corners, and there is no hiding. And even though He soils His holy hands with our dirt, He forgives our filthiness. Then He hands us a mop. With forgiveness accomplished, He gives us power to eliminate sin's sticky webs from our life. But once again, we must remain vigilant for sin, like dust, is stubborn, and it has a tendency to regroup.

Thank God that no cleaning job is beyond Jesus' power to cleanse. Brush away those sins as soon as you see them. Ask Jesus to help you shake the cobwebs loose.

143

Plan Ahead

In his heart a man plans his course, but the LORD determines his steps.
Proverbs 16:9

People who don't plan ahead often leave a happy future behind. Are you a planner? What kinds of plans have you made?

Perhaps you're plotting your future, choosing an education that will fulfill your dreams of a career. Which courses do you need? What strategy will you adopt for rising through the ranks? Whom do you need to know? How will you manage your time?

Certainly you plan ahead when buying a car. What color is most popular? How much gas will it guzzle? Where can you get the best price? Is it big enough? Who will give you the best trade-in? Which dealer is most trustworthy? Is it safe to kick the tires? How far beyond retirement must you work to pay for it?

Most of us realize that planning ahead is necessary. NASA placed a man on the moon in 1969 because it formulated detailed, step-by-step plans to accomplish its goal. Then it laboriously followed its plans, replacing or refining them when necessary. We do well to emulate NASA. We do even better if we exceed them in planning ahead.

The passage from Proverbs encourages us. Plan ahead, but entrust your plans to God. No one, not even NASA, controls the outcome of our plans. Things we hadn't planned occur at the most inopportune times. We plan, but God controls our steps. No plans are complete without Him.

Planning ahead with God's help means that we pray for His guidance, even if we question whether our goals are unimportant to God. And despite the true value of our goals, we ourselves are important to God. We're so important that He sent Jesus to plan our future. We know where we want to go, but we can't get there by ourselves, regardless of how well we plan. God controls our steps, keeping us faithful and preparing our eternal future.

Plan ahead, and trust the outcome to God. Nothing ever gets in the way of His final plan for us.

Spiritual Economics

Now when a man works, his wages are not credited to him as a gift, but as an obligation. However, to the man who does not work but trusts God who justifies the wicked, his faith is credited as righteousness. Romans 4:4–5

These days, we seem to need higher pay to pay the higher prices caused by higher pay (Economics 101). And take-home pay doesn't stay home long.

The apostle Paul imparted a critical economics lesson to the believers in Rome. Wages aren't gifts. Employers agree to pay those who work for them. They rightfully expect diligence and effort. Workers rightfully expect pay that fairly compensates them for their thoughts and actions.

Spiritual economics operates in quite the opposite manner. Let's examine the implications of this supernatural economy.

By all appearances, those who work for their eternal living should be worthy of high reward. We might expect God to commend those who toil to earn His favor and a room in His executive suite. God, however, sees things differently. He notices flaws in what others perceive as goodness and quality. He knows when we resentfully attempt to do His will rather than eagerly work to serve Him. His annual evaluation (as if He needed to wait a year!) indicates the less-than-perfect and completely unsatisfactory exertion of our thoughts and deeds. That's why we need to quit the chores of earning salvation.

Our inability to do God's will dooms us. We cannot possibly work hard enough, contribute enough money, or say sufficient prayers to earn eternal living. God saves through faith, not work. We simply trust God, who sent Jesus Christ to work for us. God credits Jesus' work to us. Talk about unearned income! Jesus made us truly wealthy, and now we have ample free time to use that wealth. Perhaps it's time to stop reading and go on a spending spree!

Take That!

Do not repay evil with evil or insult with insult, but with blessing, because to this you were called so that you may inherit a blessing. 1 Peter 3:9

You only need to drive through a metropolitan area to discover a significant urban maxim: It's easier to forgive once you've gotten even. What is it that motivates us to get revenge? Before we impulsively agree with the passage from 1 Peter, we need to assess our own R.Q.—revenge quotient. (Anyone who drives, works, or breathes should get high marks here.)

Unless you have already absorbed 1 Peter 3:9 into your temper cells, you may have already qualified for the revenge award. For example, you're exercising safe driving habits (including using your turn signal before you cut someone off, driving only five miles over the speed limit, etc.) when an impatient fool roars alongside, glares in your direction, holds the steering wheel with one hand, and delivers an emphatic hand gesture with the other hand. What is your immediate reaction?

The workplace affords ample opportunity for reprisals too. And if that's not enough, home can be the scene of the most meaningful, permanent, and satisfying retaliation. But if revenge is so sweet, why does it make life so sour?

We Christians have power to retaliate in a God-pleasing way when people mistreat us. We can repay insults with blessings; hand gestures with an apologetic wave; scowls with smiles; slights with compliments; mistreatment with kindness; unfairness with grace; meanness with mercy; bitterness with forgiveness.

At first, our reactions will surprise—and possibly anger—our antagonists. But it's a great way to share Christ's love with others.

146

Lawless

Christ is the end of the law so that there may be righteousness for every-one who believes. Romans 10:4

Although our legislature backs laws, it is powerless to bring about obedience. Crowded courts and jammed jails provide ample testimony to the efficacy of law.

Even if laws govern our actions, they never completely govern our hearts. And that's what Paul was getting at when he wrote to the Romans. Paul told them that the law is great for exposing our sinfulness and condemning us to hell, but it doesn't have power to bring the kind of obedience that God expects.

Paul knew much about the law. If ever there was a devoted law-abider, it was Paul. He was an honor student in the synagogue. He obeyed all the Jewish laws perfectly to the letter. And he vehemently prosecuted (or was that persecuted?) those who didn't. Paul thought he was perfect. But Paul's heart was bad. He didn't believe in Jesus—until God knocked him off his high horse. When Paul emerged from the blindness that accompanied his fall, he saw God's law in a brand-new light. Scrutiny under God's Law showed Paul he was fooling himself, he wasn't perfect, and that the law didn't help him one bit.

Like Paul, we need to throw ourselves on God's mercy. Any attempt to conduct a loving relationship with God is futile without Jesus. Jesus ended the law in that He saved us from the eternal consequence of our failure to keep it. He obeyed it perfectly and shared that obedience with us. Now we are judged as He is—righteous. Now we have a loving relationship with God, not because we've been so good, but because we've been so blessed. And God still empowers us to obey Him. We want to obey Him too. But salvation is already ours.

147

Get Rich Quick

He who works his land will have abundant food, but the one who chases fantasies will have his fill of poverty. Proverbs 28:19

You have about the same chance of winning the lottery whether you buy a ticket or not. Betting on the horses isn't much better—that's a game where one horse can take thousands of people for a ride at the same time. Gambling has become so rampant in some places that a portion of casino profit is pumped back into community services to rehabilitate those addicted to gambling.

The quest to get rich quick captures the imagination and wallets of millions—people as well as dollars. How sad that so many people, already impoverished by life, contribute what little they have to the false hopes of gambling. However, there is one way to get rich quick.

Faith results in instant wealth. No, I'm not speaking of the faith that people armed with cups of quarters invest in slot machines. Faith in Jesus makes us instant winners. Faith secures the biggest prize—a true case of getting something for nothing. Far from a gamble, we count on the Holy Spirit to deliver an opulent treasure chest of spiritual riches. But like gamblers on a winning streak, we're tempted to stick around hoping to become richer. Our hope is sure. The closer we remain to Jesus through faith, the more prosperous we become. Although our prosperity isn't the kind you take to the bank, it is prosperity on which you can bank.

There is no uncertainty in God's promises to abundantly bless us with abilities to serve Him. And odds are 100 percent that we're saved to live with God forever in heaven. All this without risking a cent! All this the totally free gift of our gracious Lord and Savior. God dealt us a real winner.

148

Faceless Names

"Meaningless! Meaningless!" says the Teacher. "Utterly meaningless! Everything is meaningless." Ecclesiastes 1:2

Have you ever walked through a cemetery and wondered about the people resting there? What they looked like? Where they worked? What they accomplished? Now read the Bible passage again.

This isn't starting out well if you anticipated an uplifting meditation today. Persevere. It gets better even though we read the cry of a disenchanted king once known for his wisdom and affluence. Now he believes that all his achievements and possessions are meaningless. Solomon wasn't always that way.

God blessed King Solomon with incredible peace and prosperity for as long as the king acknowledged and worshiped the one true King. As years passed, Solomon abandoned some of his wisdom. And as he approached death, his ears probably rang with a proverb still familiar today—"You can't take it with you."

Think for a moment of all the great inventors you can remember. (Unless you're a historian, it won't take long.) Who created the microwave oven, the nonstick frying pan, and the stethoscope? Who devised our monetary system, forged the first track spike, and mixed the first soft drink? As important as these events are, we've already forgotten the originators and someday society will also forget the invention.

Only a few events are meaningful for all ages. The first seven days of God's earthly creations. Christmas. Easter. And one more— the day each of us came to faith. God chose us before He created camels. He planned to send our Savior even before He hung the first apple. The Holy Spirit knew just where and when to find us well before the first brook babbled. God's love and His work are never meaningless. May God continue to fill our lives with meaning as each day He renews and strengthens our faith.

Broken Hearts

The sacrifices of God are a broken spirit; a broken and contrite heart, O God, You will not despise. Psalm 51:17

How often love results in broken hearts! For Christians, however, broken hearts result in love. Psalm 51 says so. But why would God want a lot of brokenhearted believers around?

The deepest crevice in our heart is the chasm caused by our sins. It's how we feel about our sins that Psalm 51 addresses. God is pleased by heartfelt confession, remorse, and the will to forsake sinfulness.

Confession is the first crack in a broken heart. Some of us prefer to line up in the fast-confession lane—the one for five sins or less. But if we're honest, we probably come to the Lord with a cartload of transgressions every day. How can we ever pay for what we've done? Yet we need not worry because Jesus pays the price in full.

Remorse is confession's first cousin and a second chink in sin-hardened hearts. We all know people who quickly confess wrongdoing in hopes of escaping consequences. Christians, however, experience contrition and remorse as they think about their willful, weak, or even inadvertent lapses into the very things that nailed our Savior to the cross. If our heart condition ended here, though, every Christian would be woefully depressed.

Broken hearts begin to heal when Christ comes into our lives. We abandon sinfulness when we hate the wrong that we do and ask the Holy Spirit to help us resist sins—especially our chronic ones. Of course, Jesus perfected the procedure for healing broken hearts long ago on that ugly hill. He mends our broken hearts with forgiveness and sends us to proclaim healing to others with broken hearts.

Why does God cherish broken hearts? They're the only kind that can be fixed.

150

Through the Needle's Eye

Moreover, when God gives any man wealth and possessions, and enables him to enjoy them, to accept his lot and be happy in his work—this is a gift of God. He seldom reflects on the days of his life, because God keeps him occupied with gladness of heart. Ecclesiastes 5:19–20

What do immigrants, entrepreneurs, and the Internal Revenue Service have in common? They all see America as the land of opportunity and fortune. But wealth brings anxiety whether you have it or not. But look at the words from Ecclesiastes above. Whatever happened to rich folk getting their camel stuck in the eye of a needle (Matthew 19:24)?

As the Bible indicates, money isn't evil until someone passionately embraces its beauty and value—until money becomes the god who governs life. Prosperity can be God's gift to enjoy. And we enjoy wealth more when we don't dwell on it.

Through Solomon, God urges us to work hard, be happy, and enjoy the living we make. It's much easier to be content when you remember to talk to God at least as often as you talk to your broker or banker. Satisfaction comes not from the size of the checks you endorse, but from the one who endorses you—Jesus Christ. We may work hard for our pay, but it's God's gift nonetheless.

Our greatest opulence doesn't come from hard work and healthy bank balances. Every Christian is rich beyond imagination with God's love through Jesus Christ. Neither overtime nor shrewd investments match our spiritual wealth. Whatever we have is a blessing. Our job is to avoid becoming the proverbial camel getting hung up by its hump. Go ahead, pass through that needle. God has your future all sewn up.

Collision Course

So then, just as you received Christ Jesus as Lord, continue to live in Him, rooted and built up in Him, strengthened in the faith as you were taught, and overflowing with thankfulness. See to it that no one takes you captive through hollow and deceptive philosophy, which depends on human tradition and the basic principles of this world rather than on Christ.
Colossians 2:6–8

A young girl was reciting the books of the New Testament for her Sunday school teacher. "Matthew, Mark, Luke, … Galatians, Ephesians, Philippians, Collisions …" A mispronunciation—or a profound statement?

Christian faith and the Holy Scriptures are on a collision course with the world. So much of worldly philosophy appeals to our flesh. As the entertainment industry leaves less and less to our imagination, we're tempted to minimize God's will in favor of lust.

Temptations just love to collide with us Christians, getting our attention during weak moments and when we least expect them. Should we fight with words of faith and Scripture, our smiling enemies still wound our feelings with their laughs.

Paul prods us to reach back into our memories. No, he probably wouldn't be impressed by our ability to correctly pronounce Habakkuk—or Colossians for that matter. But he does urge us to remember how the Holy Spirit gave us faith and what God created us to do.

Faith is like an airbag. It doesn't prevent collisions, but it softens the jolt. The Holy Spirit equipped us to withstand clashes with modern immorality and idolatrous philosophies. He taught us to stand up for what we believe, and He gave us an arsenal of love and good deeds to use on those with whom we collide. We may be on a collision course with the world, but now the Holy Spirit empowers us to make a bigger impact!

Caught in the Middle

But among you there must not be even a hint of sexual immorality, or of any kind of impurity, or of greed, because these are improper for God's holy people. ... For of this you can be sure: No immoral, impure or greedy person—such a man is an idolater—has any inheritance in the kingdom of Christ and of God. Ephesians 5:3, 5

Some people sow enough wild oats to feed every underdeveloped nation on the planet! Thank heavens this meditation isn't about us though. A quick check against today's Bible passage places us in good standing—or at least uttering a sigh of relief.

First, Paul excludes from God's kingdom those who are sexually immoral. ("What is immorality anyway? Doesn't society shape the concept of right and wrong? And who am I to say that certain sexual preferences are immoral? And I can have my fantasies too—just as long as I don't hurt anybody. Besides, I do go to church every Sunday.")

Justifying ourselves on sexual morality, we might proceed to evaluate our greediness. ("Not me. I've fought and scratched for everything I got. It's mine and I intend to keep it. But I'm not greedy.")

Even if we find our heavenly inheritance safe on grounds of good—or at least acceptable—behavior, we can't breathe too easily yet. We're about to get caught in the middle—the verse that comes between 3 and 5. Here it is: "Nor should there be obscenity, foolish talk or coarse joking, which are out of place, but rather thanksgiving."

Now that about does it. There is only one thing to do. Give up.

Give up figuring out how to escape God's anger and rejection. Give up to Jesus, who forgives *every* sin. Finally, give up your sins. Call on the Holy Spirit for help, and hate them out of existence. Take your wild oats to God and pray for a crop failure.

Remember Who Raised You

To Him who is able to keep you from falling and to present you before His glorious presence without fault and with great joy—to the only God our Savior be glory, majesty, power and authority, through Jesus Christ our Lord, before all ages, now and forevermore! Amen. Jude 24–25

Who raised you? Your parents? Perhaps you grew up with relatives or adoptive parents. Whoever raised you, you remember the experiences of growing up. Were you one of those children who listened to your parents only when they whispered? Much of the good we experienced came during years when our ability to remember wasn't yet well formed. (That period lasts at least until 40.)

Imagine, then, those early days when you were learning to walk. You crawled on your knees to your launch pad—a couch, easy chair, or coffee table. Flexing your wispy biceps, you pulled yourself up. Standing is half the battle. Mom or dad were so pleased they decided to help (even if you didn't ask). They reached down, took your tiny hands, stretched out your arms, and helped you hobble your first steps. How comforting to have those big hands guiding and supporting you in this exciting new phase of life!

Look at today's Bible verse again. Our heavenly Father is the "Him" who keeps us from falling. As we grow in faith, it's good to remember our humble beginnings as well as our fragile progress. Our loving Father reaches down to help us on our walk with Jesus. He provided the support that guided our first steps, and He continues to uphold us as we toddle, walk, run and stumble, limp, and trip through life. Like Jude, we thank Him for keeping us going. And like Christians throughout history, we look forward to the time we can walk completely on our own. Of course, we must wait a while longer—until our Father raises us for good.

How to Get God's Goat

Aaron shall bring the goat whose lot falls to the LORD and sacrifice it for a sin offering. But the goat chosen by lot as the scapegoat shall be presented alive before the LORD to be used for making atonement by sending it into the desert as a scapegoat. Leviticus 16:9–10

Yom Kippur is the day when Aaron got God's goat—a holy festival known as the Day of Atonement. The festival begins with two goats. One is sacrificed for the people's sins. The other is set free because of the sacrifice. This symbolic festival celebrated God's plan for His people through the sacrifice of Jesus Christ.

Christians don't celebrate Yom Kippur because Easter replaced it. But it's good to remember the symbolism of Yom Kippur as it suggests how we too can get God's goat.

We may feel sorry for the poor goat whose lot it was to die for the sins of God's people. This goat was no useless stray, nor had it committed any mischief that contributed to its death. It was a perfect specimen that could have lived a long, productive life. The goat was given to God as an offering so the people could receive the forgiveness of the Lord. How easy it is to see Jesus fitting this picture. The only perfect human, both God and man, dying an undeserved death as a sacrifice.

Perhaps we're happier thinking about the goat turned loose, living its remaining days in freedom. We're like that goat. With sins forgiven through Jesus' sacrifice, we gallop off to live as His children forever. Through God's mercy, we escape the burden of our sins. But even in our freedom, we wander through the perils of life in a desert. Like snakes and scorpions, sin either stalks us or just waits until we step on it. But God is with us just as He remained with His Son. We can call on God when sin strikes. So go ahead, get God's holy Goat anytime you need Him.

A Good Fight

Fight the good fight of the faith. Take hold of the eternal life to which you were called when you made your good confession in the presence of many witnesses. 1 Timothy 6:12

Anger normally surfaces with "fightin' words." But have you noticed that "fightin' words" often produce the best speech you'll ever regret? Most of us would agree that blowing our stack results only in air pollution. But there's nothing like a good fight to protect our faith.

A surefire recipe for a gourmet fray is to combine two young children with one ball. First, one child grabs the ball. This normally results in rapid combustion of the other child's temper. Soon, both lay hold of the ball and engage in a war of tugs, pushes, swipes, and shrill exclamations. How intently both tussle for possession!

While we don't condone battles among children, their example is similar to what Paul suggested to young Timothy. Our faith involved a bloody and deadly battle. The fight occurred on a smelly hill beyond the walls of Jerusalem. To those who witnessed the battle, it seemed the devil had the upper hand. It was all over in six hours. The one on whom generations counted for victory was dead, and the devil danced.

The devil danced with his eyes closed, though, because he didn't see God at work. The death of Jesus was God's way of winning. And to prove it, He raised Jesus from the dead. How Satan's steamy smile must have melted into a fiery frown! Jesus was alive and only sin's power remained in the grave.

The devil isn't dead, and like a vicious animal, he's dangerous when wounded. We will surely fight him before Jesus returns. We can jab with two rights and a left, but that won't be effective. What we really need are "fightin' words." What shall we say? A simple "Jesus Christ" will do.

Epic Proportions

In the beginning God created the heavens and the earth. Genesis 1:1

It's been a while since the last meditational mini-series, so perhaps you're ready for another one. During the next seven days, we'll relate God's creativity to everyday life. Ready?

We usually think that life began during the six days of creation. Actually, life never began. It always was. That's what we mean when we say that God is eternal. He has neither beginning nor end. That's impossible to understand, so we're left with what Christians have always been left with—faith. Good thing God didn't attempt to explain eternity. Instead, He explained our origins in terms even we could understand. He began with our planet and our universe. "In the beginning"—our beginning—God created the universe.

Do you suppose God enjoyed His work? God's job was so complex that scientists have spent too much time trying to discover the formula for creation. Perhaps God's awesome work should inspire us to ponder our own work.

Most readers of this book have a job at home or in a workplace. (Jobs also provide the only organized way to conduct coffee breaks!) What do you create on the job? Columns of numbers? A clean house? Loaded trucks and railroad cars? Empty trucks and railroad cars? Decisions? More work for someone else? Welded connections? Smarter students? Smooth highways? And how do you approach your daily labor? Those who rely on the quality of your work might hope that you're as conscientious and skilled as the one who created everything.

God made our universe for the same reason that we create goods or services—to glorify Him. That implies something about the quality of our work. As we conclude our coffee break, recall how God so lovingly fashioned a universe for His glory and our existence. He did everything right for us. Now we can return the blessing.

The Sky Is the Limit

And God said, "Let there be an expanse between the waters to separate water from water." So God made the expanse and separated the water under the expanse from the water above it. And it was so. God called the expanse "sky." And there was evening, and there was morning—the second day.
Genesis 1:6–8

The sky is great for holding things like clouds, sunbeams, and blimps. It also provides the air we breathe, filters out harmful rays from the sun, and insulates us from extreme temperatures. The sky is a window through which we peer into outer space with all its stars, planets, and space debris. It's clear that the sky (though not always clear) is another of God's vital, intricate, and comprehensive creations.

God spared nothing when He lavished His love on us. The sky was the limit. (Not really. Even the sky can't limit God's mercy and grace.)

I wonder how blue the sky was when Adam sucked in his first breath. Chances are, it seemed even bluer when he woke up next to the woman God gave him to love! And after 40 overcast, rainy days, I wonder how Noah felt when he saw the first patches of dry, blue sky. We even know what the sky was like some 2,000 years ago on a very particular Friday afternoon near the city of Jerusalem. Darkness covered the heavens, from 12:00 until 3:00. But blue skies brightened the bleak cemetery with a curiously empty tomb on the following Sunday.

We relate the sky so easily to our emotions. We Christians should enjoy perpetually sunny and clear skies, but gloom and gray are far too normal. Even when little dark clouds hover overhead, we have the reality of Jesus our Savior shining above it all. Isn't it good to know that He's always there, even when we can't see Him?

God's Produce Department

And God said, "Let the water under the sky be gathered to one place, and let dry ground appear." And it was so. God called the dry ground "land," and the gathered waters He called "seas." And God saw that it was good. … The land produced vegetation: plants bearing seed according to their kinds and trees bearing fruit with seed in it according to their kinds. And God saw that it was good. Genesis 1:9–10, 12

Imagine yourself back on Tuesday of God's creative week. Like a gardener anxious to plant the first seeds of spring, God wasted no time in garnishing the land with grasses, herbs, flowers, vines, and trees of all kinds. Then He gave plants the ability to reproduce themselves. He planted them, and they carried on with His blessing.

God thought of us on that first Tuesday too. Not just the collective "us" but each individual one of us. Oh yes, He knew all about us then, but that need not frighten us. Like the plants that provided veggies and fruit, He blessed us with the ability to grow and blossom. Now He wants us to carry on.

The Bible says that the gift of faith produces fruit. Confident that the Holy Spirit has planted faith in us, we're ready to bloom with what Paul called the "fruit of the Spirit"—love, joy, peace, patience, kindness, goodness, faithfulness, gentleness, and self-control (Galatians 5:22–23). This is the fruit Jesus produced so perfectly during His earthly ministry. His death and resurrection equipped us to continue His ministry. We can plant new Christians as the Holy Spirit commissions us to share our faith, and we can also strengthen spindly believers through prayer and witness.

Next time you're enjoying a juicy peach or crisp green beans, thank God for the produce He produced. But also remember to imitate what you eat. Be fruitful and feed others with the Gospel that made you grow.

159

Making Time Count

And God said, "Let there be lights in the expanse of the sky to separate the day from the night, and let them serve as signs to mark seasons and days and years." Genesis 1:14

Time probably ranks second only to money as the most valuable commodity in America. Whom can we thank for time? Why God, of course. He invented it on the fourth day of creation week. Like everything else God created, time is a blessing.

Instead of counting minutes, we need to make minutes count. God gave each of us time on earth to accomplish His will—to grow in faith, study His Word, share the Gospel, and serve other people. In so doing, we glorify Him and live a useful life. But why should we spend what little time we have doing God's will when there is so much to see and do?

God has been around a long. (No, I didn't forget to complete the sentence. Remember, time does not exist for God.) Even before time began God was thinking of us. He knew when and where we would be born. He knew that the Holy Spirit would give us faith. He also knew we would be sinners, so He sent Jesus to take away our sins. Jesus spent all His time on earth living the life we couldn't, and suffering the torment we deserve. Therefore, it appears we have sufficient motivation to spend our time serving Him who served us. How do we do that?

Making time count involves setting aside a portion of each day for prayer and part of our week for worship. More than that, we make time count when we give it all back to the Lord. But please don't quit your job and set up camp in church. We really make time count when we're out in the world on our jobs, shopping, or even traveling on vacation. Wherever we are, the Holy Spirit empowers us to declare and demonstrate the Good News about Jesus. The time is coming when our watches will stop but our joy will continue forever.

Believe It or Not

And God said, "Let the water teem with living creatures, and let birds fly above the earth across the expanse of the sky." Genesis 1:20

Every time we see a guppy or listen to a macaw, we can imagine what it was like in the beginning, when God told every kind of sea creature to begin flipping and every fowl to start flapping. It was probably the beginning of noise too, as dolphins squeaked, hummingbirds hummed, robins chirped, crows cawed, and parrots asked for crackers (which hadn't been invented yet).

You have undoubtedly noticed that the Bible doesn't provide many details about God's creativity. (Can you imagine the media hype if God had created reporters before robins?) For that matter, the Bible also reveals other important information without benefit of illustrations or blueprints. God leaves our acceptance of such biblical reports to something else He created—faith.

Most of us believe that God sent Jesus to rescue us. We believe that Jesus died to take away our sins, that He came to life again, and that He will return some day. That same faith can be applied to other biblical truths of less immediate importance—such as the six day, utterly comprehensive creation. Yet some people pick and choose which parts of the Bible to believe—especially if they think their eternal life doesn't depend on it.

Make no mistake. God expects us to believe the unbelievable— all of it. For if we doubt the creation epic, the parting of the Red Sea, or Jonah in the belly of a fish, we open our minds to doubt other portions of the Bible that deal with our personal salvation more directly. Conclude this meditation with a prayer that the Holy Spirit fill you with enough faith to believe all the wonderful, unbelievable stories in the Bible. Then get back to work. Your employer expects you to be fruitful too.

Busy, Busy, Busy

And God said, "Let the land produce living creatures according to their kinds: livestock, creatures that move along the ground, and wild animals, each according to its kind." And it was so. ... Then God said, "Let Us make man in Our image, in Our likeness, and let them rule over the fish of the sea and the birds of the air, over the livestock, over all the earth, and over all the creatures that move along the ground." Genesis 1:24, 26

I wonder if Friday left God as breathless as it leaves us. From the minute aphid to the largest dinosaur, God made all the land animals right before the weekend. If you've ever nursed aching feet after trekking through a zoo, you especially appreciate the abundance of God's living and breathing works of nature. But God also reserved the sixth day to fashion His most prized creation—people!

Did you notice the "Let *Us* make man ..."? God the Father, Son, and Holy Spirit formed a conglomerate to make humans. After all, God wanted to make people in His own image! And God wanted humans to keep busy for the life of the earth. They were to manage God's creation. That should have been enough to keep people out of trouble. But it didn't take long before sin bruised and battered the wonderful creation of God. Yet God retained His original goal for us—to be His children, manage His blessings, and be the prize of His creation. That should be enough to keep us busy!

Busy as we may be with God's business, the devil remains busy trying to disrupt us—usually with much success. Thank God that He's never too busy to continue creating—creating new hearts cleaned by Jesus' blood—creating new energy to serve Him—creating new blessings for us to manage even after we ruin the old ones. When you think about it, we've got quite an image to uphold.

Rest Assured

By the seventh day God had finished the work He had been doing; so on the seventh day He rested from all His work. And God blessed the seventh day and made it holy, because on it He rested from all the work of creating that He had done. Genesis 2:2–3

History isn't what it used to be. The way history is advancing, nearly every day is the anniversary of something terrible! Of course, it doesn't have to be that way—not when history is actually *His story.*

Even for many unbelievers, the Bible is a history book. Most history books record human achievement. It's probably safe to claim that only one history—His story—says anything about the achiever resting. God certainly deserved a rest. After all, He created everything as far as the eye could see and a few things that eyes couldn't see.

God's story is the history of love. His story reveals how He created everything perfect for His people to enjoy. God's story is the history of forgiveness, for soon after creation the apples of His eye turned sour with sin. Even while they were sinners without a clue as to what would happen next, God forgave them. God's story is a history of promises and promise-keeping. He promised a Savior who would bring humanity back into God's image, and He fulfilled that promise on a day historians call Christmas. God's story is one of sacrifice, for He came to earth in a form we humans could understand. He suffered, died, and was buried. But God's story is also one of victory because He rose from the grave, and He rose from the earth into the heavens where He remains our powerful Creator and Savior. God may have rested on the seventh day, but He hasn't rested since. He daily renews and strengthens our faith. The comfort we get from knowing that God is still active helps us rest assured that His story will continue throughout history.

Christian to Christian

*I pray that you may be active in sharing your faith, so that you will have
a full understanding of every good thing we have in Christ. Philemon 6*

God prepared a smorgasbord of spiritual goodies for His
children, but some people seem to be on a diet. Most of
us haven't discovered all the goodies available because we never
make it to the end of the table the Lord prepared for us. Paul seemed
to address that issue in his letter to Philemon, especially in the verse
printed above. Paul might have said it this way: "Keep growing in
Christ. The more you grow, the more you know. The more you know,
the more you show. The more you show, the more you grow."

Paul's intimate letter asked and encouraged Philemon to take
his Christian reputation one step farther. And it had to be a difficult
step. It seems that one of Philemon's slaves had run away.
Apparently, this slave, Onesimus by name, met Paul in Rome. By the
power of the Holy Spirit through Paul, Onesimus became a
Christian—just like Paul and Philemon. Now Paul asked Philemon
to accept Onesimus back, not as a piece of property, but as a brother. We don't know if Philemon responded with a leap of Christian
love or a bitter reunion.

The letter to Philemon is an example of what may be required
of practicing Christians. We're not asked to be judicially or legally
fair, but we're also not asked to do anything God wouldn't do.

We're an awful lot like Onesimus. We often seek to escape our
Master, but He always welcomes us back. And because we've experienced His mercy repeatedly, we have an opportunity to respond in
kind to the Onesimuses in our life. As we practice this very personal kind of Christian love, we will uncover even more "hidden blessings" of faith. It's as Paul says. We begin to understand the blessings
of our Christ-filled life. Give a lot. Get a lot.

164

Reform School

Let us examine our ways and test them, and let us return to the LORD.
Lamentations 3:40

Okay, so it's an outdated term—reform school. But we all know someone who belongs in one. Christ-centered people spend their entire life in reform school. Like many schools, reform school schedules a quiz daily. Here's yours for today.

1. **T F** The book of Genesis reports the creation of the world.
2. **T F** The book of Noah tells about the flood.
3. **T F** You can obey the Ten Commandments if you try really hard.
4. **T F** Methuselah lived a record 965 years.

Check your answers. Only the first statement is true. Noah had his own boat but no book, and we cheated Methuselah by four years. Number 3 is why all Christians need reform school. (You have a chance to improve your score with number 5 at the end of this meditation.)

How futile our spiritual education when we realize we can never achieve the perfection God demands. As hard as we might work at reform, we never entirely achieve it. Futile, indeed. But because the Holy Spirit gave us faith, our futility leads not to dropping out or giving up, but into the arms of our Teacher and Savior.

Christ reforms us daily. He removes impediments to our growth and teaches us all we need to know for salvation. Our minds wander, and our consciences doze more than a few times every day. But Jesus never gives up on us. He died to give us all we need to "commence" with eternal life. He renews our energy to resist temptation and fight the "classroom bully." He even whispers the answer to the only question that counts:

5. **T F** I believe that Jesus is my Savior.

Getting Directions

May the Lord direct your hearts into God's love and Christ's perseverance.
2 Thessalonians 3:5

You've probably participated in a discussion like this:
"Why don't you stop and ask directions?"
"No, I think I'll just turn right at the next corner."
"You said that the last time we turned right. Didn't you look at the map?"
"No, I couldn't get it unfolded."
"If you can't even unfold a map, how do you expect to find the expressway?"
"Oh, you never trust my judgment. I'll turn right, and we'll be okay. You'll see."
(Three right turns later.) "Why don't you run into that donut shop and ask directions?"

We Christians face a similar dilemma. God tells us that we're strangers on earth, far from our home in heaven. As we travel through life, it's easy to get lost. That's why Paul left the Thessalonians—and us—the words of blessing in today's Bible passage.

How we need God's direction in our life! Only God creates faith that leads us to know Jesus as our Savior. Only Jesus paves the way to heaven through His death and resurrection. And only the Holy Spirit delivers directions clearly and accurately.

Certainly, we can read God's Word by ourselves. But it's also good to hear it from others who have studied it and meditated upon it. They can tell us about landmarks that make unfamiliar surroundings more familiar—things like the cross and the empty tomb. Things like the bread and wine and river of life. Things like forgiveness and living God's way. All these make our trip to heaven smoother and more enjoyable, though long nonetheless. Don't you feel like reverting to your childhood and asking, "Are we there yet?"

Paul turns to us and says, "Be patient. We'll be home soon."

A Long List

I urge, then, first of all, that requests, prayers, intercession and thanksgiving be made for everyone—for kings and all those in authority, that we may live peaceful and quiet lives in all godliness and holiness. 1 Timothy 2:1–2

On occasion, we may remember to include the president or the local mayor in our prayers, especially when their administration is particularly stressful. Our prayers may take a different tone when we find our representatives doing things we don't like! The best example of prayer, however, comes from Jesus Himself. Even as He suffered the most unjust judgment a government ever made, He prayed, "Father, forgive them, for they do not know what they are doing." Take a moment now to silently pray for your government. What does it need most right now?

While many Christians have lengthy prayer lists taped to the refrigerator or the cover of their Bible, most every home has an even longer list at its disposal. It's called the telephone book. It's easy to pray for those whom we know or with whom we can identify. But what about the thousands of people we don't know? Don't they too contribute to living what Paul calls peaceful and quiet lives?

The task of praying for all those people may seem impractically large, but it's not so formidable if we break it down to smaller steps. Start with the page on which you find your name. Go to the top and pray for one person each day. (Don't be discouraged. Even Methuselah didn't live long enough to pray for every person in a large city!)

How do you pray for those you don't know? Won't you repeat yourself? Probably. But that hasn't stopped you before, has it? Perhaps the following will help:

Lord Jesus, I don't know if _____ knows You, but I know he/she needs You. Come close to _____ and live in his/her heart. Bless _____. I'd like to meet her/him in heaven someday. Amen.

Bare-Bone Existence

He asked me, "Son of man, can these bones live?" I said, "O Sovereign LORD, *You alone know." Then He said to me, "Prophesy to these bones and say to them, 'Dry bones, hear the word of the* LORD!' " *Ezekiel 37:3–4*

Most people have a skeleton or two in their closet, but the prophet Ezekiel had a whole valley full of them. Just what he needed when his people were already filled with despair as a defeated and captive nation! Why does Ezekiel's experience in the valley of dry bones remain important to modern Christians?

Let's go back to the beginning—when God Himself looked at the soil in Eden's garden. He took a handful and breathed on it. Suddenly, the soil had body and soul. If God could do that with ordinary garden dirt, Ezekiel believed that the scattered skeletons would come alive if God willed it. So Ezekiel trusted God and did what others might consider useless. He talked to the bones. By God's power they came to life.

Sometimes, living the Christian faith seems pointless to believers. So many others don't believe, perhaps even in our own family. Every day we may pray "Thy will be done" only to witness what appears quite contrary to God's will. Or perhaps our faith has become so routine that it's dull and nearly lifeless. We aren't really aware that it's operating as we sit at our desk, assemble our designated piece, make lunch for the kids, enter our data. At times like that, we need to remember Ezekiel, who went about his daily business—even talking to dry bones—trusting God to bless his work. And remember God, who empowers us to practice a godly work ethic and to witness to family, friends, and co-workers. If you think you're talking to deaf ears, just think again about Ezekiel.

Big Brother Is Watching You

I am with you and will watch over you wherever you go, and I will bring you back to this land. I will not leave you until I have done what I have promised you. Genesis 28:15

How do you react to this: Jesus always knows where you are and what you're doing? Even if you're the most devoted and ambitious worker this side of Father Abraham, there are probably times when you do things you wouldn't want Jesus to see. Big Brother's ever-present watchfulness isn't always welcome. That's the Law side of God's watch over us. When you think about it, even that side of God's care is a blessing.

Have you ever done something wrong and just waited to get caught? Maybe it was that time you skipped school. Or maybe it was that misplaced decimal point that cost your company so much. Just how can these experiences be a blessing?

If God already knows what you've done wrong, what reason is there to hide it deep beneath piles of guilt? Like Adam and Eve after their deliciously sinful snack, God knows all, but He wants us to tell Him about it. Only then are the doors to forgiveness open and the onus of guilt relieved.

On the Gospel side of God's watchfulness, His children also experience great comfort from knowing their Brother's care. When storm winds rattle windows and sweep trees to the ground, it's surely good to know that Jesus sits out the storm with us. When we are so sick we think we're going to die (or afraid that we won't!), it's reassuring to know that Jesus promises to stay close. When we don't know where to turn for help, it's encouraging to realize that Jesus turns even the worst things to good for His brothers and sisters.

Get back to whatever you were doing, unless of course … And smile. Big Brother is watching you.

On-the-Job Training

"Ah, Sovereign LORD," I said, "I do not know how to speak; I am only a child." But the LORD said to me, "Do not say, 'I am only a child.' You must go to everyone I send you to and say whatever I command you."
Jeremiah 1:6–7

Sometimes we feel inadequate to do God's work. Do you feel qualified as a missionary? How about a pastor? Sunday school teacher? Witness? While God didn't intend everyone to be missionaries or pastors, He has equipped each of us for some kind of work. And you're in pretty good company if you feel incapable. Jeremiah, the prophet, felt the same. Did you notice what God said to him?

God provides on-the-job training when we work for Him. It's a good deal too. Where else can you get all the benefits and your entire compensation before you even start the job? You may not become a manager or supervisor, but you will contribute to His glory.

Regardless of the skills and interests God gave you, every Christian has the ability to witness. God commissions us to both live and speak the Gospel. We don't need a theologically impressive vocabulary to witness. We simply need to tell others what we know—in our own words, using terms that others like us understand. But words aren't the real problem. Courage is. Many of us squirm if someone asks why we go to church, why we avoid foul language and dirty jokes, why we pray before eating lunch, or why we're reading this book. Even Jeremiah worried about people's reaction to what God wanted him to say. It's unlikely that anyone will toss you into a mud-filled cistern as they did Jeremiah. But they may sling some dirt at you. How can you witness then? The answer isn't always clear, but God will give you an answer. Just ask Him. He can do what you can't.

170

What Sacrifice?

I know, my God, that You test the heart and are pleased with integrity. All these things have I given willingly and with honest intent. And now I have seen with joy how willingly Your people who are here have given to You. 1 Chronicles 29:17

The word *sacrifice* conjures up many images. We might think of Old Testament days when God's people burned the best of their harvest to honor and worship Him. We may shudder at the Passover celebration when rivers of blood flowed from thousands of lambs slaughtered and cooked for the festival. And yes, we also remember God, who sacrificed His Son, Jesus, to pay for our sins. We rightly associate the word *sacrifice* with loss.

Christ's sacrifice mercifully ended the requirement for all other sacrifices. Yet how else can we thank Jesus for His extraordinary sacrifice on the cross except by making a few sacrifices of our own? We see an example of generous sacrifice in today's Old Testament text, which was part of King David's prayer after he collected special contributions for the temple. The people responded unselfishly to God's love. They gave until it hurt—and they were happy about it!

Giving until it hurts really isn't a true measure of generosity. Some people have a very low tolerance for pain! True giving comes from a happy heart.

Modern Christians still thank God with sacrifices. Sometimes we give our time to manage or maintain our church or to visit the sick and lonely. Sometimes we sacrifice a generous portion of our income for missions or charities. Sometimes we offer our voices to sing praises or tell others what Jesus did for us. Prayer qualifies as a sacrifice too—especially when we talk to God about the needs of others. If someone commented about our sacrifices, we would probably respond, "What sacrifice? I was glad to do it." And that's the whole point of sacrifices.

171

Drop in Anytime

Dear friend, you are faithful in what you are doing for the brothers, even though they are strangers to you. 3 John 5

Have you ever looked for a helping hand? We can usually find one at the end of our own arm!

Most of us are in the same position as Gaius, whom John addressed above—able to help and support our Christian brothers and sisters. A good place to start is at God's house. At times, it's easy to snipe (either verbally or within the privacy of our own thoughts) at the choir or the pastor as they display occasional inadequacies. And then there are all those people who aren't paying attention to the sermon. And that noisy kid in the front row! How much did Mr. Hobbs put in the offering basket? Just what would John say if he wrote a fourth epistle to us?

He would probably tell us to drop in on Gaius. Better yet, he might tell us to drop in on Jesus—anytime. Jesus always showed up where He was needed. Once it was among some outcast lepers. He dropped in on them, and they ran off completely cured. Another time, He dropped in on a mob about to stone a promiscuous young lady. And then there were the hours after the resurrection when Jesus strolled alongside two men discussing the recent tragic events. He dropped in at their home for supper too. He not only said "grace" at the table, He *was* grace!

Now it's our turn. Remember the best place to find a helping hand? How might we show kindness and love to others? A phone call and an open ear sometimes meet the need. And the pastor isn't the only one qualified to visit the hospitalized and lonely. How about a little book to keep that noisy kid occupied, and another voice for the choir to savor? Oh yes, one more thing. Sometimes the best helping hand is the one that is folded in prayer.

172

Just What the Doctor Ordered

A cheerful look brings joy to the heart, and good news gives health to the bones. Proverbs 15:30

One survey indicated that children laugh an average of 500 times daily. Adults, 15 times. If God created humor, I hope it doesn't become extinct. He made us able to smile, grin, chuckle, giggle, laugh, or even howl. He also helps us laugh at our troubles (probably so we never run out of things at which to laugh). He enables us to laugh at ourselves too—a wonderful source of amusement. Proverbs tells us that joy is good medicine whether we're sick or not.

Like everything else God created, humor can be misused. We're often eager to laugh at sin. Jokes about sex or race, especially when told in confidential whispers, often prompt fits of laughter when they should really move us to tears. And sometimes cruel laughter escapes our mouths as we enjoy the misfortune or faults of others.

Forgiveness makes humor possible. When life becomes troubled, it's hard to laugh. But as God's forgiveness and comfort begin to soothe and heal, we can look back and laugh at our troubles. It doesn't take much imagination to hear Peter enjoying a shoreline dinner with his friends, recalling the day he almost drowned. *"Ha, ha.* I was *so* brave. I stepped out on those waves, and I was really going to show you guys how much faith I had. Then I thought, 'What am I doing out here?' I thought I'd have to sink to the bottom and run for shore!"

Always be ready to laugh. And when you laugh, make a note of what was so funny. Maybe you can share it with someone who really needs a laugh. Enjoy a good grin a few times each day. A good howl will get your heart pumping too. And you know what they say about he who laughs last. (He didn't get the joke.)

Prophet Sharing

And the glory of the LORD will be revealed, and all mankind together will see it. For the mouth of the LORD has spoken. Isaiah 40:5

A banquet speaker once said, "My job is to speak and yours is to listen. I hope we stop at the same time." In Old Testament days, the prophet's job was to speak. Often, the listeners quit before the message ended. What do you suppose would happen if men like Isaiah, Jeremiah, and Elijah returned to address modern society? We can't meet them in person, but we can rejoice that God recorded and shared their words in His book.

It's easy to see the parallels between Old Testament depravity and today's events. We, like our Old Testament counterparts, tremble to think that God's judgment remains upon us as He punishes sin. It's good that God shared these prophecies with us, for they still show us our sinfulness and need for repentance. They warn us to fear, love, and trust God, as Martin Luther was so apt to say as he explained the commandments.

The old prophets also had Good News. Isaiah shared the Gospel even before anyone knew there was a Gospel! The entire 40th chapter offered welcome relief to his prophecies of doom. For the ancient believers, it pointed toward a Savior who would re-create a right relationship with God. We modern believers know Isaiah's prophecy came true on the first Christmas. But we also share the prophet's words for our future.

Christ will come again. No one will mistake Him for a poor, helpless baby next time. He will come in glory, not humility. He will destroy everything evil, but we need not fear for we are God's people now. He will come to take us home. Isaiah gives us something to hope for as he promises, "those who hope in the Lord will ... soar on wings like eagles" (40:31).

174

Love Is ...

And this is love: that we walk in obedience to His commands. As you have heard from the beginning, His command is that you walk in love. 2 John 6

Many would-be poets attempt to define love. Few have succeeded as famously as Shakespeare or the Brownings. And when the songwriter wrote, "Love makes the world go 'round," did he really mean that love makes people dizzy? Think for a moment, how would you define love?

John wrote a loving letter "To the chosen lady and her children, whom I love in the truth ..." (2 John 1). He explained love with the verse at the beginning of this meditation. Take a moment and read it again. John's insight about love came from the King of Love Himself—Jesus Christ.

We often fail to consider that obedience and love are synonymous. The relationship between these words might be easiest to understand when we think of parents and children. But how many children feel they are loving their parents when they obey them? And how many parents cherish a homemade Valentine card more than their children's obedience? Then there are "modern" wedding vows. The word *obey* is often deleted because obedience is tantamount to giving up too much of self. But isn't loving obedience really a victim of distrust—often well-deserved?

Thank God we can always trust Him. It makes obedience so much easier! As Jesus obeyed His Father during His earthly ministry, so we want to obey God. We can obey God's two-dimensional plan for love—loving God and loving other people—even the unlovable, despicable, and spiteful ones. (Who is the most loathsome person in today's news? How can you love that person?)

A word of caution: Our walk in love and obedience might wind through valleys of derision, scorn, contempt, loneliness, accusation, and even death. But those conditions are only temporary—as Jesus proved. And after all, lovers even enjoy walking in the rain.

175

Once Upon a Time

I want you to recall the words spoken in the past by the holy prophets and the command given by our Lord and Savior through your apostles.
2 Peter 3:2

Call it what you want—recall, recollection, reminiscence, or memory. It's one of those fleeting things in life. Memory is that function of the mind that suggests you've probably forgotten something.

Some things are unforgettable. They constitute a treasury of "once upon a times" for us. Perhaps it was a special birthday surprise, a wedding, or the birth of a child. Maybe it was a once-in-a-lifetime trip or first car or family reunion. Like fine wine, recalled events get better as they age—even if a few sour grapes contaminated the original version.

The apostle Peter knew the value of memory too. Far from just an ingredient of sentimentality, he considered memory a vital link between God's Word in the past and life in the present and future. The Bible provides indispensable "once upon a time" stories still valuable today.

Once upon a time—actually before there was a time—God created a splendid place to live.

Once upon a time, God was so angry with the evil world that He flooded it, destroying all but a few lives. In His incredible mercy, He rescued a few faithful people and a boatload of animals. Then He placed a rainbow in the sky to remind people that He still loved them.

Once upon a time, God took the form of a common man so He could live a holy life for hopeless sinners. He obeyed all the laws perfectly. He loved people unselfishly and unconditionally. Then He carried our sins to the cross, suffered, died, and was buried. He showed Himself victorious over the devil when He rose back to life.

Once upon a time, He will also return and take us to heaven where we'll live happily ever after. And that's no fairy tale.

Hypocrites and Other Sinners

Meanwhile, when a crowd of many thousands had gathered, so that they were trampling on one another, Jesus began to speak first to His disciples, saying: "Be on your guard against the yeast of the Pharisees, which is hypocrisy." Luke 12:1

Are you a hypocrite? Consider the following questions:
1. You smile contentedly as you write a large check to the IRS.
2. You must always think before putting the best of your two faces forward.
3. You stay away from church because too many hypocrites are there.
4. You know 27 people other than you who should read this meditation.
5. You agree with everybody.

A real hypocrite is one who simply pretends to be a Christian. A real hypocrite may attend church and recite the creed but deep down inside does not believe Christ is the Savior. A real hypocrite is a nonbeliever. We also act like nonbelievers whenever we do that which is inconsistent with our faith—sin. So in other words there are times when nonbelievers act like Christians, and there are times when Christians act like nonbelievers. No wonder things get so complicated.

The difference between Christian sinners and the nonchristian hypocrite is that Christians recognize two faces of their faith—the perfect face that is a gift of the Holy Spirit and the beaten face, scarred by wars with the devil and our own natural desires. Those around us may see only the beat up face of a sinner. They make us feel guilty—like hypocrites—if they point out inconsistencies between what we believe and how we act. Should Christians guzzle one too many? Should Christians curse when cut off by a motor moron? Should Christians laugh hysterically at filthy jokes?

Jesus is the cure for hypocrisy. And while scars remain, we're also cleansed of our sins as well. And even though we stumble and fall repeatedly, our clumsiness as saints is only a stage from which we'll pass someday. God forgives when repentant sinners run to Him for healing, even when we're repeat offenders.

177

A Tender Kiss

An honest answer is like a kiss on the lips. Proverbs 24:26

You'll probably agree that the verse above is better than the old adage about honesty being the best policy. As of this writing, kissing remains one of the more pleasant ways of spreading germs. And honesty still pays more than it costs. Or does it?

Here are some times when you may be tempted to be less than truthful: Completing a resume; filling out any form with the number 1040 on it; answering questions about sex; reporting last Saturday's golf score; telling children how well you did in school; selling your car with 212,000 miles on it; describing your athletic heroism before you injured your knee (falling off the bench); how many oysters you can eat; and how fast you thought you were going in that 25 MPH zone. You could probably create additional paragraphs about honesty, but then kissing might take on a bad flavor. Or become extinct.

One reason people resort to dishonesty is to protect their image. Or their income. Or their freedom. Or their eternal life? Wouldn't you know it? The only time the devil is truly honest is when he's telling God about us. Before the divine throne the devil accuses us. (And he's proud of it!) He's not very discreet either. The devil tells all. But God made it possible to beat the devil at his game. God makes it possible for us to be honest with Him. There is nothing He can't or won't forgive (except not believing in Him). He forgives even the most appalling sins.

God's response to our repentance is indeed like a kiss—especially as one psychologist defines a kiss: It's when you're so close that you don't see anything wrong.

178

Now I Lay Me Down to Sleep

Do not be anxious about anything, but in everything, by prayer and petition, with thanksgiving, present your requests to God. And the peace of God, which transcends all understanding, will guard your hearts and your minds in Christ Jesus. Philippians 4:6–7

If you're like most people, the average amount of sleep you need is 30 minutes more. Millions of people, however, can't even get to sleep or remain asleep for any length of time. According to the *Chicago Tribune* (Oct. 1, 1995), a study by The National Center on Sleep Disorder Research estimates that 70,000,000 Americans suffer some type of sleep disorder. (I wonder if counting sheep two at a time would make you fall asleep twice as fast.)

Guilt alone could keep us sleepless every night of our lives. No day passes when we can sink a guiltless head into our downy pillow. And if we didn't seek God's forgiveness before we closed our eyes, we probably couldn't keep them closed. It's easier to fall asleep counting on your Shepherd rather than calculating sheep.

Worry is a great sleep robber also. Normally, it's useless to advise worried people not to worry. Yet it's comforting to hear Paul's words to the Philippians. And living by them provides lasting solace and unfailing contentment. Paul counsels us to place all our anxieties in God's care.

In every uncertainty and risk, we do well to trust God. He may not dissipate that tornado, banish the drunk driver, protect us from disease, or provide miraculous escape from accidents. But He does promise to make good out of even the worst situations. He promises to strengthen us and be at our side when we must cope with trouble or tragedy.

We can count on the Shepherd. Remember that next time you're sleepless. And put a new spin on that old prayer. "Now I lay me down to sleep, I pray the Lord my *life* to keep. Amen."

179

No God

Oh, the depth of the riches of the wisdom and knowledge of God!
How unsearchable His judgments, and His paths beyond tracing out!
Romans 11:33

An 18-year-old girl once said she couldn't believe in God. Her friend's mother suffered an excruciating death from cancer. A friend had AIDS. Another friend was killed on his way to school. All this seemed sufficient evidence that no God existed. You probably hear similar stories from other skeptics.

God doesn't always make sense. The truth is that *we* often have no sense—not His kind anyway. That's what Paul told the Romans. Comparing God's thoughts and actions with those of humans is like comparing apples and orangutans! How sad it is when people bring God down to their level of understanding. It's even worse when they blame God for something He hasn't done.

God didn't bring sin into the world. Adam and Eve's first sin so defiled the world that sin has been epidemic ever since. Sin is a random terrorist and killer. Sin's greatest promoter loves to have us believe that there is no God because there is so much sin! Isn't that just like shrewd old Satan?

God never promised to keep sin from hurting us. But He does promise that should sin even take our life, He won't let it defeat us. We have the hope of eternal life even when earthly life seems like a living hell. There is only one way to be sure that God's promise is stronger than sin's grasp. Faith is the answer. Faith is trusting God to make the best of every situation. Faith drives us to read the Bible where we find many stories of God's love in the lives of His suffering and dying people. And the only way we can respond to declarations like "No God" is to say, "Know God."

Upward Mobility

In My Father's house are many rooms; if it were not so, I would have told you. I am going there to prepare a place for you. John 14:2

This is the first in a series of seven meditations on Jesus' promises as recorded in John 14. The first promise involves moving—moving to a better location. In fact, the move is into a mansion.

If you're like most Americans, you've moved several times during your life. People move often and for various reasons, mostly work-related. But did you hear about the man who read that most accidents happen within 25 miles of home? He moved 50 miles away just to be safe! Some people move so often they don't even feel at home at home. And anyone who has ever packed and unpacked their own moving boxes probably yearns for the day they can stay put. The day is coming.

Jesus knew His followers didn't want Him to leave. Even after His Easter return, the disciples wanted Him to stay longer. This time He would withdraw His physical presence until the world ended.

Jesus went ahead of all His friends to get a new place ready. It's spacious enough for all His friends to live together. No ordinary house, our new home will be a mansion with many rooms. And our life there will add new depth to the phrase "happy home."

We often think of our future heavenly happiness in terms of what makes us happy now. Perhaps that's a good way of visualizing the joy that still awaits us, but nothing we enjoy now will come close to what we will enjoy at our new home. The greatest earthly pleasure is likely to be the simplest heavenly pleasure—if it even ranks! Our most exalted ecstasy will involve living in the presence of our Savior—actually seeing Him and worshiping Him. And as we settle in for an eternity of bliss, we'll praise God that we never need move again.

Get Moving

And if I go and prepare a place for you, I will come back and take you to be with Me that you also may be where I am. You know the way to the place where I am going. John 14:3–4

Has this ever happened to you? You approach the stop sign and dutifully obey. You wait. And wait. And wait. Suddenly you realize the sign will never turn green.

We sometimes act the same as we travel the road to our heavenly home. As Jesus promised in the text above, He's returning to take us to heaven. We may want to sit back and patiently wait for that moment when the sign turns green—when the sound of trumpets announces His second arrival. Christians, however, can't sit around and wait.

We can become so preoccupied by our blissful future that we fail to move toward that goal. Furthermore, we sometimes fail to realize that our eternal life already began when we were baptized. Like most roads, the one to heaven isn't always smooth. But at least we know the way.

God cleared the way for us when He sent Jesus to take away our sins. Then the Holy Spirit delivered faith in Jesus as the only way to heaven. Now He's honking at us to get moving. Sitting still and waiting around makes us prime targets for getting rear-ended by the devil.

The pages of our Bibles provide a road map that makes clear the way home. And when the road is suddenly filled with forks, dangerous intersections, and steep grades, we need to slow down and go over God's map again. Going the wrong way has tragic consequences; there is only one way to go.

One more thing—as we travel to the place Jesus prepared for us, we need to be alert for others who need a lift. Sometimes, the Holy Spirit makes us the vehicle for a spiritual hitchhiker's trip to heaven. Maybe it's the driver who should hold up his thumb!

Promise of Success

I tell you the truth, anyone who has faith in Me will do what I have been doing. He will do even greater things than these, because I am going to the Father. John 14:12

The secret of success remains a secret to many people. Not that there's any lack of formulas, especially those that follow the familiar injunction "If at first you don't succeed ..." Here are some you might enjoy.

If at first you don't succeed ...

- read the directions.
- retrieve the directions from the wastebasket.
- do it the way the boss told you.
- give up. Why make a fool of yourself?

Promises of success are usually misleading. God's promises, however, are reliable and true.

At first glance, Jesus' promise recorded in today's Bible passage seems astounding—or at least too good to be true. But His promise is also built on a premise. Faithful Christians do what Jesus did. Like many premises, this one is slightly flawed, but it's not God's fault. We do as Jesus did, but we don't do it nearly as well. Sin often messes up our work, but God's forgiveness patches up the problem and enables us to copy the Savior's behavior. And rather than focus on our shortcomings, Jesus promised that we will do "greater things." How can sinners—even forgiven sinners—possibly do that?

It's not easy. But Jesus meant that we're here on earth, surrounded by needy sinners, while He's up in heaven getting things ready for us. We continue the work He started. Oh, we're not alone. Not when we pray. And just wait till you see tomorrow's promise.

193

Tomorrow's Promise Today

And I will do whatever you ask in My name, so that the Son may bring glory to the Father. You may ask for anything in My name, and I will do it.
John 14:13–14

You've heard it before. It's not *what* you know, but *who* you know. And how would you like to know someone who could and would give you whatever you asked? Dream a moment. Just what *would* you ask?

Back to reality now before your garage is overcrowded with Rolls Royces or your job begins to interfere with exotic vacations or … Jesus' promise, as it appears above, is in context of the preceding meditation. Remember? Jesus told believers they will not only continue His work on earth, but they will also do great things when they pray in His name.

Praying in Jesus' name means more than simply adding a few words at the end of our prayers. When our prayers harmonize with everything that Jesus was, did, and is, then we are praying in His name. So forget about luxury cars and a multimillion-dollar income. They aren't important—nor are they covered under the terms of this promise. In fact, this promise promises more than most of us can dream.

Now that we have the promise in focus, what would you ask for? Want to be another Billy Graham? Would you like to feed 5,000—no, make it 15,000—with only the contents of your lunch? Just ask. Right? Great things lurk within the sound of your prayers!

Once again, we need perspective. The greatest thing we can do for God may be far less great in our minds than it is in God's will. That's why we pray not only in Jesus' name but according to God's will.

Great things don't always mean startling statistics, dramatic deeds, or fabulous fame. Yet God challenges us, and we can ask His help to succeed. Why not ask Him right now? Then watch for the opportunities.

194

Faithful Friend

And I will ask the Father, and He will give you another Counselor to be with you forever. John 14:16

How many friends do you have? You'll never really know until you buy that new home with a guest house, swimming pool, and tennis court. Of course, we're talking about good friends—faithful friends—here. We all could use a good friend. (And we often do!) The fifth promise in John 14 is about just that—a friend whom Jesus called "Counselor."

A good friend is someone who listens to us. And a good friend will counsel us or tell us what we need to know—even if it momentarily offends us.

The Holy Spirit is the Counselor whom Jesus mentions. Notice that the Counselor offers a forever friendship. Jesus spoke these words to the disciples just before He was captured and killed. He knew that even after He rose from the dead and visited with them, He would finally leave them to work without His physical presence. Jesus didn't want to leave them friendless though, so He sent the Holy Spirit. The Counselor's solid friendship rests on Christ's forgiveness and God's power.

Sad to say, we don't always return the Spirit's friendship with much enthusiasm. We're too tired or embarrassed to pray. Worship isn't as important as reading the Sunday paper or sleeping late. We consider Christian witnessing just too risky. And at times, we are downright hostile. "Get thee hence, Spirit! Leave me alone."

In our loneliness, the Spirit is still there—a forgiving friend. The Spirit gently nudges and sometimes powerfully prods us to act out our faith. As much as we allow, the Spirit guides us to know God's will, and we accept His wise counsel. He remains close by, listening to our deepest thoughts and feelings—ready to respond with compassion and love. He's a friend just waiting to be used.

185

The Best Thing to Leave Behind

Peace I leave with you; My peace I give you. I do not give to you as the world gives. Do not let your hearts be troubled and do not be afraid. John 14:27

A move is afoot to eliminate laws about disturbing the peace. Worldwide wars and skirmishes make us wonder if peace is only a period of discontent and perplexity between wars. There isn't much peace left. In fact, about the only sure place to find it is in the dictionary.

Before you slink behind your coffee cup and curl up into a ball, true peace isn't totally out of reach. The sixth promise in John 14 has Jesus telling us that He leaves peace as a legacy for us to share and enjoy.

To take advantage of His peace, we totally surrender to Him. That's both good news and tough news. Good in that the Holy Spirit has already given us the gift of faith, which gives us God's peace. Tough in that we sinners are prone to breaking the peace with God as well as between others and us. Yet the truly peaceful heart remains in Jesus, and Jesus always forgives and maintains the peace. But His peace goes beyond human relationships and into our own personal life as we face our own troubles, failures, sickness, and mortality. Then we begin to understand the nature of peace with God even though our world falls apart around us.

Jesus said, "Do not be afraid." That pretty well sums up His peace. We have nothing to fear because we trust God to bring something good out of everything. We're willing to wait for His mercy and love to show itself too. We're also willing to accept the fact that His peace passes all understanding. And all misunderstanding too.

Glad to See You Go

You heard Me say, "I am going away and I am coming back to you." If you loved Me, you would be glad that I am going to the Father, for the Father is greater than I. John 14:28

What would you like engraved on your tombstone? What words would you like to leave behind? Dream big because you probably won't be able to afford much engraving. (Blame it on the cost of living!) I prefer the idea expressed by Jesus in John 14: I'm going, but I'm coming back again. And when we truly understand death, we can also share this comment that might seem strange to some: Be glad to see me go.

You've heard the funeral talk before. "It's such a blessing that Aunt Edna died. Now her suffering is over." And sometimes the conversation isn't so easy. "What a shock about Bobby! He was so young. I guess when your time is up, your time is up."

Did you notice anything missing in those words? It might be considered bad taste to say so, but something is missing if we don't at least think the phrase "Glad to see him go." Why? Not because the suffering is over or because God's love is hard to perceive. We're glad to see Christian people "go" because now they live in heaven where they experience a perfect relationship with God the Father. They've been welcomed by Jesus as if He'd known them all His life. (He did!) And they might even see the Holy Spirit breezing around, delivering faith to that young child, inspiring the words of this preacher, and warming the hearts of believers everywhere. They might even see the Spirit working in us right now as we renew our trust in Jesus and as we confirm our own faith that someday we're "going" too. But not for long—not as God counts time. We'll be back as good as new—even better—in heaven. Meet you there. And that's a promise too.

Hot Heads

If your enemy is hungry, give him food to eat; if he is thirsty, give him water to drink. In doing this, you will heap burning coals on his head, and the LORD will reward you. Proverbs 25:21–22

It's been said that conscience keeps more people awake than coffee. It's also true that we live in an increasingly decaffeinated world—both in coffee and conscience.

Most people would agree that it's good to know your enemies. Fewer people would agree that it's also good to love your enemies, but that's a well-known admonishment straight from God's Word. Regardless of how others feel about enemies, our task is to know our enemies so we can love them. That may leave us asking, "What good will it do?"

First, identify "the enemy." It might be a co-worker, a competitor, a family member, someone at church, or a neighbor. Then ask yourself how you know that person is your enemy.

Second, think about ways to love your enemy. Way down deep, we might want to literally love our enemies to death. But that's not the idea God means in the "heaping coals" image. God's plan for dealing with enemies is to prick their consciences with our own good behavior. We are to make them feel guilty by returning good for evil, kindness for meanness, mercy for cruelty, forgiveness for revenge. We are to make them feel guilty enough to repent! That's God's goal for them and for us.

We bring others to repentance the same way Jesus brought us there. True, our Savior did tell us to repent, but in gentle words and actions. He demonstrated His love not by beating the devil out of us, but by loving us to death—His own. That's exactly the kind of love we need to practice on those who hate us. They may never change, but they'll wonder about us. And someday, maybe they will figure it out.

Shots That Miss

Do not be afraid of those who kill the body but cannot kill the soul.
Rather, be afraid of the One who can destroy both soul and body in hell.
Matthew 10:28

Drive-by shootings are no longer confined to squalid streets in sprawling metropolises, and victims aren't restricted to gang members. Terrorism no longer happens only in other counties. It may strike just across the street. Horrific diseases like AIDS no longer afflict only those with risky lifestyles, but it stalks the innocent as well. All these things scare us, and make us fear for the future of those we love.

Even as dread and apprehension drip from daily headlines, we're tempted to miss even greater dangers. As Jesus said in today's text, life-threatening danger goes beyond bullets, dynamite, viruses, and steering wheels. Certainly, those physical things can put us in an early grave. More perilous are those less-visible perils that can put us in an eternal grave.

How does Satan stock his arsenal for spiritual terrorism? It's no real secret. We might even help him. The devil's goal is to lure us away from God. It's not hard to accomplish that satanic intent when intended victims get lazy about regular prayer and worship.

The devil also plots our demise by enticing us away from the way God wants us to live in relation to others. He merrily envisions warehouses full of body parts as we get eyes for eyes, teeth for teeth, toes for toes, elbows for elbows—well, you get the idea. And we all too often comply with his ambitions. Soon our desire to forgive and be forgiven has been erased. Then we drown in a lake of trespasses and sins.

It doesn't have to be that way if we're on our guard. We can't whip the devil with karate chops or 9mm semi-automatic handguns. But we can slash away with the pages of our Bibles and the pleas of our prayers. God will protect us and keep us safe. Even death won't defeat us.

Apple Polisher

In a desert land He found him, in a barren and howling waste. He shielded him and cared for him; He guarded him as the apple of His eye. Deuteronomy 32:10

A literal rendering of the phrase "apple of His eye" would be "little man of His eye." I guess I prefer apple. A little man— even if he's a pupil—trying to keep his balance on my slippery eyeball sounds painful. Besides, this meditation is more about apples than eyes.

Apples—especially large, crispy, shiny red ones—capture our imagination as well as our taste buds. Many of us probably retain the appetite for applesauce that we first developed as a child. And in our mind's eye we can feel our teeth stick to the nutty caramel on our first taffy apple. (Now our teeth might stick better to the taffy apple than to our mouth!) Of course, we can't forget steamy vapors rising from the flaky crust of apple pie with ice cream on it either. Apples are, indeed, something special and a true delight to our eyes.

Apples, however, don't always retain their positive image. You probably know someone who is rotten to the core or the one bad apple that spoiled the bunch. And even great apples, when you get down really deep, are seedy, and they have those little shavings of core that taste like cellophane. Makes one wonder if "apple of His eye" is a good metaphor for our special relationship with God.

Good thing God loves even rotten apples. How often aren't the "apples of His eye" soft, bruised, and moldy? Like apples fallen from the tree and attacked by bees and worms, we apples sometimes feed what seeks to consume us. Yet we remain the apple of His eye. He doesn't concentrate on the soft spots or decay. Jesus polished us through His victory over sin, which He earned hanging on the tree from which we fell. Jesus, the apple of His Father's eye, waxed us with forgiveness and created a whole new saying: One Good Apple saved the whole bunch!

Don't Ask

"But what about you?" He asked. "Who do you say I am?" Peter answered, "The Christ of God." Luke 9:20

When is the last time you expressed an opinion? We probably share opinions more frequently than we realize. Most liberal thinkers believe that opinions must be pliable and that only fanatics maintain their views without compromise. My opinion is that opinions are sometimes foolish. Millions of opinions shared by millions of fools are still foolish opinions. So there.

Whoops. We can really get caught up in our opinions, can't we? Sometimes we confuse them with facts. Sometimes we mistakenly label facts as opinions too. Take the matter of Jesus and Peter recorded in the passage from Luke above. Did Jesus seek fact or opinion from Peter?

Today, as always, facts must be based on proof. Opinion, on the other hand, is often what we think about facts. When Jesus asked Peter that famous question printed above, Peter answered with a fact. In those days, as well as today, people expressed diverse opinions about Jesus. Some thought He was a great prophet. Others, no doubt, thought Him a silly fool. His enemies thought He was a heretic. Only Peter correctly identified Him. Jesus was the Savior sent by God. Fact.

We can claim that the Bible clearly identifies Jesus as our Savior, the Son of the only true God, who is still active today in the Holy Spirit. But others also convincingly claim other gods. So what makes Christians right and everyone else wrong?

Faith is the answer. Believing an opinion doesn't make it right unless the Holy Spirit has planted that belief in our hearts and minds. He did. Thank God for faith to believe what otherwise would be an incredible opinion!

The One and Only First of Many

For God so loved the world that He gave His one and only Son, that who-ever believes in Him shall not perish but have eternal life. John 3:16

You're probably not alone if today's title leaves you puzzled, so perhaps I owe a quick explanation. You're embarking on a series of meditations built on significant Bible passages known as the 3:16s. During the next several days we'll consider the third chapter, 16th verse of several books, but today's 3:16 is a universal favorite.

God so loved the world that He didn't form a committee to plan it, hire a consulting firm to improve it, or look the other way and pretend not to notice its problems. God so loved the world that He didn't send someone else to save it. He did it Himself.

Now God appointed Himself to deal with sin from the very beginning. He made promises, and He also made threats. Quite often people forgot His promises and ignored His threats. It seems that people had difficulty putting their trust solely in one God. So God put some flesh on His promises by taking the form of a human so the world He loved could actually see Him.

As you know, much of the world didn't like what it saw. (It still doesn't.) Jesus was humble, gentle, forgiving, and law abiding. He had power to overpower, but He didn't use it except in cases where someone needed healing or help. As might be expected, He was arrested on trumped-up charges and executed. God died. Think of that. The second person of the Trinity was actually dead. But not for long. He came back to life and promised that we would do the same. Now He's waiting for us.

God so loves the world that His Holy Spirit is still with us. God so loves the world that He will keep us with Him until the end of time. And even longer.

Wisdom 316

Long life is in her right hand; in her left hand are riches and honor.
Proverbs 3:16

Wouldn't it be great if you could enroll in a college course numbered Wisdom 316? Some claim that age brings wisdom, but age sometimes travels alone. And when it does come with old age, it's too late to do us much good! A course to teach wisdom? Hardly possible. You can buy an education, but wisdom is a gift from God.

Some define wisdom as knowledge at work. Others claim wisdom is learning from our foolishness. The writer of Proverbs had his own definition of wisdom. He said that trust in God was wisdom (3:5). In that verse, he also advised the "wanna be" wise not to "lean on their own understanding." That seems to warn that our own life experiences can be misleading or useless.

Life may teach us to keep quiet, save our money, and otherwise look out for Number 1. Keeping quiet is fine when we have nothing good to say, but wise Christians just can't be mute when it comes to sharing the Gospel. It's not always the popular thing to do, and some will think it unwise, but we can trust God's wisdom in His command to proclaim His Word.

Saving or investing money is a wise way to approach retirement, but spending some of that money on God's work is an even wiser practice. After all, there is no mandatory retirement age for Him, and His work needs to proceed. Spending money on God's work requires the trust Solomon wrote about too. Did it ever strike you that he was exceedingly rich even though he spent fortunes for God's work?

Looking out for Number 1 is a wise thought too. As long as we remember who Number 1 is! True wisdom comes with recognizing God as Number 1 in our life and trusting Him more than we trust ourselves. He provides plenty of guidance in His Word and through His Spirit. We're wise when we trust Him. If we don't, we're otherwise.

Accounting 316

Then those who feared the LORD talked with each other, and the LORD listened and heard. A scroll of remembrance was written in His presence concerning those who feared the LORD and honored His name.
Malachi 3:16

Business students must take several accounting classes before they graduate. Some, like me, took the same accounting course several times before we graduated! My liabilities always exceeded my assets. I guess I just wasn't cut out for Accounting 201.

All Christians qualify for Accounting 316, though. We should probably add verse 17 to really profit from the prophet. He said, "'They will be Mine,' says the LORD Almighty, 'in the day when I make up My treasured possession.'" We should probably remember Revelation too, in which John sees God looking for the names of believers in the Book of Life—the heavenly ledger.

Life is a liability. Filled with sin, we stubbornly cling to the debit side of life's balance sheet. All our numbers seem to be in the left column with no earthly way of paying the debt we accumulate. But God marks the largest number to our credit.

All the credit, of course, goes to Jesus Christ, who paid for our sins with His life. When God looks into that Book of Life on the last day, He'll see one entry that dwarfs the others. Not that we earned that asset ourselves. It was a gift, and it covered all that we owed God for a life of weak faith, unwitting mistakes, and broken commandments.

As we count our daily sins, we need to confess our inability to balance the Book of Life. But this is no time to be timid. God offers free forgiveness. He takes away our sins, and we're able to begin the next day with a clean account. In fact, we really have a credit balance when you think about it. Just count your blessings. They far surpass your troubles.

194

Quality Control 316

John answered them all, "I baptize you with water. But one more powerful than I will come, the thongs of whose sandals I am not worthy to untie. He will baptize you with the Holy Spirit and with fire." Luke 3:16

Quality-control departments provide assurance that every product is the best that it can be. But with God, quality control is different. He starts with the best and makes it even better.

Today's Bible passage mentions two baptisms. Now before you run out to get another one, be assured that one baptism is all it takes to make you a Christian. Our baptism with water is the only one necessary. When John the Baptist, who did the talking here in Luke, said that his baptism was only with water and that Jesus baptized with the Holy Spirit, he wasn't putting down baptism by water. Baptism is a means of grace—a way of receiving God's love, mercy, and forgiveness. Jesus did everything necessary to bring all the benefits of baptism our way. He made us holy. The other baptism of which John spoke referred his listeners to an event yet to come, namely Pentecost. Those already-baptized believers would receive the Holy Spirit, thus enabling them to proclaim the Gospel and baptize even more people.

We start with the best—holiness through the blood of Jesus, which washes away our sins. Then we become better—better people living Christ-centered lives, telling others about Jesus, and applying faith to everyday life.

But there's more to this idea of best and better. John the Baptist indeed was great, but He knew Jesus was greater. In the same way, we Christians have the best right now. We're saved. God is faithful to us. The Holy Spirit keeps the fire in our faith. Yet something better remains in the future. Jesus will come again. Then, together with all the saints, we'll celebrate with an eternal party.

What's Your Doctor's Name?

By faith in the name of Jesus, this man whom you see and know was made strong. It is Jesus' name and the faith that comes through Him that has given this complete healing to him, as you can all see. Acts 3:16

Medical specialization dominates the health-care scene. If your head cold moves down into your chest, you have to change doctors.

The names of certain doctors carry status and prestige. If your doctor's name is Salk, Barnard, Menninger, or Mayo (how about Luke?), you probably wonder if he or she is related to THE physician who made that name famous. A doctor's name is also a doctor's reputation. This was always true, even in the days of the early Christians.

Today's Bible verse comes from the story of Peter healing the crippled beggar. People wondered about this medical miracle, and they probably wanted to note the attending physician's name—just in case they needed similar help. Peter bypassed his moment in medical history when he gave all the credit to someone else. Jesus was the specialist, and faith in His power brought true and complete healing.

All of us are disabled and impoverished—in dire need of healing. No covey of specialists has a cure, and even if they did, no insurance company could afford the price. Our sickness is sin. We're hobbled by its power to separate us from God. Thankfully, God isn't paralyzed by it's power. He sent the Great Physician, Jesus Himself, to eliminate sin's power to kill us. Oh, we have our relapses, but the Great Physician has long office hours. He's always ready to hear us describe our despair, and He offers the remedy of His forgiveness. He never sends us a bill either, for He has already paid the price to cure us once and forever. Even more astounding, He writes a perpetual prescription. Just think—no limit on refills and we can even read His writing! So call the Doctor often and be sure to take all His Word too.

Church Bodies

Don't you know that you yourselves are God's temple and that God's Spirit lives in you? 1 Corinthians 3:16

Some people think God lives in church buildings. You can tell by the reverence they show while in the sanctuary. But our latest 3:16, from Paul's first letter to the Corinthians, indicates that God's sweetest home is in the hearts of His people.

Don't you know that you are a place in which to worship God? Don't you know your body is home to the Holy Spirit? Real churches are places of forgiveness, and so it needs to be in the walking, talking variety.

Just as members of churches serve God, so must the members of church bodies serve Him. Let's take a look at the body of our church. Starting at the bottom, we have feet. Isaiah called them beautiful—when they belong to someone who delivers Good News and peace. Working our way up, we arrive at the knees—God's great invention for bending. Knees and prayer seem especially good companions. Moving on, we reach the place where we seem to spend most of our time—our rear end. God gave us some decent padding, which makes reading our Bibles a comfortable proposition, but He doesn't expect us to spend all our time there.

Heading north again, we migrate past the vital organs. While they might not play tunes like the one in church, they do keep our service to God moving along. Our church body has an especially warm heart as well as the most vital organ—one that doesn't show up on x-rays—our soul. Home sweet home for the Holy Spirit! And off to the sides reside our arms and hands, willing servants for the more physical service to Christ. Finally, we reach the top. Ears to hear God's Word as it admonishes and blesses. Eyes to see the wonders of His creation. Mouths to house disciplined and kind tongues, and brains to think of even more ways to serve the Savior.

Who needs stained glass when we have such beautiful churches so close by?

Dwell on It

Let the word of Christ dwell in you richly as you teach and admonish one another with all wisdom, and as you sing psalms, hymns and spiritual songs with gratitude in your hearts to God. Colossians 3:16

For many years, the Bible was a best seller. It was also the best buy. We may rightfully suspect, however, that if all Bibles were waved in the air at the same time, we would experience the worst dust storm in history!

The only way to let Christ's Word "dwell in you richly" is to dwell on it richly. Yet so many obstacles have us dwelling elsewhere. The biggest impediment is time. If clocks had little pitchforks instead of hands, perhaps we would realize how well the devil uses time. We so cram our calendars that when we have time to rest, that's all we want to do.

God blesses us with several ways to let the Word of Christ dwell in us. In addition to the Bible, there is music. Humming "Jerusalem the Golden" may not be in everyone's repertoire, but nearly everyone enjoys some type of music. Music with Christ-centered lyrics comes in so many varieties that nearly every taste can be satisfied. Have you ever had a tune in your head that just kept coming back? That's the way it is when Christ's Word dwells in us. We live and breathe and speak and hum it without realizing what we're doing.

The indwelling of God's Word enables us to "teach and admonish one another with all wisdom." Note that this is not a one-dimensional activity. "One another" suggests that each Christian is both giver and taker. As we gather with and listen to other Christians, the Holy Spirit opens our souls and minds to new possibilities for living out our faith. When we read our Bibles and sing our spirituals, the Holy Spirit is there too, helping us perceive the awesome majesty of God's power and love—even if a small dust cloud chokes us as we sing off-key.

Nothing Like a Good Mystery

Beyond all question, the mystery of godliness is great: He appeared in a
body, was vindicated by the Spirit, was seen by angels, was preached
among the nations, was believed on in the world, was taken up in glory.
1 Timothy 3:16

Mystery stories remain popular both in books and on tele-vision. Of course, the mystery is only a mystery until the hero or heroine figures out the puzzle. The same is true for certain mysteries in the Bible.

Paul revealed some important mysteries about God when he wrote to young Timothy. Notice how Paul explains the mystery of Jesus. In doing so, Paul also delivers a brief creed that well capsulizes the life of Jesus. And in explaining the mystery, Paul is careful to avoid any explanation of how God did all these things. That will remain a mystery. Instead, Paul reveals the mystery of who God is.

If you're reading this meditation through the eyes of faith, you may ask, "What mystery?" It doesn't puzzle you because God already revealed the mystery through the Holy Spirit. God chose to give you faith, and now you have received and developed that marvelous—and even mysterious—gift.

But to unbelievers, God's love and the identity of the Savior are a mystery. Without the Holy Spirit's work in uncovering the mystery, the truth remains hidden. To make matters worse, the devil loves mysteries too. Even when the Spirit exposes the truth, the devil tries to hide it, urging us not to believe.

Rejoice that you comprehend the mystery of everlasting life with the Savior. Keep your faith strong in prayer, study, and medita-tion. Be ready to disclose the mystery to others. You'll have some good opportunities when you find others frustrated, sad, lonely, or sick. They're prime candidates for the Holy Spirit and you. Tell them the truth—even if it hurts.

Good for Everything

All Scripture is God-breathed and is useful for teaching, rebuking, correcting and training in righteousness. 2 Timothy 3:16

The Bible is good for everything. Sure proof of the Bible's value is in the nature of those who dispute it! By the same token, it has survived some of its fanatic and ignorant "friends" as well!

How do you like the phrase "God-breathed"? Older readers may recall that "inspired" was once the word. But perhaps God-breathed is more inspiring. After all, Shakespeare, Louis L'Amour, and Danielle Steel could be considered inspired writers too. But for something to be breathed by God—well, that's another story. Not really a story at all, but divine truth useful for all occasions. Because the Bible's words are God's actual words, we don't have to worry if Paul or Moses or Matthew was having a bad day—perhaps a day when writer's block forced them to leave out some important details or motivated them to fantasize some fiction. We take comfort knowing that God's Word is God's Word!

Writing the Bible, like speaking God's Word, must have been difficult at times, especially when God talked about sinfulness. He told us what we need to know; namely, that we deserve His anger and punishment. But we have Good News in the Bible too. God loved sinners so much that He didn't want them spending eternity in the fiery depths of hell. Jesus brought us close to God through His death on the cross and His victory over sin and Satan. An incredible story but nonetheless believable because God says it's so.

What do we do when someone challenges our belief in the Bible's value and authority? There's no use arguing or trying to prove our point with human logic. Our only ploy is to insist, "God says so." Too simple? Probably. But isn't that what faith is all about? Even children know the answer. Just listen to them sing "Jesus loves me, this I know ..." They'll tell you why.

200

Faith Full

See, he is puffed up; his desires are not upright—but the righteous will live by his faith. Habakkuk 2:4

Nearly everyone remembers the old saying "Pride goeth before the fall." Yet pride still thrives. We all know people who strut around inflated with themselves. And we've heard pride exert itself in those whose heads have been turned by success. Of course, the real problem with a "turned head" is that it leaves one facing the wrong direction.

Who would you name if asked to identify someone who could be proud of his faith? Maybe it would be Abraham, who believed God's promise of having many descendants—even while he was elderly and childless. But to save his life, Abraham once told an Egyptian pharaoh that his beautiful wife was his sister (Genesis 12:10–20). The problem? Abraham trusted his own cleverness rather than God's protection.

Now that we've demoted Abraham, who else had a faith of which to be proud? David, for sure. Remember his confrontation with Goliath (1 Samuel 17)? David praised God rather than himself for the victory. But is this the same David who decided that adultery and murder were means to satisfy his desires (2 Samuel 11–12)?

Two heroes down. Did any heroes of faith remain strong through every trial and temptation? Only one name comes to mind—Jesus. Not fair, you say? Yes, Jesus is God. But He is also a real man who faced temptation not just from the world and His own human flesh, but also from the devil, who gave Jesus some really personalized attention. Jesus' faith in His Father's plan motivated Him through 30 years of life and also through a grossly unjust trial and torture. Even on the cross, Jesus showed His faith. He placed Himself in God's hands. And just as important to us, He remained faithful to sinners too. Because of that, we'll meet Abraham and David someday. We won't flaunt our faith, even though we'll be more full of it than ever.

201

Well Oiled

The Spirit of the Sovereign LORD is on me, because the LORD has anointed me to preach good news to the poor. He has sent me to bind up the brokenhearted, to proclaim freedom for the captives and release from darkness for the prisoners. Isaiah 61:1

How true it is that the Lord loves cheerful givers! Maybe that's why so many people enjoy handing out free advice. But Isaiah said that we should give counsel only to those who really need it. In fact, Isaiah indicates that God makes Christians well-oiled machines (Isn't that what *anointed* means?), fully capable of dispensing mercy and grace.

When God anointed people to fulfill a task, it was a sign that He would be with them, giving them power and wisdom to carry out His holy will for the people He loved. That's precisely what He has in mind for us too. Let's take a closer look at two of the tasks He "oils" us to undertake.

First, we're told to "bind up the brokenhearted." What interesting language! God commissions us to mend broken hearts—bind the pieces together again. If you look around, you'll probably find lots of hearts that need repair.

Quoting a Bible passage may seem to be the right bandage for a broken heart. But as much as people need God's Word, they also need good listeners. They need someone willing to hear gut-wrenching emotions spend themselves in words. Then they need someone willing to say, "Jesus loves you in good times and bad. Trust Him to bring you through."

Next we're told to "proclaim freedom for the captives." Some captives are imprisoned by drugs, sex, or alcohol. Others are prisoners of greed, gossip, or hate. We can share what it's like to be a forgiven child of God, freed from guilt and condemnation by our loving Savior. Only words? Yes, but we need not feel guilty or inadequate. Just as we might not understand how glue bonds objects, we don't need to know how Christ's love binds broken hearts and frees captives. What we do know is that it works.

Dead and Buried

For, "All men are like grass, and all their glory is like the flowers of the field; the grass withers and the flowers fall." 1 Peter 1:24

Does the name Johann August Eberhard ring a bell? He was an author who lived from 1739–1809 and wrote a book entitled *Neue Apologie des Sokrates*. Certainly, Johann was acclaimed in his family and hometown. For most of us, though, his name doesn't even jingle, much less ring a bell. He is dead and buried. Gone and largely forgotten.

We're probably headed for the same degree of renown, and most of us will leave behind only a headstone. One hundred, five hundred, a thousand years from now, will anyone know or care about who we were and what we did? Most of today's population can't remember the name of the first person to walk on the moon, and that was in 1969!

The apostle Peter's first letter confirms the dismal truth. He compares us with flowers. As beautiful as they are, they all must wither and die. They return to the very ground that nourished them from tiny seed to fruitful adult. Dead and buried. Forgotten. How pathetic for Peter and for us if the end were really the end.

Cemeteries are filled with people who may be anonymous in history and unknown to us personally. But God remembers each of them. He could no more forget than a mother could forget each of her children! God created every one of them and invited them to call Him Father. He sent His only Son, Jesus, to redeem the world, and to record the names of believers in a special book. The book is called The Book of Life. (Read Revelation if you want to know more.) Your name is in it even though you haven't died yet. Maybe Johann's is in it too. Certainly, we'll find Abraham, Samuel, Ruth, Mary, Lazarus, and Peter there. They're all dead and buried. Gone, but not forgotten. Jesus remembers. And our names will live on forever.

Set Apart

May God Himself, the God of peace, sanctify you through and through.
May your whole spirit, soul and body be kept blameless at the coming of
our Lord Jesus Christ. 1 Thessalonians 5:23

It sure beats "Have a good day." Of course, if we used the farewell that Paul left with the Thessalonians, people might look at us funny. They might think that we are "different" and they might set us apart from themselves in the future. They would be right in one respect. We are set apart.

Paul says the God of peace sanctifies us. To be sanctified means to be set apart. God set us apart to be His own children. He chose us to receive faith from the Holy Spirit so we could believe the extraordinary story of what Jesus did for us. Because God has set us apart, our lives have special meaning.

As much as we might like to bask in the blush of peace and glow of glory that accompanies our status, we don't have time to sit back and admire ourselves. We are set apart to do God's work. So as sanctified Christians, we roll up our sleeves and get busy.

First, it is important to regularly study and reflect on God's Word. Next, we practice His Word in our daily activities and routines. As sanctified Christians we let the Holy Spirit control our lives, and we willingly desire to serve God and our neighbors—both local and global.

Good works are the job of those set apart by God. The possibilities are too numerous to mention, for good works include everything believers do, say, or even think to God's glory or the benefit of others. And the Spirit doesn't let us tackle this work alone. He gives us "tools" to accomplish His will. So what are you waiting for? Quit reading and get back to work. Oh yes—be sure to use some of your new tools.

Show It

In the same way, let your light shine before men, that they may see your good deeds and praise your Father in heaven. Matthew 5:16

To turn on a light, you must flip a switch. The Holy Spirit has "flipped our switch" and now our purpose in life is to remain bright beacons of Jesus Christ. This undoubtedly makes us happy, but perhaps we haven't told our faces about it.

We let God's light shine when we let our teeth shine. Yes, smiles qualify as good deeds. Not that we have to be giddy or silly. Some take a smile as an invitation to generously dump their troubles on you as if you were an old, close friend. Still others might wonder what you're after—especially if it's the opposite sex. Lighting up your face with God's love can illuminate a whole lot more than you expect. But Jesus loves us, and He expects us to show it.

Consider the "dumpers." It's only natural for people to assume that if you're friendly on your face, you're also friendly in your heart. And your ears. Your tongue goes along with it too. What better opportunity for witnessing do we have than with people who are hurting? Even annoying, whining, selfish people who are hurting. Maybe you've noticed this on a night ride through a rural area: the darker the dark, the lighter the light.

Finally, nothing makes a suspicious person more suspicious than a smile. These people need our sympathy—and our witness—too. Most suspicious people act that way because they've been misused, abused, or simply used. As Jesus showed unconditional love even to the worst of His tormentors and the best of sinners, our light needs to shine even on those who prefer the shadows. *Unconditional* is a key word. Give everything, expect nothing. Not exactly the way of the world, is it? That's what makes it so good. So leave the light on for someone today.

But I Thought You Said ...

Be careful not to do your "acts of righteousness" before men, to be seen by them. If you do, you will have no reward from your Father in heaven.
Matthew 6:1

The previous meditation dealt with "letting our teeth, er, light shine" as one of many good deeds in our Christian life. Now we read a passage that says we should keep our good deeds hidden!

Good deeds are susceptible to corruption, and the contamination usually comes from within. When it comes to good deeds, it's the motivation that really counts. Rather than contradicting Himself on the "shining lights" verse, Matthew 6:1 is Jesus' comment on those who do good deeds for bad reasons. Only one pure motivation exists for serving God: loving Him. And even that's not enough.

We love God only when, by faith, we realize how much He loves us. As we meditate daily on His Word, we remember that He sent Jesus to live and die for our sins. We continue to sin, and He continues to forgive. But our vast experience as sinners helps us relate to other sinners who need to know Jesus' love and forgiveness. That's where good deeds—or "acts of righteousness"—come in. And they can't come in from our own hearts and desires. They are totally a reaction to God's grace and mercy. Therefore, we have no reason to boast of our own goodness.

So what would you say if someone asked, "Why are you always so helpful (friendly, peaceful, etc.)?" No call for false modesty here. Real modesty is best. Confess that you're good (And you are!) because Jesus made you that way. Now He wants us to do good for others—to His credit. He expects us to testify on His behalf, and He gives us the power to make a good name. Not for ourselves, of course. We don't need it. We've already got the best name on earth. Don't we, Christian?

A Short Space

Here is a trustworthy saying that deserves full acceptance: Christ Jesus came into the world to save sinners—of whom I am the worst. 1 Timothy 1:15

Sometimes there's only a short space between an atheist and a_theist. You probably know a few atheists. They're the ones who shake their fists at the God they claim doesn't exist. Atheists can't find God for the same reason that criminals can't find police officers. Atheists have almost as long a history as believers do, which makes one wonder. How could the early inhabitants of our planet not believe in God? They had so much evidence. But then, as now, evidence doesn't make believers. Faith does, and they refused it.

Take the case of Paul, a.k.a. Saul. He was the promoter and supervisor of many persecutions of early Christians. Two thousand years ago, Saul's famous name brought cheer and encouragement to those who hated Jesus. They didn't believe Jesus was God's Son even if they believed in God Himself. They believed in a God they couldn't see, but they couldn't believe in a God they could see! Worse, they wanted to silence forever any lips that confessed Jesus as God and Savior.

Had anyone predicted that Saul's fame as a persecutor would be dwarfed by his fame as a Christian, they would have been laughed all the way to Damascus. But we know what happened (Acts 9). The Holy Spirit performed the miracle of conversion. Paul talked about it in his note to Timothy. If it can happen to Paul, it can happen to anyone.

Pray for all atheists—even successful ones. Pray that they accept the Spirit's invitation to join the worst of sinners who acknowledge the Savior as Lord and King. Pray that the Spirit put some space between them and their unbelief—that they go from atheist to a_theist. The Holy Spirit can do it, and Paul is living proof!

Don't be surprised if Christmas displays mysteriously appear on courthouse lawns some day.

Unforgivable

And so I tell you, every sin and blasphemy will be forgiven men, but the blasphemy against the Spirit will not be forgiven. Anyone who speaks a word against the Son of Man will be forgiven, but anyone who speaks against the Holy Spirit will not be forgiven, either in this age or in the age to come. Matthew 12:31–32

Do you know the best way to get back at your enemies? Forgive them. Jesus did that repeatedly. Some of His enemies, however, preferred not to be forgiven. Those who chose to be condemned are unforgivable.

Have you ever heard of the deadly Pharaoh Syndrome? Its most conspicuous symptom is hardening of the heart. Given numerous opportunities to repent of his sins and to release God's people whom he enslaved, Pharaoh refused. Years later, Jesus would tell the disciples to forgive 70 × 7 times. Yet Pharaoh only had nine chances. Why? The answer, of course, rests (uncomfortably) with Pharaoh himself. He refused to believe the true God.

While large numbers of various sins get forgiven each day, the Bible also cautions that one sin will not be forgiven. Jesus called it the sin against the Holy Spirit. Before you check back to see if you've inadvertently committed it, stop and breathe a sigh of relief. It's unlikely this sin belongs to anyone who takes time to read this meditation. The sin against the Holy Spirit is refusal to accept the faith He freely gives. Naturally, those who reject faith reject God and all that He offers.

We Christians don't need to worry. Our sins were forgiven on a dark hill 2,000 years ago. Each day we come before God and ask Him again to forgive us for the sake of Him who died on that hill. And each day we can be certain we are indeed forgiven. As long as you know that and believe it, you can be sure that you haven't fallen to the unforgivable—and unforgettable—sin.

Sweet Dreams

We believe that Jesus died and rose again and so we believe that God will bring with Jesus those who have fallen asleep in Him. 1 Thessalonians 4:14

The call from the hospital came at 3 a.m. The doctor said, "I'm sorry, but your father expired just moments ago." Makes it sound like he was a credit card or a store coupon. Expired?

Many Christians prefer what some consider a euphemism. Death is only sleep. But just as surely as you awoke this morning, you will also awaken after death. Isn't that one of the great comforts we Christians share? Death may extract loved ones from our life, but not forever.

Two things are certain in life—death and taxes. Since we can't escape either, we must live with both. At least death only comes once. And when it comes, it's helpful to use Bible language for death—sleeping. Critics may laugh or think us too soft to face finality. Some people just prefer to think of death as the end of life's story. The truth is that it's only a phase. It'll pass.

If death is sleep, then it's possible to construct some parallels to our limited knowledge about the subject. Some people fear falling asleep because of recurring nightmares. (I had that problem once myself, but it disappeared as soon as I left Latin class.) Cold sweat is a good way of describing such experiences. Christians may experience such discomfort during earthly sleep, but they certainly have nothing to fear as they wait out the death phase of eternal life. In fact, it probably wouldn't be out of order to greet the dying with a sincere "sweet dreams." As John Newton said in his famous hymn, "How sweet the name of Jesus sounds/In a believer's ear!" And as for ourselves, we find comfort in this coming nap too. And this time we'll be eager to wake up when the alarm rings!

Life Insurance

So do not worry, saying, "What shall we eat?" or "What shall we drink?" or "What shall we wear?" Matthew 6:31

At one time, many Christians considered purchasing life insurance a grave (really bad pun!) sin. Others refused to obtain policies because they wanted everyone to be sad when they died! But back to the sinfulness issue. If we take today's Bible passage seriously, are things we do to enhance or protect our future contrary to God's Word?

Like anything else we allow to control our lives, planning for the future can be sinful. But God has also given us resources to use wisely for ourselves and our families when we can no longer work. Death being one of those times when we can no longer work, life insurance can also be classified as wise planning, not outside of God's will. And there is another kind of planning that we can do as an investment against the future. In fact, you're doing it now.

Wise planning for the future involves Bible study, meditation, prayer, and worship. It's a lot cheaper than conventional insurance, but it's also more valuable. As an added benefit, we can enjoy it even before it's paid in full. As our relationship with Jesus deepens through these investments, we begin to comprehend what Jesus meant by His words about the future. But like any insurance policy, we need to read the whole thing to completely understand it. So here is what follows Jesus' words in Matthew 6:31: "But seek first His kingdom and His righteousness, and all these things will be given to you as well" (6:33).

Jesus placed everything in perspective. As we "seek first His kingdom," we take care of our spiritual needs first. With that in place, we continue to live confidently, knowing God will always care for us.

Our future is well protected thanks to Jesus' investment on our behalf. And His coverage is a vast improvement on life insurance, which is misnamed anyway. Thanks to Jesus, we have life assurance!

210

Perfect Score

Praise be to the LORD, who has given rest to His people Israel just as He promised. Not one word has failed of all the good promises He gave through His servant Moses. 1 Kings 8:56

Some people spend half their time making promises. Then they spend the other half making excuses. Not so with God. He has the 300 of bowling, the 0.00 earned run average, perfect 10s of skating, and 100 percent free-throw average all rolled into one. God's perfect record in keeping promises has never been and never will be equaled.

Unfortunately, people have been testing God's promises since Adam and Eve. But even after their unfaithfulness, God offered another promise—a Savior to take away their sins.

Throughout the Old Testament, God's promises continued to roll right along with His wrath over people's unfaithfulness and immorality. Each time His righteous anger flared, so did His compassion. He promised various things to His Old Testament people, but His foremost promise remained that of a Savior. And when He finally delivered on His promise, hardly anyone believed it.

Jesus made promises too. He promised to return to life after He died. Even His disciples didn't believe *that!* He kept His promise anyway. Then came the time for Jesus to return to His rightful place in heaven. As He left, He promised to return.

We live in a promising age. It's the same era in which Paul, Peter, and John preached about Jesus' promise to return. We've waited 2,000 years for Jesus to fulfill this most important vow. In the meantime, we're blessed with Jesus' other promises, like the ones to be with us and answer our prayers. Like the ones to keep His forgiveness equal to our sins.

Yes, the time approaches when God will give rest to all His people. We can count on it happening any day now. Or any decade now. Or any century now.

Eat, Drink, and Be Merry

A man can do nothing better than to eat and drink and find satisfaction in his work. This too, I see, is from the hand of God, for without Him, who can eat or find enjoyment? To the man who pleases Him, God gives wisdom, knowledge and happiness, but to the sinner He gives the task of gathering and storing up wealth to hand it over to the one who pleases God. This too is meaningless, a chasing after the wind. Ecclesiastes 2:24–26

Solomon's words from Ecclesiastes would be widely accepted today—especially if taken out of context. Skeptics may smirk over these verses. They view them in the "Eat, drink, and be merry for tomorrow we die" category. While the opening verse sounds similar initially, the words that follow add spiritual depth unsurpassed in Epicurean epitaphs.

God used Solomon to tell us to eat and enjoy life. Surprised? Hey, isn't that what Thanksgiving is all about? Of course, the only way we truly enjoy life is by knowing God. Who can eat, drink, and be merry fearing the good life will end someday? Eating, drinking, and otherwise having fun is so much better when we're satisfied with the present and looking forward to the day when life gets even better!

The banquet of blessings doesn't end with physical merriment. Did you notice what God provides for those who please Him? God gives us wisdom, knowledge, and joy too. But, if we're really honest, we must ask, Who can please God? Isaiah said we're like filthy rags to Him (Isaiah 64:6). Even the local mechanic doesn't like filthy rags!

Eat, drink, and be merry anyway. Jesus put those rags through a three-cycle cleaning with His perfect life, sacrificial death, and victorious resurrection. We can please God because Jesus made it possible. We are wise and happy because we know Jesus. And while unbelievers sadly chase the most temporary of pleasures, our joy never ends. So eat, drink, and be merry. For tomorrow we live!

It's History

But blessed are your eyes because they see, and your ears because they hear. For I tell you the truth, many prophets and righteous men longed to see what you see but did not see it, and to hear what you hear but did not hear it. Matthew 13:16–17

Old Testament prophets, even those who preached doom and destruction, lived on hope. You know how hope works. Hope is what we have on the first day of our new diet. And like those ancient prophets, we may die long before our hope is fulfilled.

We probably have little reason to envy those Old Testament men of God, even though they had direct, two-way communication with their Lord. Jesus Himself commented on how much better off we are than they. The prophets had visions of the future, but they didn't get to see what they foresaw! How blessed we are actually to see prophecy accomplished in the life of Jesus Christ!

Sometimes, however, sin blinds us to the Savior. We may find sinning so enjoyable that we wonder how anything so great can be so bad. Usually, we create plausible excuses like "It's just a little harmless fun. I'm not hurting anybody." Or we might write sin off as invalid iniquities. "Oh, that *used* to be a sin, but not anymore. Everybody does it."

Thank God that sin doesn't blind the Savior to sinners. While the prophets could only hope for the day when the Savior would revitalize the relationship of God's people with Him, we know it's history. We live in an age the prophets only dreamed about. We have the cross before us. And it's empty! So is the tomb. Jesus lives and we know all about it. In a sense, we no longer need to hope. Why would anyone hope for something they already have?

Hope does play a role in daily life, however. It's the certain hope that we'll see the Savior sometime in the future. In a way, we also hope like the prophets did—that Jesus will come. It's comforting to know that He's been here once, and He knows the way back. Then we'll live with Him forever.

Leftovers

For this is what the LORD, the God of Israel, says: "The jar of flour will not be used up and the jug of oil will not run dry until the day the LORD gives rain on the land." She went away and did as Elijah had told her. So there was food every day for Elijah and for the woman and her family.
1 Kings 17:14–15

Nothing lasts longer than that jar of pickles shoved to the back of the refrigerator. (Well, maybe that box of bulgur bran cereal lasts longer.) The world record leftover, however, belongs to a widow's jar of flour in the town of Zarephath. Her tiny urn of flour fed her, her son, and Elijah for many days while the rest of the country suffered though a severe famine.

No, this meditation doesn't encourage you to stock your cabinets like Mother Hubbard's in hopes that God will keep your jars (pickle or otherwise) filled. But the story does help us focus on trusting God. And even beyond the trust issue, it serves to remind us of God's power, patience, and forgiveness.

We live in famine-stricken times. Our lives are parched and starved by sin. But God comes to our rescue. He furnishes a perpetual supply of nourishment. As Elijah became a house guest at the widow's place, Jesus came to live in us. For His sake, God gives us all we need to survive. *Survive?* That word isn't good enough. *Thrive* is more like it!

Like the food that supported the widow's household, God's love through Jesus nourishes us daily. As we sin each day, we draw on the forgiveness God gives through Jesus. We dip into the jar repeatedly, yet an ample reserve always remains. God's forgiveness for Jesus' sake is the only source of spiritual sustenance that we can trust.

Next time you clean out the refrigerator, move that jar of pickles to the front. Let it remind you that God's forgiveness is always there.

214

The Garden

"No," he answered, "because while you are pulling the weeds, you may root up the wheat with them. Let both grow together until the harvest. At that time I will tell the harvesters: First collect the weeds and tie them in bundles to be burned; then gather the wheat and bring it into my barn." Matthew 13:29–30

Every year my yard is covered with thousands of pretty yellow flowers. Actually, I would pull them out given some time and ambition. But then my front yard might look like a strip mine! One gardener, whose lawn has nary a speck of yellow, told me the best way to eradicate weedy pests is to choke them out with good plants.

Weeds caused problems in Jesus' day too, as you can see from the passage above. Any veteran weed-puller knows that when weeds entangle their evil tentacles with the roots of the innocent, pulling them is risky. Jesus' solution to the problem was simple and eventually drastic. But Jesus wasn't giving advice to mere green thumbs.

We should always allow a few dandelions on our lawns to remind ourselves about life as Christians. Most of us prefer the company of other Christians, even if they aren't perfect. But if we are to make the most of life, we repentant sinners must live with sinners of the other variety too. And as my gardening friend suggested, we need to choke out their evil with our good—a job we can't do alone.

Our goodness comes from Jesus Christ, whose death and resurrection provided fertile fields in which to grow. As we bud with good deeds and display the beautiful blooms of the Gospel, we show our "beholders" the beauty of Jesus. He works through us to choke out evil with kindness and replace thorns with forgiveness. So don't be afraid to nestle next to some weedy characters. Maybe some of your beauty will rub off on them—or at least choke the sin from their spindly stalks.

Think Again

But when Jesus turned and looked at His disciples, He rebuked Peter. "Get behind Me, Satan!" He said. "You do not have in mind the things of God, but the things of men." Mark 8:33

Intelligence is highly overrated. If you like to fish or know someone who does, you'll probably agree. We pit human intelligence against the modest brains of our quarry and often loose the battle of wits!

Often, opinions are more overrated than intelligence. God's Word provides some excellent examples. Jesus spoke today's verse when Peter didn't like what Jesus said about His divine future. No doubt Peter wanted Jesus to look on the bright side rather than predicting His own death. And then to say that He would return to life … Well, that's just more than intelligent disciples can tolerate. But Peter was mistaken. He tried to pit human intelligence against divine will and wisdom.

Jesus' reprimand may seem harsh, but He needed to set the record straight. After all, if Peter's way of thinking prevailed, Jesus wouldn't die. Jesus knew the Father's plan for Him, and He knew why He needed to die. He also knew that temporary death was better than temporary joy—not that anyone would disagree. But Jesus knew He would defeat the power of death in a way that human brain power would never evaluate, assess, or statistically prove. Clearly—and thankfully—Peter's opinion didn't count.

We do well to listen too. When God says He created the world; almost obliterated it with a flood; brought plagues on Egypt; and sent Jesus to suffer, die, and rise to save us from our sins; we don't need to form an opinion. We have His Word, and it presents the facts. To rely on our own intellect is like believing that somewhere, someplace we'll figure out how to snag that world record bass.

Me, Myself, and I

Praise be to the LORD my Rock, who trains my hands for war, my fingers for battle. He is my loving God and my fortress, my stronghold and my deliverer, my shield, in whom I take refuge, who subdues peoples under me. Psalm 144:1–2

My mother had a pet expression for those who incessantly talked about themselves. "Me, myself, and I," she would say. "That's all they can talk about." The unholy trinity of self-centeredness!

But look at the excerpt from Psalm 144 above. Ten very personal pronouns weave their way into David's words of praise. Very clearly, David wants us to know that God cared about him. And there is no reason not to adopt these words as our own.

Me, myself, and I. That's who God cares about, and that's who God strengthens and protects. Isn't it thrilling to know how much God loves *me*? It's one thing to be included in a crowd, like the time presidential-hopeful Eisenhower waved to a bunch of us outside the NBC studios in Chicago. Just think how we would have felt had he approached and actually shook our hands—or called us by name! But God—our awesome, holy, omni-everything God—knows me, myself, and I personally. He knew my name long before my parents picked it. He knew about that episode of puppy love that left me whimpering and whining—and He comforted me. He knew about that time in English class when I cheated—and He accepted my repentance for Jesus' sake. He knew my unspoken needs for a wife and family—and He supplied just the right one for me. He saw the drunk driver snaking through traffic behind me and led me safely away—even though I never knew it happened. Yes, He cares for me, and it's VERY PERSONAL.

Enough about me, myself, and I. What about you, yourself, and you? You know, that's one of the best things about being God's chosen child. Me, myself, and I is something everyone can say.

Open 24 Hours

All that the Father gives Me will come to Me, and whoever comes to Me I will never drive away. John 6:37

Twenty-four-hour service seems to be a trend. All-night truck stops are indispensable, and hospitals need to offer round-the-clock service, but do we really need ATMs when we're short of cash at 3 a.m.? (Only if our car is laid up at a garage for repairs at 2 a.m.!) Convenience and service have come a long way. One thing hasn't changed, however.

God was always open for business 24 hours a day. What service! No matter how early or late we get up, God patiently waits for us to begin our day in conversation with Him. And we don't need to worry that He got up on the wrong side of the bed! The same is true when we retire, fatigued with the day's labor. God is wide awake and all ears. Even if we fall asleep while talking to Him, He isn't insulted or hurt. In His magnificent mercy, He addresses even our unspoken needs.

We aren't limited to talking with God by appointment only. The regular times are important, but He's ready for emergency interruptions too: Junior hasn't returned from his date yet. It's snowing, the streets are slippery, and he's only had his license for eight months. Or the baby wakes up every fifteen minutes all night. The fever just won't break. She begins to convulse. That's when God's spiritual 911 swings into action. Before you even call, He's with you, meeting your needs, and giving you strength to cope.

God invites us to pray anytime. He promises never to be too busy. In His grace, God even listens to those who have never talked to Him before and to those who only do it when they are in trouble.

Be sure you talk to God today. Any time. Even if it's just to say, "I love You."

218

Keep the Change

This is what the Lord *Almighty, the God of Israel, says: Reform your ways and your actions, and I will let you live in this place. Jeremiah 7:3*

Most people welcome change—especially at the grocery store. But this really isn't the subject of today's meditation. The kind of change we shall consider is the change synonymous with reform.

Babies provide a good example for change in our own lives. Babies always know when they need changing, even though their parents sometimes practice the art of distraction and delay. (This clever ploy sometimes gets the *other* spouse to notice the predicament and act.) With the removal of the soiled (isn't that a polite word?) diaper, the child becomes more comfortable and happy. Until the next time.

Our own sins have us wallowing in a mess too. Those around us may react in ways similar to dirty diaper episodes. For example, there's the "maybe if I ignore it, it will go away" syndrome. Conversely, there's also the "Aggggh! That baby needs changing" reaction that brazenly points out what is already obvious. We sometimes react to our sinfulness in ways that excuse it, indicate that it's nobody's business but our own, or accuse others of being equally sinful or worse. Jeremiah tells us that we better acknowledge our sinfulness and then do something about it.

Reform isn't easy. In fact, it's impossible without the Holy Spirit, and then it still takes spiritual perseverance. The initial ingredient of reform is a repentant heart. That too comes from the Holy Spirit's urging. We respond with both sorrow and sincere aspiration to abandon our sinfulness. Then the Holy Spirit gives us the essential element of reform, namely His power to fight sin.

Empowered by the Spirit, change may not be easy, but it is possible. Like that baby in a fresh diaper, we find comfort in the cleansing Jesus brought into our lives. It brings change worth keeping.

What Muscles!

The LORD will lay bare His holy arm in the sight of all the nations, and all the ends of the earth will see the salvation of our God. Isaiah 52:10

Americans spend a fortune developing muscles. Perhaps you remember the time when really muscular boys rolled up their sleeves—their short sleeves, at that—to grace the girls and send potential male challengers onto their backs in submission.

Isaiah painted an impressive picture for our minds when he spoke of the Lord's bare arm. This wasn't the scrawny, tortured arm of Christ sagging on the cross. This was the holy arm of Jesus in all His glory. Think of the last exercise machine commercial you saw on TV. What arms, rippling with muscles, glistening with sweat! That arm belongs to a wimp compared to the arms of our glorified Savior.

What our Savior did with His arms is far more important than how they looked. For those of us who like action and adventure, we can picture Jesus flexing His muscles right before He gets to the good part where He sends the devil tumbling head-over-heels into an inferno of molten sulphur. No one else could do this. And we need not glibly revel in righteous revenge. Instead, we breathe a sigh of relief. Jesus rescued us, helpless as we are. It was a life-and-death conflict, and it ended happily.

Strong arms need to be tender arms too. Once again, Jesus is the perfect model of strength. Can you feel the firmness of His hug as He comforts you when you're down in the dumps? Have you felt Him hold you close when you were very sick? Have you sobbed on His brawny shoulder after a loved one died?

Next time you talk to Jesus, ask to see His muscles. Ask Him to carry your sins and protect you. Then give your folded hands a gentle squeeze. Jesus is there.

Deep in Debt

Let no debt remain outstanding, except the continuing debt to love one another, for he who loves his fellowman has fulfilled the law. Romans 13:8

In the United States, repayment of the national debt is passed on from generation to generation. That's probably why babies scream when they're born.

Jesus once told a parable about a kindly creditor and a loan shark (Matthew 18:21–35). In those days, failure to repay loans meant certain imprisonment and even loss of family. No wonder Paul urged people to "let no debt remain outstanding." He probably had the moral obligation of repaying debts in mind too. Of greater interest (forgive the pun) is Paul's exhortation to let a certain debt remain.

Perhaps, like the Jews of Paul's time, you've worried about keeping God's laws. Some Christians place too much emphasis on that aspect of faith! Paul tells us the easy way to keep the Law—love one another. Easy? Hardly. As much as we may want to love our neighbors, they do so many unlovable things. And that's nothing compared to some of our global "fellowmen" who would prefer seeing us fried in a nuclear fireball. Love is hard. If only others could be more like us …

Paul based his entreaty on Christ's love for us. If anything, Paul knew how badly he sinned. He claimed to be the worst. Sinners are God's enemy, right? That makes you and me no better than our worst enemies. But Christ changed all that, and that's where the debt comes in. Because Jesus died for our sins—even while we were still sinners and therefore His enemies—we owe Him a debt of thanksgiving and gratitude, which we address through our treatment of others.

Our debt is longer term than a house mortgage, but it's a rewarding debt to pay. In loving others we find the true expression of our faith in Jesus. How satisfying to forgive others and pray for them! And how wonderful to know that others are doing the same for us!

Ouch! Thank You

Dear friends, do not be surprised at the painful trial you are suffering, as though something strange were happening to you. But rejoice that you participate in the sufferings of Christ, so that you may be overjoyed when His glory is revealed. 1 Peter 4:12–13

What makes you happy? Most of us realize that happiness is where you find it, although rarely where you seek it.

New Christians enjoy a spiritual high unattainable by any other means. Well they should! But experienced Christians know that faith will lead them through life's uncomfortable and perhaps painful experiences. Peter says to be thankful for it.

Persecution is far more subtle and far less physical for Christians living in developed countries. Most people reading these pages have never encountered threats of jail because they are practicing Christians. And it's doubtful that any of us have been chased out of town or whipped because of our faith. It's hard to understand how Paul could thank God for such experiences. How Peter could say we should rejoice in such treatment is incredible!

Peter's counsel is well advised nonetheless. He says that such persecution is a way of participating in the oppression Christ suffered. When Jesus tells us to take up our cross, this is one experience He had in mind. And "suffer with me" isn't such unusual advice. Ask anyone who has endured a terrifying tragedy about the bond that develops among victims. We come closer to Christ through suffering for His sake. That's reason enough for rejoicing!

Thank God next time someone ridicules your honesty, mocks your prayers, derides your morality, or taunts your faithfulness. It's a healthy sign that you are living your faith right out where people can see it. We can put up with some suffering now. After all, we have an eternity of bliss ahead of us.

Banner Year

He has taken me to the banquet hall, and His banner over me is love.
Song of Songs 2:4

Everybody enjoys a good love story. Television cameras pan a stadium filled with cheering sports fans as a skywriter inscribes the sky with "Allison, I love you. Will you marry me?" Here's a concrete representation of our verse for today. The banner over Allison was love!

Think for a moment. Over whom would you fly your banner of love? Why would you do it? Now think again. Who would sail their banner over you? Spouse or special friend? Co-workers? The boss? Your next door neighbor? It probably hasn't happened, but that doesn't mean you're not loved.

Love is a funny thing. Young lovers often think it's a feeling. Old lovers know it's actually commitment, forgiveness, self-sacrifice, tolerance, contentment, and service. The banner may become tattered and discolored, but it soars high just the same. Such is the banner that Jesus hoists over us.

It's not unusual for Christians to yearn for spiritual feelings. You might hear, "I'm a believer, but I just don't feel close to Jesus." Or someone will ask, "Can't you just feel God's love here among us?" And your honest answer, if you dared, would be, "No. I wish I did." Love, be it human or divine, may or may not be accompanied by strong emotions. And Christ's love, not unlike the love of a couple married many years, is present whether it's consciously felt or not.

Christ's banner over us is love. He showers us with it when we're mourning and when we're whooping it up. It's there when we're sleeping or trying to stay awake during the sermon. It's at the assembly line, computer terminal, classroom desk, steering wheel, and behind the vacuum cleaner. His banner flies when we do His will, and it dips to half-mast when we're sinful—but it continues to fly. Sometimes His love is pretty routine, and other times it's downright sensational. His love promises us a banner year. Every year. For all time.

Golden Rules

Do not seek revenge or bear a grudge against one of your people, but love your neighbor as yourself. I am the LORD. Leviticus 19:18

Neighbors are those people who sometimes motivate us to keep up, thereby causing huge losses of savings, hair, and common sense. Neighbors are those who really listen to you—especially when you're arguing with your spouse or offspring. Neighbors are those whom the preacher talks about at church. In short, it's often easier to love some lost jungle tribe on another continent than it is to love the family in the next apartment or house. Despite all that, we are able to love our neighbor as ourselves—and that's direct from God Himself.

Maybe we should ask if we really love ourselves. We confess in church that we're "sinful and unclean." So what's to love? The answer, of course, lies in God, who loves us despite our sinfulness. In fact, we're probably safe in saying that He loves us as He loves Himself—maybe more. God loves us enough to sacrifice His Son to save us from our sins. If God loved us that much, then we can certainly love ourselves. And if we can love ourselves, we can love our neighbors too.

In the previous devotion, you read that love isn't always accompanied by intense feelings. But love is always accompanied by concern and service, compassion and prayer, mercy and kindness. We can love our neighbors a variety of ways. It takes some work, though. We need to keep an eye on our neighbors—not to catch them doing something, but to see what they need. They need waves, smiles, and a call to see if everything is okay after the storm. It may even mean cutting the grass an extra few feet on your neighbor's side of the property line or keeping the TV volume a little lower for people on the other side of the wall. And you can't expect neighborly love to be returned. Not everybody plays by the same rules.

What Are You Worth?

Jesus looked at him and said, "How hard it is for the rich to enter the kingdom of God! Indeed, it is easier for a camel to go through the eye of a needle than for a rich man to enter the kingdom of God." Luke 18:24–25

Back in the '70s, salespeople offered me an opportunity to invest in Wisconsin wilderness land that would someday become a popular ski area. They said I could realize my financial fantasies. I had been to Wisconsin, and aside from a few places with cliffs, I hadn't seen any hills worthy of skiing. Being no fool, I refused to invest. (You still have a hard time seeing the hills in that area these days. Too many skiers.)

The passage above is another of those we like to apply to other people. Few folks are as wealthy as they desire. On the other hand, if you don't consider yourself prosperous, you can ignore such words from the Bible, and use them to threaten others. Wealth, however, is relative, and Jesus *is* speaking to us.

Note please, that Jesus didn't say it was impossible for rich people to enter heaven. He said it was hard. Far from being a curse, wealth of any degree is actually a blessing. God gifted certain individuals with money so they could use it to His glory—just as He gave some people good voices, the ability to teach, or skill at making things. Jesus understood how easy it is for the devil and our own evil natures to distract us from what really counts. The trouble comes only when the gifts become more important than the giver. That's what Jesus was talking about.

What are you worth? Whether you need a calculator to figure it out or you can do it with a pencil and scrap of paper, you're worth more than you can imagine. Jesus died to take your sins away. Believe that and you really have a good investment.

Take a Number

But many who are first will be last, and the last first. Mark 10:31

Does it ever fail? You're at the grocery checkout, approximately in the middle of 19 customers. The store manager orders another cash register to open. The line peels off, and now you no longer occupy the middle. You're at the end. Proof that the last shall be first and middle shall be last! The first? They're still first.

Jesus didn't shop at grocery stores, but He was right anyway. His remarks came in response to Peter who asked what the disciples could gain by following Him. A couple of them wanted to be first in line for the blessings of heaven! And while Jesus had already hinted that His closest followers could expect harsh treatment, He also reassured the disciples they would have a special place in heaven.

That answer wouldn't please anyone interested in immediate gratification. At the time, Peter had no idea how he would suffer because of his faith. Rather than rising to either political or popular heights, he would eventually be raised on a cross. Peter would be considered the lowest of low before God transformed him into a victor.

We Christians are tempted to arrogance. Those who demonstrate higher and greater Christian characteristics might also begin thinking highly of themselves. "I serve on three church boards, teach Sunday school, and send money to missions. How great I art."

That's when Jesus' words need to slap at us. Jesus' idea of being first involved being the first to serve others, the first to forgive, the first to care. The worldly equivalent happens when Grandma serves Christmas dinner. Who does all the cooking and is the last to sit? First to serve; last to fill her plate.

The "me first" practitioners are in for a few surprises come Judgment Day. They may succeed in pulling low numbers from the machine. But Jesus will call them backwards!

Unfair Labor Practices

"These men who were hired last worked only one hour," they said, "and you have made them equal to us who have borne the burden of the work and the heat of the day." Matthew 20:12

Rule number 1 for arguing with the boss: Make sure you're right. Then stifle the urge. Rule number 2: Look at both sides—the boss' side and the outside.

Today's passage reports a labor grievance. The problem was that a vineyard owner paid everyone the same wage regardless of hours worked. Although it sounds unfair, the owner's reply was logical to any self-directed business owner. (But it does make you wonder how many showed up on time for work the next day!)

Jesus is definitely unfair according to human standards. A person can be a Christian her whole life, living in accordance with God's will, suppressing worldly desires, boldly striving toward obedience. Another person can live a wild, undisciplined, rebellious life and repent minutes before she dies. Both go to heaven. Or consider the Christian who has a weak faith. He vacillates between reading the Bible and studying the daily horoscope. He often doubts that Jesus would bother with him, and he is afraid of dying. He goes to church only once a month. Next to him on the same pew that Sunday is another Christian who occupies this space every week. He tithes, meditates, and reads devotional books daily. He's eager to meet the Lord in person. Should he be surprised to see the other man in heaven? Certainly not.

All this isn't to encourage practicing faith as little as possible because you can get away with it. The point is that faith in any quantity saves. Before we mutter about fairness, we should remind ourselves that if God were fair, none of us would get to heaven. So let's join the angels who shout "Hip, hip, hooray" every time someone is saved. And let's ask Jesus to continue His record of unfairness.

Private Eyes

Keeping a close watch on Him, they sent spies, who pretended to be honest. They hoped to catch Jesus in something He said so that they might hand Him over to the power and authority of the governor. Luke 20:20

People hire private investigators when the police can't or won't investigate some suspicion for them. It happened to Jesus, as Luke reports.

Luke didn't mince words—or titles. He called the investigators dishonest spies. They came to Jesus asking what seemed like legitimate questions, but they hoped for answers that would doom Him. Jesus' answer was so starkly honest that they abandoned their spy mission.

Common people like us probably breathe a sigh of relief knowing we're not important enough to warrant a spy's interest. But that's dangerous. The devil spies on us constantly. His eyes see everything we do in private, and he takes notes. He's saving the evidence to present on Judgment Day when we stand before God. The devil probably won't need to lie much about our activities. We're quite sinful enough without his embellishment or exaggeration. He wants us to plead guilty without any defense.

As guilty as we are, our only defense is to throw ourselves on the mercy of the Judge. We should freely confess all we've done wrong because His own investigation revealed the same evidence as the devil's. Yet God is certain to agree when we ask Him to save us for Christ's sake. We will testify that Jesus died to save us and that we know He accomplished that mission. The verdict will be swift and very partial. We'll join the throng of other saved sinners at God's right hand.

Until that time of judgment, we need to be on the lookout. Not for spies, but for our own sinful behavior. Let's not wait for Judgment Day to throw ourselves on God's mercy.

Dark Days

Today in the town of David a Savior has been born to you; He is Christ the Lord. Luke 2:11

Merry Christmas! Even if it's not. Christmas, that is. If you have any "child" left in you, Christmas is delightful to think about any time of year. Besides, Christmas really does last all year—especially if you have credit cards!

Have you noticed God's history of taking really drastic action when days seem the darkest? For example, just when it seemed that wickedness was so overwhelming that it would wipe out heaven's future population, God washed away the evil with a flood, devastating to all but a handful of believers and animals.

Another example: Just when it seemed that more than four centuries of slavery would blend Israelite faith with Egyptian myth, God miraculously emancipated His children so they could serve Him without distraction and receive His blessings without interference.

We don't know the exact date of Christmas, but it is certainly celebrated at an appropriate time in the northern hemisphere. December 25 is close to the shortest day of the year—the first day of winter. So much darkness! The Romans were so acutely disturbed by this phenomenon that they celebrated the "return of the sun"—*Io Saturnalia*—as soon as the days began getting longer, if only by minutes. What a great time to celebrate Christmas!

Jesus is the return of light to sinners living in darkness. We no longer live in the dark days of sin because Jesus took our sins away on the darkest of Fridays. We live, instead, in times of light and hope as we look forward to the day when Jesus returns. We'll never be in the dark again.

Pray for a Blizzard

"Come now, let us reason together," says the LORD. "Though your sins are like scarlet, they shall be as white as snow; though they are red as crimson, they shall be like wool." Isaiah 1:18

It's only natural to think of snow the day after talking about Christmas. Children are especially enchanted by snow. (Perhaps that's because they don't have to drive in the stuff!)

Fresh snow turns ordinary sunshine into dazzling light, and when a full moon falls on a carpet of flakes, darkness transforms into a romantic, silvery glow. And there's so much you can do with snow. Even the most frigid snowman warms the hearts of its creators. Snow skiing is a favorite pastime of many too. And some relish the swish of a toboggan or tube racing downhill. Sometimes the thrills are as simple as friendly snowball fights or soggy snow angels dimpling clean, white fields.

God talked about snow, as you can see from today's verse. He knew that people liked its color together with its symbolic purity. What a fitting comparison to think of our bloody sins transformed into exquisite drifts of snow! However, anyone who lives in a snowbelt city knows what happens to pearly white snowbanks. They soon turn ugly, soiled by dirt and pollution. Then we wait for the next snowstorm to restore beauty to our world.

So it is with our life! Though Jesus died only once to take away our sins, our sins must die daily. That sparkling blanket of snow that covered the sins of the world becomes tainted over time. Our daily sins inflict ghastly stains on the purity and righteousness that Jesus provided for us, so each day we pray for another blizzard of forgiveness. Then we can enjoy life again. We can ski into valleys where the shadows of death once lurked, and the whole concept of snow angels takes on a richer meaning. And while we're enjoying the snow so much, maybe we can even fling a few snowballs at the devil.

Cost of Living

Then what was spoken by Jeremiah the prophet was fulfilled: "They took
the thirty silver coins, the price set on Him by the people of Israel."
Matthew 27:9

You probably feel the impact of escalating costs every time
you drive—if not your car, then certainly your shopping cart.

Judas received a handsome price for betraying Jesus, a price
predicted in Jeremiah long before the heinous act. I'm not sure if
inflation existed in those days, but it didn't affect what Jeremiah
prophesied. God's Word is immune to such things. But the issue
isn't inflation. Rather, it's the high cost of living.

True to form, God turned evil into good. What we still view as
"blood money" was at the same time the cost of living—and Jesus'
enemies paid it! Jesus paid the price too. At the cost of His life, Jesus
made life worth living. And living and living and living and …

God's gift of eternal life was ours the moment the Holy Spirit
worked faith in our heart. While faith was a free gift, we owe a cost
of living nonetheless. The cost is painless for some and a challenge
for others. To put it another way, some Christians find their service
to God a complete joy. As affluent people barely notice increases in
the cost of living, some Christians enjoy such abundant faith that
they don't consider good works an imposition. Sometimes they even
fail to perceive the good they do for Christ's sake. Would that all of
us possessed such lavish faith!

Other Christians have lesser measures of faith. Serving God in
prayer, worship, and good deeds is more difficult. Sometimes they
feel sorry for themselves due to their persistent indebtedness.
Sometimes they forget the alternatives. But they worship and serve
anyway because that's the cost of Christian living.

Wherever you find yourself on the faith scale, you can be sure
that the cost of living is worth the price.

231

Star Studded

Do everything without complaining or arguing, so that you may become blameless and pure, children of God without fault in a crooked and depraved generation, in which you shine like stars in the universe.
Philippians 2:14–15

I heard on the radio that for the reasonable sum of $45, I could buy a star and name it for a loved one. Its name would be registered and sealed in a vault. As an additional benefit, I would receive a chart showing me just where in heaven my loved one twinkled.

Maybe having a star named after you isn't as ridicu ... er, unusual as it sounds. Did you see what Paul told the Philippians? He said that we Christians shine like stars in an otherwise dark and depraved universe. And because our names are on those stars, we might also be inclined to heed the first part of today's note to the Philippians. "Do everything without complaining or arguing."

Perhaps Paul meant that we should avoid church meetings. No. Disregard that last lapse into sarcasm. (But if your congregation holds regular meetings to discuss its "business," you know what I mean.) So many jobs await eager Christians. They also await those who aren't so eager. But doing God's work means pitching in together even when we're tired and don't feel like pitching. Doing God's work requires unity rather than disparity, hidden agendas, private prejudices, and self-centeredness.

God helps us do His work. Perhaps we should think of ourselves like that star God sent over Bethlehem—the one registered to Jesus Christ. It showed the Wise Men where they could find their Savior. God put us on earth for the same reason. He makes us glisten with the Gospel and glitter with grace. And our names won't be secured in some musty vault. They will live forever in God's International Registry of Saved Sinners.

Quiet Times

When He opened the seventh seal, there was silence in heaven for about half an hour. Revelation 8:1

If silence is golden, why are so many books written on how to speak and so few on how to be quiet? Silence, at the very least, offers protection. You don't have to explain what you haven't said. Besides, it's better to remain quiet and be thought dense and witless than to speak volumes and remove all doubts.

In the expression of faith, time for silence is advisable too. Sometimes, we need to do nothing but think and leave our hearts and minds open to discovering God's will for us. Of course, "doing nothing" isn't natural for many Christians, so here are two hints on how to keep silent before God.

1. Think for a moment about the last time you were left speechless. Maybe you were afraid or so awestruck that you were at a loss for words. Or maybe someone said something so profound (or painfully true) that your usually quick wit slipped to half speed.

God is awesome; therefore, it's natural—and wise—to be awestruck in His presence. The very fact that God listens to our prayers, meets our needs, and accepts our love is enough to stir such strong feelings of respect that we're temporarily silent. Silence is faith's exclamation of respect. And God listens to it!

2. Silence is golden in the presence of those who know more than us. God knows everything, and He wants us to know part of what He knows. Listening to God, however, is futile if you expect to hear voices inside your head. (If you do hear voices, ascertain that you removed the earphones from your portable radio.) God talks through the Bible. As we quietly meditate on His Word, He fills us with the Holy Spirit. It's good to conduct some silent, informal conversation with the Spirit at these times. Tell Him you want to do God's will. Then go about your business, confident that God will guide your ways and your words. Now there's something to talk about.

7: A Sure Bet

I know that my Redeemer lives, and that in the end He will stand upon the earth. Job 19:25

Much superstition surrounds the number 7. People bet on it at races, baseball pools, and lottery machines. About the only thing seven really guarantees is that the odds are long against your winning. Besides, depending on luck isn't worth the effort. Look how much luck the rabbit's foot brought its former owner!

Seven isn't a lucky number, but it's certainly a blessed one for Christians. Symbolically, the Bible uses seven to indicate completeness. And for seven consecutive days, we'll meditate on seven truths that bring blessings—not luck—to Christians like us.

Job knew the truth. (Just imagine what would have happened had he relied on luck!) Regardless of how the devil assaulted and molested him, Job knew that God would win—even if it meant Job's death (Job 19:26). Had Job been a betting man, he would have bet on God. Though his family died tragically and his personal fortune dwindled to bankruptcy, though his health was nothing to live for and he sometimes had doubts about God, Job kept the faith.

We know the truth too. One truth we never want to forget is "I know that my Redeemer lives." It's true that our Redeemer was born to a mortal woman and spent His childhood running, playing, and learning with His family and other kids. It's true that our Redeemer was falsely convicted, unjustly executed, and charitably buried in someone else's tomb. But the greatest truth is that a few days later the tomb was empty. Jesus rose from the dead, and now He lives in heaven.

It's true that Jesus will once again stand on earth. He's coming back to end our misery, and, like Job, it doesn't really matter if we're dead or alive at the time. We *will* see Jesus, and He *will* bring us into His everlasting, heavenly kingdom. Who needs luck when God's promises are a sure thing?

Know More

They said to the woman, "We no longer believe just because of what you said; now we have heard for ourselves, and we know that this man really is the Savior of the world." John 4:42

The second of seven great truths is that Jesus really is the Savior of the world. Today's Bible passage tells what happened after Jesus met a Samaritan women by a village well. She was surprised that a man—especially a Jew—would talk to her. Normally, Jews didn't exchange pleasantries with Samaritans. As they talked, the woman realized that Jesus was something special. He knew the truth about her even though she understandably couched the truth in more comfortable terms.

She had heard the Messiah was coming. Now Jesus revealed Himself to be the long-expected Savior. She believed and ran off to tell her friends. Apparently, they believed the woman's incredible story. They wanted to know more, so they came looking for Christ themselves. Jesus stayed with them a couple days, teaching everything their eager minds and hearts could comprehend. The new believers took their faith one step beyond the woman's simple witness. They now heard the great truth from the lips of the Savior Himself.

Where did you first hear of Jesus? Did your family tell you that Jesus died to take away your sins? Maybe it was a Sunday school teacher, classmate, spouse, child, or even a complete stranger. The Holy Spirit often calls people to faith through the witness of others. Thankful as we are for those whom the Spirit used to jump-start our faith, now it's time to get information firsthand. When you want to know more, there is no more important place to go than into the living pages of the Bible.

235

True Stories

And we know that in all things God works for the good of those who love Him, who have been called according to His purpose. Romans 8:28

Some people have so many troubles they're two weeks behind in getting around to worry about them! Having no problems isn't the answer, though.

We may wish that one of God's seven great truths involved an earthly life devoid of problems. Even in the best of times, it's never been that way for believers. The great truth about God is that He will work things out for our good.

God has maintained this great functional truth since sin began. And He does it so creatively! Consider those plague-filled days just before the children of Israel made their exit from Egypt. The Israelites were eager to leave, and Pharaoh had trouble making up his mind—mostly because his hard heart got in the way. Every time Pharaoh refused to let God's people go, God demonstrated His power. As the Egyptians grew to fear God more and more, the Israelites got another dose of faith-strengthening miracles. Their troubles actually brought them closer to God.

Trouble is good for that. It tends to unify. We witness a humanistic counterpart when a tornado rips apart houses but brings together people who share some common bond—even if that bond is only one of tragedy. We see it in families when distant sons and daughters gather at the bedside of a dying parent. Good as this may be, the place to go when predicaments strike is to God Himself.

History supports the truth about God. Following that fatal Friday on Calvary, a group of Jesus' followers gathered, trying to find meaning in their disappointment and grief. Suddenly, Jesus appeared, and gave them the grace to understand what Paul would someday write to the Romans. God has a history of truth. That's good to know when we face those problems that seem to have no true solution.

Camping Out

Now we know that if the earthly tent we live in is destroyed, we have a
building from God, an eternal house in heaven, not built by human hands.
2 Corinthians 5:1

The last time I slept in a tent, I awoke to a gentle nudging
from outside the tent—the place where beasts of the night
prowl, seeking whom they may devour. I could hear it breathing and
sniffing out the exact location of its next meal. Fortunately, the beast
was only a black Lab trying to root out the source of the nasal rack-
et that woke him up.

Tents are prone to sagging with rain, blowing apart in wind,
submitting easily to falling branches, and enticing nosey retrievers.
Being a tentmaker, Paul understood the perverse nature of tents.

Paul compared our bodies to tents—tents set up on earth and
subjected to all kinds of abuse. He said that someday the tent would
collapse, destroyed by sin and death. Normally, such a dire predic-
tion should worry us, but here comes another of God's great truths.
Paul says that we have a sturdy house in heaven—a new place to live
when our old place is destroyed. And there are two equally good
ways of thinking about this truth.

First, the thought of an "eternal house ... not built by human
hands" suggests heaven. Nobody has ever seen this place. Paul had-
n't seen it yet when he wrote these words either. But, like Paul, we
believe it truly exists.

Second, the tent can also be compared to our bodies.
Eventually, most of us end up with our flaps sagging and our canvas
stretching. Then things seem to get worse. Death will probably claim
us. The truth is that we'll have new "tents." Strong, fat-free, choles-
terol-impervious, death-defying bodies perfect in every way and
built to serve God person to person—or rather person to God. Now
that's one tent I won't mind inhabiting. How about you?

Our Guardian

That is why I am suffering as I am. Yet I am not ashamed, because I know whom I have believed, and am convinced that He is able to guard what I have entrusted to Him for that day. 2 Timothy 1:12

Remember the school letters that began "Dear Parent or Guardian"? During my childhood, guardians were rare. Most of us kids thought they were angels. Little did we realize how important guardians could be.

We all need a guardian—with a capital G. That's the substance of this fifth great truth from God. He guards our faith. Because overt and violent persecution of Christians is rare in America, we're lulled into a sense of safety. Maybe the devil knows that the freedoms protected in our country are best fought by doing nothing. When believers think they have nothing to fear, they tend to forget their need for God. The children of Israel were good examples of this phenomena. They lived in a cycle that began with fervent faith and moved to routine acceptance of God's involvement in their affairs. Life became so comfortable that believers took their beliefs less seriously. Before long, they ranked among the unbelievers—until God reminded them of their special relationship again.

Our greatest need today is no different. God appointed the Holy Spirit as our Guardian. In truth, He preserves our faith better than anyone else. And when we become overly contented, our Guardian sometimes jars us back to reality with a few disasters of our own. Instead of moving further away from God in times of trouble, our Guardian pushes us into the arms of our loving, heavenly Father. He takes us to the foot of the cross and the door of the empty tomb to remind us of what we believe. Of course, should the devil make bolder attempts to steal our faith, our Guardian springs into action, claiming us as children of God and off-limits to Satan. Yes, God appointed the Holy Spirit as our guardian. "Dear Guardian" indeed!

238

Ambition

Dear friends, now we are children of God, and what we will be has not yet been made known. But we know that when He appears, we shall be like Him, for we shall see Him as He is. 1 John 3:2

When I was growing up, I wanted to be—if you'll excuse the politically incorrect expression—a garbageman. That's what we called the guys who piloted their huge orange trucks through the narrow Chicago alley behind my house. I really thought that was the job to end all jobs. I've changed my mind since then. Taking out the kitchen garbage once a day is thrill enough for me.

The fondest ambition of Christians is growing up to be like Jesus—even if we're not quite sure how that is. That's the gist of today's passage for meditation and the sixth great truth in our series of seven. Someday we will be like Jesus. It's an uncertain ambition, at that. Our imagination of that wonderful future is inadequate.

Right now we are children of God. Our faith is somewhat immature, but as we "see" Jesus in action through the words of the Bible, we want to be just like Him. That's God's will too. He told us about Jesus so that we're confident about our future even though we don't know all its details. And He also told us about Jesus so we could begin imitating our Savior in deeds of kindness and acts of forgiveness. We can't ever be as good as Jesus was at these things—at least not while we're living on earth. But someday ...

Today, Jesus lives in glory. He lives where there is no night, sadness, sickness, or sin. Sounds like a nice neighborhood. His work of sacrifice and forgiveness got Him where He is. And His same work will get us there too. After all, it's true of most jobs, isn't it? You need a little "pull" to get ahead. Jesus provided the pull for us, and it's the only way to achieve our ambition. Thank God for that. Without His pull, we would end up as nothing but garbage ourselves.

The Last Truth

We know that we have passed from death to life, because we love our brothers. Anyone who does not love remains in death. 1 John 3:14

Have you priced funerals lately? It's too expensive to die. We may find comfort in the reverse process—passing from death to life. The nice thing is that we don't have to stop breathing to do it. It's already within our grasp.

As you're reading this, you might want to check your pulse, but you can be reasonably certain you're still alive. Yet all Christians have died—died to sin, that is. Jesus took our sins to the grave. The women who peered into the tomb saw nothing, but lurking in the dark shadows were the sins of the world, dead and buried. So we have died to sin and are free to love.

Love is a major characteristic of Christians. It's what marks us as living—really living. And isn't love what the world craves? But as an old song says, we end up "looking for love in all the wrong places." Some search for it on perfumed beds while others try to drain it from a bottle. Some seek love in music, literature, or adventure. All in vain. Christ is the only source of real love.

Jesus loved sinners like us and died to save us. And while it may be imperfect, we love as we can. For Christ's sake we love our family, stock the local food pantry, do favors for neighbors and co-workers, pray every time we see an ambulance racing for the hospital, smile at lonely faces, invite someone to worship with us, or dry some tears with a tissue. That's really living, and it's all possible because of Jesus.

The funny thing about loving others is that it contributes to our own happiness. Those who love others are more content with what they have and spend less time thinking about their own troubles. Giving actually feels good. I guess that's what happens when you're really alive. Jesus gave us that gift, and it's truly a gift that keeps on giving.

What Bugs You?

He spoke, and there came swarms of flies, and lice in all their territory.
Psalm 105:31 (NKJV)

One thing universally bugs (if you'll excuse the pun) parents of school-age children: head lice. Survive one outbreak, and it's easy to understand how aggravating the plague of lice was for the Egyptians. Treatment for head lice includes what most kids regard as toxic waste in shampoo form.

Head lice, mosquitos, gnats, and biting flies are among hoards of pesky creatures that enjoy their ability to vex. They may have one positive feature, though. They remind us of sin.

Sin should bug us—and make us want to rid ourselves of it forever. Sometimes our sinfulness is like an attack of mosquitos. We feel the sting of sin as our behavior makes us miserable or sick—that "fun night out" that ends in a hangover or worse. That "harmless flirtation" that fuels jealousy and divorce. That moment of anger combined with a loaded gun. And don't forget the greatest sting—death itself.

Sometimes sinfulness is more like head lice. Sin quietly rubs off the devil, the world, or our companions and onto us. Sooner or later we'll detect the invasion. But the damage is done. To eliminate the problem, we must get to the roots, so to speak, of the predicament.

The root of sin is the devil, the world, and our own flesh. It's comforting to blame the devil or the world for our sins. But the truth is that we ourselves are equally to blame. We often crave the temptations that dance before our eyes and fall to them in preference over God's will.

Thank God for sending Jesus to get to the root of our evil. Jesus washed away our sins. His prescription is for daily repentance and forgiveness. He makes us clean each day, giving us new power to fight off that which bugs us. In fact, we don't need any stringent shampoo or deep woods repellent. Since we're armed with Jesus' power, a simple phrase will do. Try it yourself. Just say, "Bug off!" next time sin attacks you.

Finding the Key

Woe to you experts in the law, because you have taken away the key to knowledge. You yourselves have not entered, and you have hindered those who were entering. Luke 11:52

The legal experts of Jesus' time were experts in either applying the law to others or finding loopholes for themselves. For every law or rule passed, there also exists a bypass. That's the nature of the law. Except when it comes to God.

With God there are no loopholes. When He says, "You shall not kill," He includes every possible way to assassinate a person's body or character. And when He says, "You shall not commit adultery," He also means the kind that people commit in the privacy of their fantasies. Similarly, all the other commandments lack loopholes too. Even after Jesus reduced the Ten Commandments to only two, people still tried to find exceptions for loving God. And we can find even more exclusions for the law about loving other people.

God's Law most certainly condemns us. In His halls of justice, every conviction carries the death penalty. This is unheard of in the annals of justice! It has many crying, "Unfair!" because it's impossible to obey this Law.

We have something else "unheard of" in God's judicial system—getting credit from someone else who can really obey God, and receiving pardon because someone else suffered the sentence for our sins. Jesus knew the Law better than the lawyers and judges of His time. He knew the key to obeying the Law was obedience—obedience in heart, mind, and body. Jesus used that key not only to open the doors of knowledge for believers, but also to open the gates of heaven. So step around those fumbling in their pockets for the keys to knowledge. They only hinder your way. And let Jesus open the door for you.

Cutting the Apron Strings

Therefore, this is what the LORD says: You have not obeyed Me; you have not proclaimed freedom for your fellow countrymen. So I now proclaim "freedom" for you, declares the LORD—"freedom" to fall by the sword, plague and famine. I will make you abhorrent to all the kingdoms of the earth. Jeremiah 34:17

God bless America. It's a nation characterized by religious freedom. Every American is guaranteed the right to attend the church of his or her choice. Or to go golfing. Or to seek to restrain worship of the true God. Of course, only a radical would insist on worship of the one true God because any god can be true. Right? That's the nature of freedom.

Our religious freedom was granted by God. It was He who led our country's shapers to insist on freedom to worship as one chooses—a good idea, but one which we humans easily pervert or dilute. But that's God's way too. Had He wanted puppets, He would have given us strings instead of liberty. God indeed gives us religious freedom.

Jeremiah's "congregation" apparently took its liberty seriously. The people chose freedom from God rather than the freedom to serve and obey Him. Sound familiar? The most serious deficiency of religious tolerance is freedom to worship gods other than the true one. And while our country may promote such freedom, and while God allows such choice, we court disaster when we cut our apron strings to God. Under these circumstances, "Give me liberty or give me death" takes on new meaning.

Examined through the eyes of faith, religious freedom involves no choice at all. We clearly see the goodness of God. He gives unlimited benefits to citizens of His kingdom. Take health care, for example. In a day when medical insurance is a major concern, it's comforting to know that God sends healing to all who want it. Oh, there is a string attached. It's the apron one again. We must go to the doctor of *His* choice.

When You Don't Know What to Say

My dear brothers, take note of this: Everyone should be quick to listen, slow to speak and slow to become angry. James 1:19

God bless America—a land that guarantees freedom of speech. Too bad it doesn't guarantee listeners! The ability to listen is almost sure to win friends and serve them in godly ways. In fact, if you listen carefully as you read today's meditation, you'll receive a bonus tip at the end. (No fair skipping to the end to see if it's worth it. Listen to me!)

Most of us are familiar with this scene: Despite the serenity they're designed to provide, the soft, pink lighting and bouquets of flowers make us uneasy. Even the stately wooden casket can't lend genuine dignity to the young, lifeless body at rest on its cushions. The damp and reddened eyes of the family search deeply, almost desperately, into your own eyes. What can you say at times like these?

The best thing to say when we don't know what to say is to say so. The best thing to do if we're slow to speak is to be slow to speak. Chances are good that people in need don't want a speech anyway. What emotionally needy people need is for someone to be there and to listen. A hug and simple "I'm sorry" say volumes to the brokenhearted, and it invites others to open their stricken hearts to us.

But what will we hear? We'll hear memories—maybe the same ones we've heard many times before. One secret of good listeners is listening without comment to things we already know. Isn't that just what Jesus did? He knew the deepest dreads prowling the hearts and souls of all who asked His help. His words were simple, but His actions were powerful. He listened and loved.

You listened well! So here's the tip. If you want kids to listen to you, pretend you're talking to someone else. And if you don't want them to listen, pretend you're talking to them!

244

The Arsenal

The night is nearly over; the day is almost here. So let us put aside the deeds of darkness and put on the armor of light. Romans 13:12

God bless America. (Again.) Where else do people have the right to wear tank tops and sundresses anytime they want? Whoops—wrong arms. Wrong "bear" too.

The right to bear arms was born of fear that armed despots would easily overcome unarmed citizens. Unfortunately, this important freedom remains seriously abused by the very people it intended to serve. That's the nature of freedom, though, isn't it? We have freedom to be wise or foolish.

God gave us the right to bear arms, but He took it a step further. He actually armed us. We hear Paul telling the Romans and us how we're to use this freedom and power. No "deeds of darkness" allowed. We Christians wear the armor of light for the many righteous battles we fight. But aside from talk, what exactly does God give us for battle?

God's arsenal is more potent than nuclear warheads. He gave us righteousness, His Word and sacraments, and salvation. Soldiers with bad attitudes are poorly equipped even if they have a tank strapped to their back. They must believe in that for which they fight. When God made us righteous through Jesus Christ, He gave us the right attitude. He made us one with the Commander. Then He gave us the weapons of Word and Sacrament. Deceptive weapons, they are. They appear so flimsy. But these mighty weapons equip us to fight the devil. The Word tells us to resist and overcome the enemy, and the Commander Himself touches us personally through Baptism and His Supper. Then there's salvation. We can fight the fiercest battles of faith unafraid of dying because Jesus gives us salvation. God did indeed give us the right to bear arms. And for that we're eternally grateful.

Hot Pursuit

Even if I caused you sorrow by my letter, I do not regret it. Though I did regret it—I see that my letter hurt you, but only for a little while—yet now I am happy, not because you were made sorry, but because your sorrow led you to repentance. For you became sorrowful as God intended and so were not harmed in any way by us. 2 Corinthians 7:8–9

God bless America. (Kate Smith would be proud!) Our government gives us the right to pursue happiness. Most Americans are in hot pursuit. Unfortunately, a lot of money is burned trying to catch it.

Nonchristians' pursuit of happiness often differs from the Christian's. Our quest takes us through some unusual—even unhappy—places. Let's see where the pursuit begins.

The best place to start may be with Christ's disciple Peter outside the building where His dear friend was on trial for His life. Unfortunately, Peter failed miserably in returning that friendship. Before we shake a shaming finger at Peter, we need to examine ourselves, standing there next to him. How often, by word or action, do we also deny knowing the best friend we ever had? But enough of that for now. Happiness is well beyond us, and only the hottest of pursuit will help us catch up.

Breathlessly, we stop at the next station of happiness—the cross. This is happiness? The cross seems an obstacle toward happiness, and Jesus certainly didn't enjoy it there.

Our happiness, like that of the Corinthians whom Paul counseled, must begin with sadness. Not that either God or Paul enjoyed making us feel bad. Having spent the chilly evening with Peter and crouching beneath the cross, how could we feel otherwise? But that sorrow is useful, for it leads us to repentance. And repentance leads to forgiveness. And forgiveness leads to eternal life with Jesus. So sit down and rest. The chase is over. Happiness is yours. And it didn't cost you a cent.

Ignorance Is Not Bliss

The law was added so that the trespass might increase. But where sin increased, grace increased all the more. Romans 5:20

Ignorance isn't bliss. If it were, more people would be jumping for joy.

Ignorance of God's Law can either be blissful or terrifying, depending on how you look at it. One thousand years passed between the first time man (and woman) broke God's Law and the time when God gave His followers 10 rules for life. When Moses lugged the two stone tables of Law down the mountain, an era of awareness began—awareness of God's will for His people.

Now His people knew what they were doing wrong. They may have sinned anyway, but at least they knew what they were doing. With that in mind, we read Paul's words to the Romans. Does this really mean that God set out to increase our sins by revealing His Law? Hardly.

Among God's many gifts is the Law, which plainly increases awareness of our own sins. This is essential information. It's like that pain on our right side that warns us to see a doctor—before our appendix explodes. The Law tells us something life-threatening is wrong. Our relationship with God is infected with sin, and we need immediate treatment. If we didn't know about it, then … ignorance would be deadly!

Knowing our sinfulness prompts us to run to Jesus for help. His diagnosis confirms our suspicions. We are indeed sin-full. But He is forgiveness-full. The more sins we expose, the more forgiveness we receive. (Not that we should have some kind of contest to see how much forgiveness we can get!) That's Paul's message to the Romans, and it's God's assurance to us. We don't need to be ignorant of our sins, but we can be sure that God forgets them for Jesus' sake. Now that's real bliss.

247

You *Can* Take It with You

But if we walk in the light, as He is in the light, we have fellowship with one another, and the blood of Jesus, His Son, purifies us from all sin.
1 John 1:7

One big problem with the future is that it usually arrives sooner than we hope. Of course, we Christians don't concern ourselves with the future. Or do we?

There's a story about a mom and her son on a camping trip. "Nature" calls the boy in the middle of the night, so he awakens Mom and expresses his urgent need. The outhouse is in the middle of the campground—a good 200 feet from their tent. The boy isn't fond of darkness, so Mom grabs a lantern and the boy's clammy hand and heads in the direction of relief. Her son says, "I'm scared. We can't see where we're going." Mom calmly reassures him, "We're okay as long as we stay in the light."

John has similar words of reassurance. While we may be certain of our final future, most of us would admit to anxieties about the years or days or even hours ahead. The idea of a crystal ball sometimes sounds like a good idea. But who needs it? After all, we have the light.

John says we should "walk in the light." His light is far more than a lantern, but its effect is similar. When we "walk in the light"— the light of Jesus—we know we are safe even though we don't know what the future holds. Not only do we have the safety of salvation glowing around us, but we have the comforting companionship of other believers. We all know where we're going, and we have a heartening notion of the relief we'll feel once we arrive. But it surely is agreeable to bask in mutual expressions of faith and hope until we get there. Washed in the blood of Jesus Christ, we forgiven sinners can hold hands as we move through the uncertainties knowing that certainty awaits us. So continue walking in the light. And take someone with you.

248

Jail Break

[Peter] described how the Lord had brought him out of prison. "Tell James and the brothers about this," he said. Acts 12:17

Peter and Paul were painfully familiar with the justice system of their time. Both spent time behind bars. (And they weren't sipping cold beer either.)

Some readers may know what it's like to be, as it's politely put, incarcerated. Others may remember jail tours once offered to school children in hopes they would avoid a more permanent experience. I remember one such field trip. It was the first time I saw women sporting tattoos. (It was less a fashion statement in those days.) I remember the sullen looks on the inmates' faces.

Not all prisons have bars. Drugs and alcohol jail some. Lust or violence cage others. Despair and depression confine others. And still others don't even realize they're captives of money or power. Do you ever find yourself in such places? Sinners always do. And that includes Christian sinners too. That's why Jesus came on the scene. He led the most welcome jail break the world has ever known.

His work on the cross set us free. Oh, He lets us wander into prisons here and there much the same as He allowed Peter and Paul to be locked up. It won't be easy, but when we find ourselves confined to some sinful cell, we can act like Peter and Paul. They had the key. No, not the key to the door, but the key to hope and joy. They did things like pray out loud and sing hymns. Not very usual behavior for inmates. But they knew what fellow prisoners didn't. They were bound for freedom. Even if they never got to leave their cell.

We're all behind bars in some way. Every sin confines us. Pray for a jail break, and escape to tell others your story. You're sure to have a captive audience.

Strange Bedfellows

The wolf will live with the lamb, the leopard will lie down with the goat, the calf and the lion and the yearling together; and a little child will lead them.
Isaiah 11:6

Greeting card companies just love the verse above, especially at Christmas. It makes for such cute illustrations of "peace on earth."

Nobody can deny that world peace is elusive. Just about the time one hot spot cools down, another flares up and brings people to the brink of bullets and bombs. As if two warring sides were magnets, the world's nations snap into alliances, mostly in avowed pursuit of peace. Most peace comes at a cost—the cost of blood, tears, and life itself.

Think for a moment of pairs of mortal enemies. Historically, we might mention the Vietcong and the United States, Russia and Germany, Saudi Arabia and Iraq, Israel and Egypt, Catholics and Protestants, or Philistines and the children of Israel. Surprisingly, peace came for several of these enemies. Not surprisingly, some of these enemies became extinct. No list of mortal enemies would be complete, however, without mentioning sin and God.

Sin and God will never get along, nor will there be any negotiated peace settlements. Sin has contaminated and tried to destroy everything God ever made, even God's own Son. But Jesus defeated sin on the cross.

While sin and God will never get along, sinners and Jesus walk hand in hand. Jesus reaches out with His mercy and forgiveness. He loves us even though we're very different. His forgiveness brings a peace potent enough to make a calf and a lion sleeping partners. Not that Jesus loves our sinfulness or overlooks it. Instead, He takes it away and makes us His friend. Instead of devouring us with divine wrath, God invites us to be bedfellows with His Son. And He does all this while we're still sinners. Strange, isn't it? Gladly so! Thank God we're no stranger to Him!

250

The Love of Our Life

Place me like a seal over your heart, like a seal on your arm; for love is as strong as death, its jealousy unyielding as the grave. It burns like blazing fire, like a mighty flame. Many waters cannot quench love; rivers cannot wash it away. If one were to give all the wealth of his house for love, it would be utterly scorned. Song of Songs 8:6–7

Solomon had plenty to say about love. Of course, he seemed to have lots of experience on the subject.

Scholars think a woman spoke the passage above for a man she deeply loved. The "seal over your heart" and the "seal on your arm" may be ancient precursors of modern wedding rings. Some women wore pierced rocks or arm bands identifying them as property of their beloved husbands. But before you start muttering about the idea of "belonging" to someone else, let's view this passage as an expression of God's love for us.

We Christians crave God's love. If ever we wanted to "belong" to someone other than ourselves or perhaps our cherished spouse, we want to be identified with Him. We want to take His name so all the world will know how much He loves us and vice versa. And so God weds us to Himself with the mark that we belong—faith in Him.

God's love for us is "strong as death" and as "unyielding as the grave." We can think of God's love being strong as death—the death of Jesus on the cross. This was no deep coma or symbolic sleep as some claim. It was our real God who died a real death. The unyielding grave insisted on its way, but in the end, even the grave yielded, and Jesus rose to victory. Now His love continues not just to burn, but to blaze—a virtual inferno of love that defies extinguishing.

God's love can't be bought. Good love is priceless. It's unmerited. And it's free. God loves us because—well, because He loves us. What other reason could there be?

That Explains It

For prophecy never had its origin in the will of man, but men spoke from God as they were carried along by the Holy Spirit. 2 Peter 1:21

Recently, some cynical scholars have announced the "truth" about Sodom, Gomorrah, and Lot's wife (Genesis 19). (You know what cynics are, don't you? They're people who know everything and believe nothing.) You may remember the fearful story of how God demolished the sin cities with fire and brimstone. You may also remember that God spared Lot and his family, and how Lot's wife took one last, forbidden look at the hometown, becoming the first recorded victim of excessive sodium.

Now all this is hard to explain. Modern, technologically enhanced, highly educated cynics now claim that research suggests the cities were located atop a highly flammable bituminous area. As for Lot and Mrs. Lot, that was a case of mistaken identity. Their escape took them down the Dead Sea Scenic Highway where chunks of salt were known to float like icebergs, occasionally washing ashore on high waves. These scholars seem to suggest that Mrs. Lot stooped over to tie her sandal or something when Lot noticed the hunk of flotsam and ran off in horror.

God leaves no room for cynicism about His Word. Peter says that our familiar Bible stories come courtesy of the Holy Spirit, who makes the unbelievable believable. We don't need explanations about how God does things. Otherwise, how could we believe that the same God who devastated two corrupt cities would also love sinners so much that He spared their eternal lives? Our escape is through no one less than God's Son, Jesus. And when God returns to turn the whole universe into a highly flammable bituminous area, He'll lead us to safety too. Just don't look back.

413 Reasons to Thank Jesus

Jesus answered, "Everyone who drinks this water will be thirsty again, but whoever drinks the water I give him will never thirst. Indeed, the water I give him will become in him a spring of water welling up to eternal life."
John 4:13–14

When we need a little prodding to thank our God and Savior, a good place to look for suggestions is in the fourth chapter, thirteenth verse of several books. John is a good place to start. He quotes Jesus, who implies that nothing in the world completely and finally satisfies us.

Isn't it peculiar that we can be so satisfied with ourselves and so dissatisfied with others? Of course, that phenomena is easily explained. Ignorance and forgetfulness! And haven't you also noticed it's hard to be satisfied when we get what we deserve?

Jesus chose water to remind us of the temporary nature of things that satisfy us. A drink of water satisfies only until we're thirsty again. Sleep fulfills our needs only until the alarm clock rings. Even the most gratifying, long-term, human relationships end in the back of a moving van or hearse.

The only real satisfaction comes from things that last forever. Take "extended warranties," for example. We buy them in hopes of having our appliances last longer. But how satisfied can we be when we're paying in advance for inevitable breakdowns? If only we could find something that satisfies forever.

As you know, only Jesus offers eternal satisfaction. Our Savior's love and care is totally satisfying. Regardless of the multitude or magnitude of our sins, Jesus always has enough love to cover them. And while we persistently seek His forgiveness for our consistent failures, His one act on the cross was all it took to slake God's anger over our rebelliousness and unfaithfulness. And so we face each day and our eternal future knowing that whatever dissatisfies us is nothing compared to God's love through Jesus Christ. Satisfaction guaranteed.

Truly Transformed

When they saw the courage of Peter and John and realized that they were unschooled, ordinary men, they were astonished and they took note that these men had been with Jesus. Acts 4:13

History has recorded many changes over the years, and some people have opposed all of them. Others welcome change, but only if it favors them.

Some changes truly transform the way we live. Take electric transformers that adjust the power supply to your home. We're certainly thankful to whomever invented those devices. And that brings us to the subject of another Transformer—with a capital *T.*

Jesus has transformed our lives. And He's been doing it for quite a while. Go back to the days of Peter and John as recorded in Acts. People were surprised at the transformation of these two. Once they were blue-collar laborers, but now these men of God courageously told others about their Savior. Once they hoped to enjoy a few comforts, but now they withstood physical assault. Though they had little background in "book learning," now they matched the minds of educated critics. Had they joined the Toastmasters Club or earned some correspondence course diploma? Of course not. As the Bible passage says, they had "been with Jesus."

All of Jesus' transformations were truly electric! He changed the punishment that God's wrath demanded into salvation. Like the transformers you see hanging from electric poles, Jesus hung from the cross and changed the punishment we deserved into useful energy to serve Him in thanksgiving. Energy to praise Him. Energy to emulate Him. Then Jesus sent the Holy Spirit to transform us sinners into saints—even before we die. Now we can channel the love of Christ to others as we serve, forgive, and tell others how Jesus changes life. It's just another of the 413 reasons to thank God!

Inspired Performance

It was He who gave some to be apostles, some to be prophets, some to be evangelists, and some to be pastors and teachers, to prepare God's people for works of service, so that the body of Christ may be built up until we all reach unity in the faith and in the knowledge of the Son of God and become mature, attaining to the whole measure of the fullness of Christ.
Ephesians 4:11–13

When was the last time you were inspired? Perhaps you took on some creative plumbing project at home. (It probably wasn't "creative" until you started it.) Early morning showers sometime inspire musical creativity. Maybe you were inspired when you took on the career that you're in now or when you tackled certain tasks on the job.

Paul told the Ephesian Christians about inspiration—another reason to thank God. He listed apostles, prophets, evangelists, pastors, and teachers as inspired careers. Before we conclude that most of us aren't inspired in those ways, we need to realize that a little of those callings exist in whatever we do. Therefore, whatever our role in life, God inspired us to be His child and to serve in unique ways.

God inspires us to heal broken relationships, aimless wandering, lame excuses, and dead ambitions with bold forgiveness and the Holy Spirit's power. Though we may see ourselves as non-prophet in nature, Jesus inspires us to accurately predict the glorious future that awaits us and all believers. As for the evangelist, how can we keep secrets about what God has done? Pastors and teachers, as we know them today, are specially trained for their missions, but God also inspires each of us to act like a shepherd, seeking and finding the lost sheep of the world and then teaching them the formula for salvation.

You are inspired. Now get out there and give a performance that others will never forget.

The "I Can" Spirit

I can do everything through Him who gives me strength. Philippians 4:13

The best of our world's history is built on an "I can" spirit. "I can save some seeds to plant and move those rocks to grow food for my family," thought the first farmers. "I can translate God's Word into a language that ordinary people understand," said Martin Luther. "I can find a way for man to walk on the moon," figured some rocket scientist.

"I can do everything through Him who gives me strength," claims the Christian. And it's true too. It's essential to have power for love as opposed to having a love for power.

Sometimes we Christians lust for power—benevolent power, of course. We want to do great things for the Lord. Today's passage makes it sound as if we could do spectacular things to serve Him. There's just one little flaw in that perspective. It's the word *we*.

As we aspire to great service, we must also remember that the Mother Teresa in us may be intended to show compassion to a sick neighbor rather than to pitiful throngs in some pagan nation. And a desire to preach powerful sermons may need tempering down to proclaiming the Savior's love to our own children. Feeding 5,000 by God's miraculous power may seem a worthy goal too. But God may want us to work in that downtown kitchen that serves the grimy and hopeless once a week.

God's power doesn't always work in the way we normally understand power to work. The power of love that drives Christians to all kinds of service works by the Holy Spirit. And it's never a little thing to spark or strengthen faith in the hearts of others. It's a powerful thing accomplished only by the Holy Spirit working in us. We have the power to accomplish whatever God expects of us. We most certainly have an "I can" Spirit.

Consolation Prize

Brothers, we do not want you to be ignorant about those who fall asleep,
or to grieve like the rest of men, who have no hope. We believe that Jesus
died and rose again and so we believe that God will bring with Jesus those
who have fallen asleep in Him. 1 Thessalonians 4:13–14

Surely you've heard the story of the wife who accepted defeat like a man. She blamed her husband!

Consolation prizes rarely please people as much as the "first prize." "At least it's better than nothing," is the way we might comfort ourselves. Yet the only important prize—the very best prize—is the prize for losers. It's not as bad as it sounds.

Nobody can deny that we're losers. Oh, we can deny our actual status to others, but we can't repudiate it with God. He knows the truth about sinners, and we are losers. Ever since Adam and Eve disqualified themselves from the first prize of an all-expense-paid lifetime in paradise, only one person has even come close to winning.

Jesus won it all. He was a winner (even when He seemed a loser). The devil thought he had a contest when he tempted Jesus during moments when any man would be weak, but Jesus overcame every challenge. Satan couldn't nudge Jesus off the cross while He was dying, either. Instead, Jesus did as God intended. He humbly paid for our sins with His life.

Jesus won first prize. And because Jesus was a winner, all us losers got the consolation prize. What consolation it is! Though death will almost certainly claim most of us, thank God that we'll come alive again to share eternity with Him and everyone else who died in Christ.

Out of Sight and Out of Mind

As far as the east is from the west, so far has He removed our transgressions from us. Psalm 103:12

If you want to be perfectly happy, you need a lousy memory and absolutely no imagination. And have you noticed that people with the worst memories seem to remember everything they've ever done for you—and even a few things they didn't?

Out of sight easily translates into out of mind. What do you lose most often because you placed it out of sight? Car keys? Your glasses? How about your purse or wallet? Or that thing of such great value that you put it where nobody, including you, will ever find it?

Psalm 103 provides excellent comfort for those who have put something down and promptly forgotten where it was. The psalmist is talking about our sins here. While I don't remember how far the east is from the west—we must have learned that in geography—I do know it's a long way. If car keys disappear when only twelve feet away, just think how easy it is to lose something at opposite ends of the compass! And if there's anything worth losing, and losing for good, it's our sins.

Perhaps it's nothing to worry about, but it seems that God, being all-knowing and all-everything, doesn't have problems with His memory. Not by accident anyway. But He does subscribe to a policy of forgiving and forgetting. The one who died to take away our sins forgives us. And God the Father forgets every forgiven sin for His Son's sake. He packs our sins away, losing them forever behind mountains of His love. We should have such a memory!

And in Conclusion ...

But you will receive power when the Holy Spirit comes on you; and you will be My witnesses in Jerusalem, and in all Judea and Samaria, and to the ends of the earth. Acts 1:8

If you're like most readers, you're anxious to finish this book and start something new. These last three meditations will recall some "departing words" from the Bible. This one recounts what Jesus said on the day He left for heaven.

Have you ever wondered if Jesus was anxious to get on with other divine duties when He finished His earthly work? Perhaps He wanted to return to heaven so He could finish getting it ready for the millions of people He invited to live there. Certainly He understood how His dear friends felt about His departure, especially after spending those joyous and victorious post-Easter days with them. But Jesus didn't leave His followers with any sentimental farewell address. (He left that to the angels. See Acts 1:11.) Instead, He told them they could expect a different champion and companion—the Holy Spirit. And He also told them to get to work. So many people in so many places needed to hear the message about their Savior!

What about us? Are we to heed Jesus' words too? Definitely. It's as if Jesus was saying to us, "And in conclusion, My friends, spread the word about Me. Tell others the Great News about their future. And tell them the future begins right now."

The Gospel surely is Great News, but we can't just sit around reveling in its ecstasy. The Gospel has a goal, and Christians of all eras have the Holy Spirit's power to carry out that goal. Our job is to make more Christians. Our mission fields may be hallways, work stations, parking garages, hospital rooms, the middle seat on a long flight, or a child's crib. One thing's for sure—people need to hear and observe what we know. Don't worry if you're doing a good job or not. Let people draw their own conclusions.

Growth Hormones

But grow in the grace and knowledge of our Lord and Savior Jesus Christ. To Him be glory both now and forever! Amen. 2 Peter 3:18

If only our hearts would grow as steadily as our waistlines! Some people grow up and spread Gospel cheer. Others just spread. But of course, that's not the type of growth Peter spoke of in his departing words.

All Christians aspire to grow in grace. In fact, the more a believer grows in grace, the greater the ambition to grow more. Mature Christians are never content where they are; they always want more. The way to grow in grace starts—well, gracefully. We simply ask the Holy Spirit to make us more grace-full. That's just what He wants to hear, but He will also tweak our willingness to grow by more common means.

We might find ourselves praying more often—sometimes even skipping the "Dear Jesus" salutation and launching into conversation as if we're talking to a good friend. (Isn't *that* true!) We'll also have a consistent urge to worship and receive the Lord's Supper with regularity. In turn, those experiences make us more grace-full to others—believers and unbelievers, friends and foes alike. Grace grows as we experience and share it.

We need to continue growing in knowledge too. Reading through the Bible once is a fruitful practice. But fruit needs to blossom and ripen every year if the tree or vine is of any value. Once is never enough, and always is never too much. It's good to get into some Bible study with other people too. Other Christians often have new or different insights about the same passages that mean only one thing to us. And others need to hear what we've learned too. Knowledge also grows as we read books that help us understand the Bible better. (Most pastors will eagerly help you choose some.)

Peter said his farewell perhaps the best way any Christian friend can. He praised God in his time as well as for ours. Way to grow, Peter. Way to grow.

Thank You, and Come Again

Amen. Come, Lord Jesus. The grace of the Lord Jesus be with God's people.
Amen. Revelation 22:20–21

Nearly everyone wants to go to heaven, but some people hope they live long enough to see changes in the entrance requirements.

John knew the way to heaven, and his final words in Revelation tell us about it. John knew that Jesus would return as the glorious King someday, and he hoped it would be soon. So strong was his desire to be with Jesus that he implored Him to return. Is that what we mean when we pray, "Come, Lord, Jesus"? Probably not. We're likely to be satisfied with blessed food. As far as urging Him to end the world as we know it, well that may be another thing altogether.

Many people fear the end of the world. The idea even leaves many Christians shaky. It's not that we're afraid of going to hell. Jesus took care of that problem long ago on Calvary's cross. But many of us tremble at actually seeing Jesus face-to-radiant-face. And how loudly will those trumpets blast? We can probably expect to see Satan face-to-fiery-face too—and will he be mad!

What about all the saints who ever lived? Will there be room for all of us to gather in front of the King's throne? Will He remember us by name? Lots of questions, but very few answers. John got a good glimpse of Judgment Day and heaven. We can read about it in Revelation, but that often leaves us with even more questions! (Read it anyway.)

Many Christians enjoy their earthly life, which is another gift from God. But we can't begin to compare earthly life with life in heaven. We can be confident that we're ready for Jesus' return. We can be certain that it will be as sudden and as joy-filled as the first time He came. With grateful, faith-filled hearts and souls, let's join together and say, "Thank You, Lord Jesus. Come again."

Amen.

DATE DUE			